Understanding Music

Understanding Music
Philosophy and Interpretation

Roger Scruton

continuum
LONDON • NEW YORK

Continuum UK, The Tower Building, 11 York Road, London SE1 7NX
Continuum US, 80 Maiden Lane, Suite 704, New York, NY 10038

www.continuumbooks.com

Copyright © Roger Scruton 2009

First published 2009

British Library Cataloguing-in-Publication Data
A catalogue record for this book is available from the British Library.

ISBN 978 184706 506 3

Typeset by Interactive Sciences Ltd, Gloucester
Printed and bound by CPI Antony Rowe, Chippenham, Wiltshire

Contents

Preface

In the first part of this book I summarize and take forward the argument of *The Aesthetics of Music* (Oxford 1997). In the second part I apply that argument to modern music, adding some thoughts on Mozart, Beethoven and Wagner.

Versions of Chapters 3 and 4 have appeared in *The British Journal of Aesthetics*. A version of Chapter 6 appeared in Kathleen Stock (ed), *Philosophers on Music* (Oxford 2007). Chapter 7 began life as a pre-concert talk at the Bridgewater Hall, Manchester, and Chapter 8 as a pre-concert lecture at the Tuscan Sun Festival in Cortona, in 2005. A version of Chapter 9 appeared in *Prospect* magazine in 2005, and a version of Chapter 10 in Sebastian Gardner and José Luis Bermudez (eds), *Art and Morality* (London 2001). Chapter 11 appeared in Peter Davison (ed), *Reviving the Muse* (Brinkworth, 2001), and Chapter 12 in Michał Bristiger, Petra Bockholdt and Roger Scruton (eds), *Szymanowski in seiner Zeit* (Vienna 1984). I am grateful to all the relevant publishers, editors, sponsors and organizers for permission to print the chapters in this volume. I am also grateful to my publisher at Continuum, Robin Baird-Smith, for encouraging me to embark on this undertaking. It has certainly been worthwhile for me; I hope it will prove worthwhile also for him.

Malmesbury, England,
and Sperryville, Virginia,
Summer 2008.

Part I: Aesthetics

1

Introduction

Aesthetics emerged as an articulate branch of philosophy in the eighteenth century, and the study of music was made part of it by the Abbé Charles Batteux who, in *Les beaux-arts réduits à un même principe* (1746), argued that music, like the other arts, derives its significance and its appeal from the imitation of nature. Batteux's analysis was thin, and his pivotal concept of imitation unexplained. He gave few examples, and left it to the reader to nod his way to acceptance of a thesis that was more metaphor than argument. And in this Batteux was typical of his time. By the end of the century a contest was being fought on behalf of absolute music (*absolute Tonkunst*) by those who thought that music's significance as an abstract art was being diluted by ballet, opera and song. But the concepts deployed in this contest — imitation, expression, form, representation — remained as vague as they had been in the writings of Batteux, and the whole debate was conducted in metaphorical regions, seldom coming to earth in a clear example.[1]

The subdued aftermath of that contest continues to this day, and it provides one of the themes of this book. The dispute is between those who affirm, and those who deny, that music has a meaning other than itself. Words like 'imitation', 'representation', 'expression', 'content' are used fast and loose by both sides to the dispute, and only occasionally do the protagonists pause to consider what seem to me to be the true subjects of musical aesthetics: sound and how we perceive it, the relation between sound and tone, the nature of melody, rhythm and harmony, the standards of taste and judgement. Common sense would suggest that no theory of musical expression will be illuminating if unaccompanied by an explanation of those basic things. Yet even Hanslick — with Edmund Gurney the most competent of the nineteenth-century writers in this field — failed to see that he had not given such an explanation and that, without it, his theory of music as an 'absolute' art was as unwarranted as the romantic idea of music as 'the language of the emotions'.

Consider Hanslick's definition of music, as *tönend bewegte Formen* (forms moved in sounding).[2] Hanslick offered this as a literal description of what music is and does, one from which to mount a refutation of the theory—increasingly popular in the wake of E. T. A. Hoffman's music criticism and Schopenhauer's 'Metaphysics of Music'[3]—that music is an expressive medium, whose purpose is to give voice to the inner life. But what does it mean to say that the forms of music 'move' or are 'moved'? It is fairly widely recognized that, at some level, the reference to musical movement is inescapable, and I explore the consequences of this in Chapter 4. (What would it be like to abolish 'high' and 'low', 'fast' and 'slow', 'far' and 'near', 'approaching' and 'receding', from our description of musical experience? The result might still be a description of sounds, but it would not be a description of the music that we hear in them.) It is also fairly widely recognized that this reference to movement is in some sense figurative. For nothing in the world of sounds (nothing that we hear) moves, in the way that music moves.

If that is so, however, a theory which tries to explain music in terms of musical movement is not a theory of music at all: it 'explains' its subject only by blocking the path to explanation. If we allow Hanslick to get away with assuming the existence of musical motion, why not allow his opponent to assume the existence of musical emotion? For although Hanslick is right to say that what we hear is neither a sentient thing, nor anything like a sentient thing, it is also true that it is not a thing in motion, nor anything like a thing in motion.

Or consider Batteux's concept of imitation. It is well to argue that music imitates the movements of the human soul, or the gestures of the body, or whatever. But if the only grounds for saying so are that music moves in a similar way, then these are no grounds at all. For music does not move, and therefore does not move 'in a similar way'. Or rather, it does move, but only in a manner of speaking, which is just as unhelpful. (You might as well say that Batteux did prove that music imitates, but only in a manner of speaking, or that I have refuted him, but only in a manner of speaking.) At almost every point in traditional discussions this problem emerged, and in *The Aesthetics of Music* I set out to develop an account of metaphorical perception that would be a basis for a theory of musical understanding. This account informs the argument that follows, and I revisit it, and also slightly amend it, in Chapter 4.

The raw material of music is sound, and music is an art of sound. There are other arts of sound, such as poetry (the art of phonetic sound) and soundscape art (one part of garden and fountain design). Poetry depends upon the prior organization of sound as language. Fountains depend upon the relation between sound and its physical context. Music relies neither on linguistic order nor on physical context, but on organization that can be perceived in sound itself, without reference to context or to semantic conventions. The first step towards understanding music, therefore, is to understand sounds as objects of perception. This I set out to do in Chapter 2.

Sounds, I argue, are secondary objects, which is to say objects whose nature and properties are determined by how they appear to the person of normal hearing. They are produced by physical disturbances, but are not identical with those disturbances, and can be understood without reference to their physical causes. Furthermore, sounds are 'pure events', things that happen, but which don't happen *to* anything. A car crash is something that happens to a car. You can identify a car crash only by identifying the car that crashed. Sounds, by contrast, can be identified without referring to any object which participates in them, and it is precisely this feature that is seized upon by music, and made into the template on which the art of music is built. Because sounds are pure events we can detach them, in thought and experience, from their causes, and impose upon them an order that is quite independent of any physical order in the world. This happens, I suggest, in the 'acousmatic' experience of sound, when people focus on the sounds themselves and on what can be heard *in* them. What they then hear is not a succession of sounds, but a movement between tones, governed by a virtual causality that resides in the musical line. Only a rational being—one with self-consciousness, intention, and the ability to represent the world—can experience sounds in this way; hence, although *we* can hear music in the songs of birds, whales and bonobos, they themselves are deaf to it. Nothing is to be learned about music and its meaning, I contend, from studying the sounds made by animals.

That statement raises an important question however. There are people for whom music means nothing; but they are randomly scattered among populations which, viewed as a whole, accord a significant role to music. The particular musical syntax that children learn may be the product of their culture; but the disposition towards music is a trans-cultural constant. It is therefore reasonable to conclude that music, like language, is a human universal. In which case, the evolutionary psychologists argue, musicality must be an adaptation—a trait which we acquired because it enhances our reproductive fitness.

But how do human genes benefit from the musical life of their carriers? Comparisons with bird-song, conceived as an element in sexual display, give rise to the suggestion that music might have emerged through the process of sexual selection.[4] Maybe by singing and dancing a man testifies to his reproductive fitness, and so conquers the female heart, or at any rate the female genes. Or maybe through music people spontaneously 'move with' other tribal members, reinforcing the impulse towards altruistic cooperation. Or perhaps music originates in the lullaby—the sing-song with which mother and child seal the bond between them, so increasing the chances that the child will survive. Take any feature of music, boil it down until it is all but indistinguishable from a feature of animal noise, rewrite both in Darwinese and—hey presto—you have a perfectly formed functional explanation of the musical life.[5] Facts which are difficult to accommodate – that women too become attractive through their music; that music develops beyond any biological function, acquiring a complex syntax, a field of reference and an accumulating repertoire; that music comes to fruition in church and synagogue, in the concert hall, in listening quietly at home, or in other contexts far removed from our sexual endeavours—all such facts are set aside as secondary, to be brought within the purview of the theory as soon as their derivation from the primary adaptation is understood.

The evolutionary psychology of music invariably describes music as pitched and metrically arranged sound, of the kind that might be produced by a bonobo or a gorilla. However, even if it is true that music, as we know it, emerged over time from such sounds, it is not in fact reducible to them, any more than language is reducible to the warning and mating cries of the pre-lapsarian tribe. There is a metaphysical chasm—a 'transition from quantity to quality' as Hegel would put it—which separates musical organization from sequential sounds. The objection raised by Chomsky to the view that language is a gradually evolved adaptation applies equally to music: semantic organization is an all-or-nothing affair: a repertoire of noises either has it or not, and the attempts to identify 'proto-languages' which have a part of semantic order without the whole of it are doomed to failure.[6] Likewise attempts to identify a proto-music in the songs of baboons and nightingales will always end by misdescribing the phenomena. Music exists when rhythmic, melodic or harmonic order is deliberately created, and consciously listened to, and it is only language-using, self-conscious creatures, I argue, who are capable of organizing sounds in this way, either when uttering them or when perceiving them. We can hear music in the song of the nightingale, but it is a music that no nightingale has heard.

Hence, although music may have emerged from an evolutionary adaptation, it cannot be understood by referring it to its supposed genetic function. Music belongs to another order of experience and another order of explanation from the cries of animals. It is to be understood in terms of the life that moves in it—a life that is perceivable only to a rational being, who can organize sounds in terms of the spatial metaphors that transform them from inert events to actions, joined by a virtual causality in an imagined space of their own. Such, at any rate, is the thesis that I defend.

I claim that sounds heard as music are heard in abstraction from their physical causes and effects, and assembled in another way, as individuals in a figurative space of their own. Sounds heard as music are heard as tones, and tones are animated by a continuous movement in a one-dimensional space. I describe this 'acousmatic' experience as central to musical understanding. Even if we are aware that music is a performance, and that in listening to music we are hearing the real actions of real people, putting themselves into the sounds that they produce, this awareness must be registered in the musical movement if it is to be musically significant. When a violinist strains to produce Bach's great D minor Chaconne, it is not the strain in producing sounds that we appreciate, but the legacy of that strain in the virtual world of tones.

That approach to musical aesthetics has been doubted. Certain commentators—notably Andy Hamilton[7]—have objected that the account does not give sufficient emphasis to the way in which the physical reality of sounds enters into the experience of them, when we hear them as music. The acousmatic experience does not, it is suggested, account for timbre. It does not give sufficient weight to the performers and their physical actions or to the ways in which we must attend to the physical location of sounds if we are to hear their full musical potential. Fully to understand music, Hamilton suggests, we must hear the sounds both acousmatically, in terms of the virtual causality of the melodic and rhythmical line, and also acoustically, in terms of their physical place and causality. It is no more correct to say that you can understand a musical work purely in terms of the virtual movement contained in it, and without reference to its physical 'embodiment' in a sequence of sounds, than to say that you can understand a Van Gogh as a figurative image, and without reference to the brush-strokes that compose it and which implant in its surface the visible residue of human action.

It is of course true that the acoustical properties of the sounds in which we hear the organized tones of a musical line are relevant to our experience, just as the brush-strokes are relevant to the experience of a painting. Someone who saw the image in a Van Gogh but took no interest in the brush-strokes and the way in which the image is deposited by them, would have missed something truly important. But compare the person who sees *only* brush-strokes, and no image, with the one who sees only the figurative image, and no brush-strokes. The first is not in fact understanding what he sees, however aesthetic his attitude, while the second is *seeing figuratively*, and therefore with the kind of understanding to which the medium is addressed. Likewise, compare the person who hears only the acoustical properties of sounds—their position, loudness, physical causes and effects—and is deaf to the virtual causality of the musical line, with the one who is absorbed in the musical line, but has no idea of where the sounds are coming from or how they are made. The second is hearing music (even if also missing something), while the first is not. Such considerations suggest the centrality of the acousmatic experience to the understanding of music. And it is only from the premise of that centrality, I argue, that we can build a true theory of music.

It has been said in this connection that the emphasis on *what we hear* imports a cultural context, and that this context is by no means the universal condition under which music has been produced and enjoyed. At a certain moment there arose in European society a habit of organized listening and—as a by-product of this habit—the establishment of public and private concerts. In other words there was a point in history when audiences *fell silent*. Thereafter music took on a new meaning, as an act of solemn communication, occurring in another space from the space of everyday life. Instead of being a background, something that was never more prominent than when being danced to or sung, music became an object of attention for its own sake, a 'real presence' before its own hushed congregation. And with this transformation came another, which was the shift of attention from performer to composer, and from improvised songs and dances to fixed musical works. The emergence of the 'work concept' has therefore been described as distinctive of 'Western art music'.[8] Other cultures see music as a kind of performance, improvised around recurring material, but not organized into distinct musical works, certainly not works to be listened to as unique acts of communication between composer and audience. By confining our attention to musical works we not only fail to see what is common to music in all traditions; we also misrepresent the music of those who lack that concept or treat it as marginal.[9] And we give undue prominence to our own tradition—or to that part of our tradition which is contemporary with the Romantic movement and its aftermath—misleading ourselves into thinking that a transient application of music is really the essence of music in all its forms.

That argument lends itself to a certain kind of *political* dismissal of musical aesthetics. It is argued that by elevating the concert-hall experience to the paradigm of musical appreciation, and the musical work to the paradigm musical object, we confer a kind of necessity on the listening culture. And to make permanent and unassailable in this way, what is by its nature transient and questionable, is not philosophy but 'ideology'. By 'privileging' the concert-hall experience we make 'bourgeois' attitudes part of the very fabric of music, and so protect them from criticism—a criticism ever more necessary now that most music exists outside the concert hall.

That kind of argument might be levelled by the defender of popular music against the classical tradition; by the advocate of 'mechanical reproduction' against the traditions of musical performance; by the ethnomusicologist against the defender of 'Western art music'; by the believer in song, dance and improvisation against the denizen of the concert hall. In all its forms the argument adopts and adapts a standard move in the Marxist criticism of culture, exposing as 'ideology' what claims to be disinterested thought. And it shares this move with what in other respects is the polar opposite of those critical responses to the listening culture: Adorno's radical defence of atonal music against the 'ideological' products of the tonal system.

In giving a theory of music we are accounting for a certain human experience and the interests that have grown from it. This experience is an aspect of our rationality. It can be educated, brought under conscious control and emendation, subordinated to religious, moral and social uses. It may therefore be subject to cultural fluctuations, and the interests that have grown from it may not be everywhere the same. There is improvised music, as well as music written down and ring-fenced against change. There is music for dancing and marching; music for listening, music for worshipping and 'music while you work'. There are traditions like ours, in which the repeatable work has emerged as all-important, and in which a developed system of notation enables people to compose without performing, and to leave permanent records of what they have invented. And there are traditions like the Indian, in which melodies and their elaborations are memorized, but in which notation is schematic and incomplete.

This does not mean that there are no 'works' of Indian classical music. There are plenty of them: but they are not identified through scores. The Indian raga comprises four elements: a mode, a rhythmic cycle or *tâla* which allots time-values to successive notes, a melody occupying an entire cycle, and a sequence of diminutions or *raginas*, born from the basic phrases of the work. Traditional notation was never sufficient to encompass the result, which might last for an hour or more, and astonishing feats of memory were required of traditional musicians—feats made possible only by the absorption of the raga into religious worship, and by the religious discipline of the musicians. Nevertheless, even though imperfectly notated, the ragas have existed, some of them for centuries, as individual works, realized, to be sure, in contrasting performances but, like musical works in our tradition, the foundation of a listening culture. And although many of these works are anonymous, not a few are attributed to specific composers like Tyâgarâja (1767–1847), whose works, memorized by his pupils and disciples, have been passed on and revered not merely as interesting musical objects, but as the creations of an interesting soul.[10]

When the first attempts were made to write down some of the ragas in Western notation they were already on the verge of being lost, however, and the All-India Musical Conferences were established in 1916 in order to rescue and perpetuate the classical repertoire. This episode in musical history is of considerable importance in illustrating the inner connection between memory and musical structure. Complex musical structures require strenuous acts of recuperation; and outside a religious discipline and the contemplative state of mind that it induces, the Indian style of melody would be difficult or impossible to memorize.

The collective failure of memory which threatened the survival of Indian classical music threatened also the survival of plainchant, and until the work of Dom Prosper Guéranger and his monastic community at the Abbey of Solesmes in the first half of the nineteenth century, there was no real agreement as to how the medieval manuscripts should be read. Here too the efforts of the Benedictine communities have been devoted to recovering not just a tradition of performance, but the *works* which have been and—thanks to recent scholarship—still are performed in it. Jazz too makes room for the work concept, even if the work is often used as the starting point for a series of improvisations. The jazz standard, in which a strophic song is reduced to a melody and a chord sequence, and notated in a lead sheet, is still a work of music, though one that can be performed in many different ways.

We should therefore respond with a certain measure of scepticism to those who dismiss the work concept as a fleeting and in some way accidental imposition on the endless flux of musical inspiration.[11] It is of course true that the status of the musician has changed over the centuries, that musicians are of many kinds, and that other epochs have been more interested in performers than composers and often barely able to distinguish the two. Nevertheless, even if it is true that other traditions either marginalize or make no mention of the 'work' concept, the distinction between work and performance grows spontaneously in the practice of acousmatic hearing. There is a peculiar experience of 'same again' which is fundamental to musical organization. There could not be meaningful improvisation without this experience, and the emergence of works from a tradition of spontaneous performance is exactly what we must expect when people listen, and therefore recognize what they hear as 'the same again'. 'Play it again' is the mark of acousmatic joy, and one that is by no means confined to 'Western art music' or the concert-hall culture.

Almost all musical traditions therefore have named melodies —named usually from the song that is sung to them. Many have notated classics. The notation may be (like that of the Indian ragas and much classical Chinese music) more ambiguous than the Western classical tradition would countenance. But in all traditions, ours included, notation under-determines performance and identifies works of music only when read in the context of a performance tradition. Many 'baroque' classics—and most of the Bach cantatas—are notated with a figured bass, leaving the instrumentalists to work out the accompanying voices for themselves. Nevertheless we love and admire these works as *works*, make the same distinction between work and performance as we would in the case of a Strauss tone-poem or a Schubert song, and study the sources in order to know how best to compose out the middle parts.

Of course, when improvisation by the performer is a fundamental component in what the audience enjoys, the work takes on another character—less the music itself than a template for producing it. And since the invention of recording, and the mass reproduction of the result, individual performances can acquire a kind of eternal and transcendent character comparable to that of the classical masterpieces. There then arises a new kind of work—the work composed *as* a template for improvisation, of which perhaps only a few recordings achieve the status of classics. An obvious example is Thelonious Monk's *'Round Midnight*, rightly esteemed for its authoritative harmonic sequence and soulful melody, but existing in countless performances, some by Monk at the piano, some by the Monk Quartet, some by other musicians using other forces, all differing in every respect that the tradition of jazz improvisation allows and encourages. Only some of the extant versions of 'Round Midnight achieve the heights, or depths, of melancholy soulfulness that Monk coaxed from the piano, and all listeners will have their favourites. Nevertheless there really is a musical work which is 'Round Midnight, and the work concept is as usefully applied in such a case as in the case of a Mozart symphony. In the case of 'Round Midnight, however, much more is left to the performer's discretion than is left by the score of a Mozart symphony, and a talent *of the same kind* as the composer's is needed, if the performance is to be truly successful.[12]

Hence we might usefully distinguish template works, like the jazz classics and the classical Indian ragas, from 'filled in' works, such as those of the Western concert-hall tradition. Questions of musical ontology arise from this distinction—questions every bit as scholastic as those which animate so much of musical aesthetics in America.[13] But they have no bearing, it seems to me, either on the centrality of the work concept, or on that of the listening culture. From its very inception jazz has been as much part of the listening culture as has the symphonic tradition. And as for the Indian raga its whole *raison d'être* is to be listened to, with the kind of rapt attention that requires years of training if it is to be perfected, and which is not fully separable from a tradition of meditation and worship.

Indeed, even if there are sound ethnological reasons for believing that music originated in dance and song, listening, I maintain, is the heart of all musical cultures. You cannot sing or dance if you do not listen to the music that you are singing or dancing to. Maybe listening *in motionless silence* is a sophisticated latecomer to the repertoire of musical attitudes. But it might, for that very reason, provide us with the laboratory conditions, so to speak, in which we can best study what is involved, when rational beings *hear sound as music*. Such, indeed, is my contention, and I have found nothing in the writings of those who advocate 'other musics', or who dismiss the Western classical tradition as deviant, to persuade me that I am wrong.

But this raises a question of great importance, namely, the question of tonality. In *The Aesthetics of Music* I defended tonality, not as the only way in which music can be organized, but as a *paradigm* of musical organization. The account I gave of tonality was not intended to exclude modal music, nor did I mean to imply that atonal music is impossible. What I did imply is that, if atonal music is addressed to the same interest as tonal music, then it must be heard as moving forward in a similar way, unfolding an audible argument that moves in a perceptible direction. Moreover, I tried to show that successful experiments in atonality recreate, often in defiance of the theory which allegedly inspires them, quasi-tonal melody and harmony, moving towards definite points of closure that are understood in terms of their tonal resonance. Nevertheless, I freely admit that my discussion was incomplete, and it left many readers wondering as to the precise connection between tonal order and the acousmatic experience which I identify as the heart of musical understanding.

There is a way of arguing for the primacy of tonality which I think arrives too easily at its foregone conclusion. This is the argument from 'natural' harmony—an argument that has its roots in Pythagorean mysticism, and which achieved a resounding endorsement from Helmholtz's researches into the overtone series. Whenever a string or a column of air is made to vibrate—as in the instruments that are familiar to us—then subsidiary vibrations are set up, whose frequencies are whole-number multiples of the frequency of the fundamental tone. As one ascends the overtone series the subsidiary vibrations become ever fainter, and as a rule only the first four are noticeable, and even then only by the trained ear. However, these first four overtones spell out the notes of the major triad on the fundamental tone. The theory of overtones, beating, and undertones can be elaborated to form something like a complete physics of natural harmony,[14] and the fact that it coincides at so many points with our Western chord grammar has sometimes been taken as proof that the system of triads is a system of 'natural' harmony, independent of musical convention. Even in musical traditions that avoid triadic chords the octave, fourth and fifth are recognized as defining the space in which the notes of music move. There is no musical culture that I know of that does not recognize the octave as equivalent to its fundamental, and most traditions acknowledge the fifth as a metastable position on the scale, and the drone on the fifth as a stabilizing harmonic accompaniment.

There is another route, equally astonishing, and equally fertile, to the idea of a natural music, and this route lies through melody rather than harmony. The interval of the fifth, when inverted, gives a fourth: from these two intervals we construct the major second, by subtracting one from the other. If we then fit into the scope of an octave all those tones which are no less than a major second apart, and which are related as fifth or fourth to other tones in the octave, the result is the pentatonic scale. It is a scale that never inflicts a semi-tone or a tritone on the ear, so all its notes stand in genial

Example 1

relations to their neighbours. Ethnomusicologists have found that this scale exists almost everywhere as a primary melodic resource, familiar in Celtic folk songs, in Negro spirituals, in the music of the Australasian aborigines, in Burmese temple chants and in the old country music of China. Once again, therefore, we seem to have arrived at a 'natural' music, and one which respects the intervals familiar to us from our tonal tradition.

It doesn't need much critical thought, however, to realize that this search for natural music is already on a collision course. The most important tone in any melodic scale, after the tonic, is the leading tone—the tone which leads upwards to the tonic and so facilitates closure. If we arrange the pentatonic scale so that its intervals permit the tonic to be harmonized with the 'natural' triad on the tonic, then the result, as in the first scale in Ex. 1, is the pentatonic scale without a leading tone—one that permits only hollow melodies. If we allow the leading tone, by contrast, the result is a pentatonic scale in the minor key, in which the minor third takes on dominating melodic significance, as in the second scale. Combining this natural melodic scale with the natural harmonies of the overtone series, we arrive at the 'blue' notes that emerged from the American Negro spiritual tradition: notes which result from the clash between the melodic demand for a minor third and the harmonic demand for the major interval that conflicts with it.

Of course, in one way those facts could be seen as confirming the underlying pressure towards 'natural' tonal order—a pressure which here produces the clash that was so happily resolved by the Blues. But it also suggests that, as soon as people begin to sing creatively, convention displaces nature, and shapes what we hear according to laws of its own. The 'natural' relations among tones are at best raw material, from which scales, modes and harmonic devices emerge by habit and experiment. The order that we learn to hear is permeated by the traditions that have shaped our ears. And these traditions vary from culture to culture, as is evident not only from the findings of ethnomusicology but also from the theoretical texts on music that have come down to us from ancient Greek and Arabic sources, many of which endorse the Pythagorean system of natural harmonics, while imposing on that system scales and modes that are all but unintelligible to the modern Western ear.[15]

True though that observation is, it does not imply that there are no limits to musical conventions. There are *a priori* constraints on musical syntax that derive from the very nature of musical movement. Pitched sounds present us with the experience of musical space, of up and down, rising and falling, fast and slow, towards and away, hollow and filled. These are inevitable features of the musical *Gestalt*. We cannot hear musical movement without seeking for points of stability and closure—points towards which the movement is tending or from which it is diverging, and to which it might at some point 'come home'. We inevitably distinguish phrases that 'follow on' from those that make a new start; phrases that 'answer' from phrases that question; phrases that imitate, repeat or comment from phrases that stand alone. These audible relations are the raw material of musical order, and are furthered by the syntax of tonality in ways that justify the belief that tonality is a kind of paradigm. In his attempt to break with tonality Schoenberg ended by imposing a serial organization on the twelve tones of the chromatic scale. But this search for a permutational order in place of the elaborational order of the familiar tonal syntax is profoundly anti-musical. Schoenberg's music, whose merits I would be the first to acknowledge, is almost invariably heard *against* the serial organization, by listeners who search for closure, repetition, imitation and elaboration, and who strive to hear harmonic progressions rather than sequences of 'simultaneities'.[16]

This does not mean that all music is tonal, or that tonality is a single, unitary system, the same in every epoch and every style. Tonality is an evolving tradition, arising from the modes of medieval music and evolving through medieval and Renaissance polyphony to the contrapuntal idiom of the Baroque and thence to the four-square triadic syntax of the classical style. It is a tradition in which there have been genuine *discoveries*, such as the well-tempered scale. This scale reconciled triadic harmony with the chromatic intervals, and thereby facilitated what has perhaps been the greatest advance in all music, which is the emergence of tonal centres, and persuasive modulations between them. All this is familiar to the historian, and there is no need to emphasize it. However it is worth pointing out that the serial organization introduced by Schoenberg is entirely dependent on the well-tempered scale, whose rationale lies in the harmonic vistas that are opened with each successive semi-tone. These vistas are there in the melodic line of the Violin Concerto, in the agonizing tone-row of *Moses*

Example 2

und Aron, and in the delicate textures of the last two quartets. And it is only by an effort of will that Schoenberg was able to close them off.

Although tonal music is not the only music that there is, therefore, tonality should not be regarded as a fleeting, arbitrary or merely *stylistic* episode in the history of music. It tells us something essential about music—in particular about the nature of musical movement, about the dimensions in which movement operates, and about the way in which vectors combine, so as to change music from a monologue to a conversation. It is not tonality, but the seeming rejection of tonality by Schoenberg and his followers, that should be seen as fleeting and merely stylistic. At the very moment when Schoenberg was dismissing tonality as an 'exhausted' idiom, a wholly new form of it was breaking forth on the musical horizon—one influenced not only by the principles of classical harmony, but also by the modes and rhythms of Negro music, by the harmonic experiments of Debussy and Ravel, and by the discovery of sequences consisting entirely of dissonant harmonies, in which nevertheless progression towards closure could be heard. Adorno, as is well known, hated this new tonal idiom, and had outraged things to say about it. But—while reserving judgement for the moment as to the merits and deficiencies of jazz—I am convinced that it provides a perfect illustration of the centrality of tonal thinking in the understanding of musical order. Moreover, it shows the way in which tonality *remakes* itself, by proposing new relations between voices, and new kinds of voice-leading from chord to chord.

To take a very simple instance. The first chord in Ex. 2 is, in the contrapuntal tradition of classical music, the tail end of a suspension, in which one voice—the high G—has yet to move to its 'proper' place, something which, as a rule, immediately happens as G moves to F sharp and the chord resolves on to the major triad of D in root position, as shown in the second part of the example. But that is not how jazz musicians treat the chord. For them it is, and has always been, a new harmony, one in which the third is replaced by a fourth so that each note stands bold and clear and affirmative, and none is subject to the gravitational pull of the tonic. In due recognition of its classical origin they call the first chord of Ex. 2 the 'sus' chord on D, but they construe it as a stable harmony, with a pungent quality all of its own. Moreover, add the 7th and 9th, and the sus chord on D becomes identical with the A minor 7th over a D pedal, as in the third chord of Ex. 2 — in other words not a tonic chord at all, but a chord on the dominant. A completely new harmonic perspective then opens, as we come to understand sus chords on the tonic as supporting improvisations on the dominant. Moreover, sus chords do not, in the jazz idiom, demand resolution, so a piece might consist entirely of sus chords — as in Herbie Hancock's *Maiden Voyage*. One simple emendation to a classically occurring harmony, therefore, opens the way to another kind of music. Yet it is music that shares the ruling characteristics of tonality in all its forms: voice-leading, polyphony, melodic closure, harmonic sequence, and scales in which a tonic and a dominant exert their controlling influence.

Much contemporary pop music is modal — using the various church modes as melodic devices, supported by stacked chords, such as the so-called 'phrygian' chord (a minor ninth on the tonic) which incorporates a flattened supertonic into the melodic minor scale. This device is familiar from Heavy Metal, and can be heard at its most exhilarating in Metallica's 'Master of Puppets'. The minor scale with flattened supertonic is identical with the Phrygian mode. But the mode, introduced in this way, is contained within an adverse tonal template, emphasized by the phrygian chord, which anchors the deviant super-tonic to the tonic and forbids its escape. Once again we see the force of tonal thinking, and the way in which tonality lends order and closure to new idioms, new ways of singing, and new uses of the musical line.

Perhaps the greatest mistake involved in the marginalizing of tonality, however, has been the failure to perceive that tonality is also a *rhythmic* system. This I argue at greater length in Chapter 6, but folk songs and pop songs make the point sufficiently clearly. All such music is strophic in organization, and strophes can be understood only in terms of the experience of closure, which divides the music into repeatable sections. The presence of a tonic generates the background rhythm of a song, by permitting the singer and the listener to come home to a specific pitch, and to seek refuge in a particular harmony. It is from that background sense of 'home' that the small-scale closures derive their force, and without scales, whether diatonic or modal, strophic organization is virtually impossible to achieve. And scales, even when modal, provide both tonic and the leading tone that points to it.

To invoke jazz and pop as proof of the enduring relevance of tonality opens me to the objections made by Adorno. If your only examples of a renewed tonality, he would say, are the improvised and grammarless sequences of jazz and pop, then you merely confirm my point—that tonality has become 'fetishized', part of the 'ideological' approach to music which prefers sugar and spice to real musical thinking. It is not *this* that will vindicate tonality as a rival to the 'developing variation' made possible by Schoenberg's new musical grammar.

It is impossible to proceed far into the aesthetics of music without encountering this argument, and it is the aspect of Adorno with which I am most in sympathy. In the last chapter of *The Aesthetics of Music* I tried to say something about the difference between musical culture and musical kitsch. In Chapter 13 I return again to this theme, conscious of the enormous dangers it presents to an author, in a world where pop-addiction is all but universal and where the tedious tapestries of routine jazz muffle the walls of so many communal spaces. Even if nothing else in Adorno deserves our sympathy, we must surely admire his courage in pouring scorn on mass culture. The strange thing is that he believed American popular music to be the enemy of the people, when it is was the people who had produced it, and who had found in its glittering surface the true mirror of their soul. To understand this episode in cultural history is, I think, essential, if we are to theorize about music as it is today. And if I tread warily across this territory, then this is not because I share Adorno's contempt for the old American songbook, but because I feel its pull too strongly, and know that there are deep questions to be asked, concerning the nature of musical temptation, and the discipline that might help us to resist it.

Notes

1 The leading texts have been collected and extracted by Peter Le Huray and James Day in their *Music and Aesthetics in the 18th and Early 19th Centuries*, Cambridge 1981.

2 E. Hanslick, *Vom musikalisch-Schönen* (Leipzig 1854, revised 1891; *The Beautiful in Music*, tr. Payzant, New York 1974.) Edmund Gurney's *The Power of Sound*, London 1880, has been reissued by the University of Chicago Press, 2003.

3 See Schopenhauer, *The Word as Will and Representation*, tr. E. J. F. Payne, New York 1969, vol. 2.

4 See Geoffrey Miller, 'Evolution of human music through sexual selection', in Nils Wallin *et al.*, *The Origins of Music*, Cambridge, Mass. 2000.

5 This process of reducing explanandum to the terms preferred by a favoured explanans has been eloquently ridiculed by David Stove in *Darwinian Fairy Tales*, New York 2002.

6 See especially *Language and Mind*, New York 1968, p. 62, in which language is described as 'an example of true emergence—the appearance of a qualitatively different phenomenon at a specific stage of complexity of organization'. Chomsky has been taken to task by, for example, John Maynard Smith and Eörs Szathmáry, *The Major Transitions in Evolution*, Oxford and New York 1995, pp. 303–8. However, it seems to me that the arguments of such writers miss

the point, which is that the emergence of language involves a transition from one ontological predicament to another—like the emergence of a face from an array of dots when the last dot is added. Of course the process is one of gradual change: but one that leads to the emergence of a new order of experience and a new kind of explanation. See Roger Scruton, 'Confronting biology', in Craig Titus, ed., *Philosophical Psychology: Psychology, Emotions and Freedom*, Arlington, Va. 2009.

7 *Aesthetics and Music*, London 2007.
8 See Charles Rosen, Review of the *New Grove Dictionary of Music*, reprinted in *Critical Entertainments*, Cambridge, Mass. 2000; Carl Dahlhaus, *Esthetics of Music*, tr. W. Austin, Cambridge 1982, and *The Idea of Absolute Music*, tr. R. Lustig, Chicago 1989; Edward Saïd, *Musical Elaborations*, London 1991; Lydia Goehr, *The Imaginary Museum of Musical Works*, Oxford 1992.
9 See Lydia Goehr, 'Being true to the work', *The Journal of Aesthetics and Art Criticism*, 1989.
10 Some of Tyâgarâja's works are set out (in embryo form) in Ethel Rosenthal's excellent treatise *The Story of Indian Music and its Instruments*, London 1929, Chapter 4. This book also contains Sir William Jones's prescient essay 'On the musical modes of the Hindus', written in 1784 but not published until 1799 in the Transactions of the Asiatic Society, Bengal. It is worth mentioning this work as indicating (*pace* Edward Saïd and others) that Indian culture today owes much to the British Indians and their enthusiasm for things 'other' than themselves.
11 Further pertinent observations are made by some of the contributors to Michael Talbot, ed., *The Musical Work: Reality or Invention?*, Liverpool 2000; see especially the contribution from Reinhard Strohm.
12 Peter Kivy has gone further, arguing that, in every tradition, the performance is a work of art, independent of the work of art that is performed. See '*Ars Perfecta*: Towards perfection in musical performance', in *Music, Language and Cognition*, Oxford 2007.
13 See, for example, the disputes surrounding the question whether works of music are or are not types, universals, sound structures, sound structures as specified by a person at a time, compliance classes specified by notation, and so on: see Nelson Goodman, *Languages of Art: An Approach to a Theory of Symbols*, Oxford 1969, Chapters 4 and 5, and Jerrold Levinson, 'What a musical work is', in *Music, Art and Metaphysics*, Ithaca NY, 1990. I have discussed these theories in *The Aesthetics of Music*, Chapter 4, where I argue that they all make an impregnable molehill out of an easily conquered mountain.
14 See Hermann von Helmholtz, *On the Sensation of Tone*, tr. Alexander J. Ellis, London 1885.
15 See M. L. West, *Ancient Greek Music*, Oxford 1992; Al-Fârâbî, *Kitab al-mousiqi al-kabir* (Big Book on Music), Cairo 1923.
16 Of course, it would be begging many questions to suppose that the debate over atonality and serialism, and what they require of us, is in any way closed. The debate about this issue is never ending, as can be seen from the pages of *Musical Analysis*. See in particular, Julian Horton, 'Schoenberg and the "Moment of German music"', *Musical Analysis* 24 (2005), 235–62.

2

Sounds[1]

Sounds are like secondary qualities in that their nature is bound up with the way they are perceived. However, they are not qualities, either of the objects that emit them or of the regions of space in which they are heard. Sounds, I suggest, are objects in their own right, bearers of properties, and identifiable separately both from the things that emit them and the places where they are located. If you ask to what category of objects they belong, then I will say, first, that they are 'secondary objects', in the way that colours are secondary qualities (though what way is that?); secondly that they are events (though is there a relevant distinction between events and processes?); and thirdly that they are 'pure events'—things that happen but which don't happen *to* anything (though how is that possible?).

In ordinary physical events, such as crashes, physical objects undergo change: a car crash is something that happens to a car and to the people in it. But a sound is not a change in another thing, even if it is caused by such a change. Nor does anything participate in the sound in the way that the car participates in the crash. You could accept those thoughts on the supposition that sounds are not particulars but universals. However, my claim in this chapter will be that sounds are particulars, but particulars of a special kind. In my view their two most puzzling features—that they are secondary objects and pure events—are fundamental to the art of music. These features are also both curious in themselves and the source of interesting philosophical puzzles.

The theory of sounds as events has been defended by others, notably by Roberto Casati and Jérôme Dokic in their pioneering study *La philosophie du son* (1994), and in more recent work by Casey O'Callaghan.[2] But those authors take a resolutely 'physicalist' approach, repudiating all suggestion that sounds might be essentially connected to the experience of hearing things, and identifying them instead with physical events in or around the objects that emit them. Sounds, they argue, are identical neither with the waves that transmit them nor with the auditory experiences through which we perceive them. They are identical with the events that generate the sound waves—physical disturbances in physical things, such as those which occur when the string of a violin vibrates in air. In other words, sounds involve changes in the primary qualities of physical objects. On this view a sound happens to the thing that emits it, in the way that crashes happen to cars, and the happening consists in physical changes that could be measured in other ways than by hearing.

'Physicalism' is not confined to those who defend the view that sounds are events. Robert Pasnau, for example, who thinks of sounds as properties of the objects that emit them, is also a physicalist in my sense. He argues that an object 'has' or 'possesses' a sound when it vibrates at a particular frequency and amplitude: in other words, that sounds are primary qualities of the objects that are heard to emit them (in contrast to Locke, who describes sounds as secondary qualities).[3] I do not explicitly argue against this form of physicalism, since I am persuaded that sounds are events, not properties.[4]

Physicalists can admit that sounds have secondary qualities, and that it is by virtue of these qualities that we discriminate them. In themselves, however, so they will say, sounds are primary-quality events involving the bodies that emit them. Why should we deny that? Here are some of my reasons:

(i) I want to hold on to the view of sounds as 'objects of hearing' in something like the way that colours are objects of sight. Sounds are 'audibilia', which is to say that their essence resides in 'the way they sound'. Hence they are absent from the world of the deaf person in the way that colours are absent from the world of the blind. The physicalist view has the consequence that deaf people could be fully acquainted with sounds (for instance by using a vibrometer which registers pitch and overtones), and also that people could see sounds without hearing them. There is nothing incoherent about either suggestion: however, both suggestions seem to relegate to the 'purely phenomenal' level everything in sounds that distinguishes them—not merely their relation to hearing, but (as I go on to argue) their internal order, their ability to speak to us, and much of their information-carrying potential.

(ii) I believe that we do not attribute the secondary qualities of sounds to the bodies that emit them, or to events that occur in those bodies. We attribute them to the sounds themselves, conceived as independently existing events, located in a region of space. When I hear a car passing what I hear is the *sound* of a car passing, an event caused by the car's passing but distinct from any event involving the car. The sound made by the car is not an event in the car or a change in which the car participates. It is an event in itself.

(iii) The information conveyed by sounds is not, typically, information about a vibration in any object, nor do we usually group sounds together by reference to their source. Psychologists have studied auditory grouping, asking themselves what evolutionary function it might serve.[5] For example, we tend to group quiet sounds interrupted by bangs together, as though they formed a continuous sequence, just as we continue in imagination the lines on a page that are interrupted by blots. In general, sequences of sounds are 'streamed' in our perception—each allocated to a temporal *Gestalt,* formed according to temporal analogues of the principles for *Gestalt* formation in vision. Proximity in pitch, duration, timbre, loudness and so on lead to streams which endure through silences, interruptions, competing streams and unstreamed events. Albert Bregman, perhaps the most noted researcher into these phenomena, is of the view that 'the perceptual stream-forming process has the job of grouping those acoustic features that are likely to have arisen from the same physical source'.[6] However, as I go on to argue, streaming involves attributing to sounds an identity distinct from any process in their source, and involves the creation of a world of coherent sounds, rather than a world of coherent spatio-temporal objects. Unlike the visual field, which shares its structure with the objects that are displayed in it, the auditory field is incongruous with the physical events that it records. It is only *because* of this feature, indeed, that sound can fulfil its evolutionary function, of providing an auditory map of the surrounding physical world.

(iv) Sounds can be detached completely from their source, as by radio or gramophone, and listened to in isolation. This experience—the 'acousmatic' experience of sound—removes nothing that is essential to the sound as an object of attention.[7] The striking thing is that sounds, thus emancipated from their causes, are experienced as independent but related objects, which form coherent complexes, with boundaries and simultaneities, parts and wholes. They can be divided and combined, prolonged and curtailed, and much of the art of music consists in using them to compose forms in which they appear as identifiable and repeatable parts.

For those reasons it seems to me that there is every reason to reject the physicalist view. In espousing physicalism Casati and Dokic bravely accept the consequence that sound is essentially non-phenomenal, in other words that what a sound essentially is has nothing to do with how it sounds.[8] They are prepared to accept that sounds have secondary qualities, but believe that the idea of a secondary object—an object, all of whose properties are ways in which it appears—is *extrêmement contestable*. But they do not say why, and their own account of sounds, which attributes to sounds only the most uninteresting of intrinsic properties, leaves us with no basis from which to explore *what we hear* through the organization of the auditory field. It seems to me that what we hear, both when we hear sounds in our day-to-day environment and when we listen to sounds acousmatically, is not merely a subjective impression but a real part of the objective world. That is what I mean by describing sounds as secondary objects.

Before substantiating those points, it is worth addressing the question whether there are other examples of secondary objects? It seems to me that there are, and that they include two extremely important instances: rainbows and smells. I shall concentrate on rainbows, since they so closely parallel sounds. First, rainbows are *visibilia*, objects of sight which are not objects of any other sense. You cannot touch, smell or hear a rainbow, and if, when rainbows occurred, there were also sensations of touch (e.g. wetness in the air), of hearing (e.g. a fizzing sound) or of smell, we should feel no compulsion to say that we are feeling, hearing or smelling the *rainbow*. (Lightning is always followed by a thunderclap, sometimes by a scorched smell, and often by rain but we do not say that we hear, smell or feel the lightning.)

Rainbows are secondary objects in the following sense: their existence, nature and qualities are all determined by how things appear to the normal observer. That there is a rainbow visible over Sunday Hill Farm follows from the fact that a normal observer, located here, would have just such a visual experience if he looked towards the hill. This does not mean that rainbows have only secondary qualities: on the contrary, rainbows have many primary qualities, such as shape, size and duration. But their having these qualities depends upon a counter-factual about experience.

Rainbows are located, but not precisely. There is no pot of gold at the end of the rainbow because there is no place which is the end of the rainbow; nor is there a stretch of sky that the rainbow occupies. In this case location too is experience-dependent. To say that there is a rainbow visible over the hill is to say that a person located in a certain

place and looking towards the hill would see the arch of a rainbow lying over it. Rainbows don't take up space, and don't exclude other objects from the spaces where they appear. Nevertheless there is a distinction between the places where rainbows are and the places where they are not.

Rainbows are real and objective. Someone who claims to see a rainbow where the normal observer could not see one either is under an illusion or has made a mistake. He is wrong about the way the world is. Rainbows can be other than they seem, and seem other than they are. There were rainbows in the world before there were creatures to observe them, for the truth about rainbows consists in the truth of a counterfactual, concerning what normal observers *would* see were their eyes to be turned in a certain direction. The rainbow, like the photon, is an ungrounded disposition, and it illustrates the way in which ungrounded dispositions can be part of the fabric of reality.

None of that implies that we could not give a full explanation of rainbows in terms of the primary-quality structure and changes of normal primary objects. The explanation is indeed familiar to us, and invokes light waves and their refraction by water droplets in the air. This explanation of rainbows is very similar to the explanation of the experience of sound, in terms of the transmission of a vibration by sound waves. But it will not mention any particular object that is *identical* with the rainbow, in the way that the physicalist urges us to consider the vibration of the source as *identical* with the sound. Hence it will leave us free to locate the rainbow in the area where it appears, and not at some place chosen for its prominent role in the theory of rainbows (for instance the patch of water drops in the air, the sun, the eye of the beholder). Of course, the rainbow appears to be in place X only from place Y: someone standing at X might not see it. But this illustrates once again the peculiar relation of rainbows to the space in which they are situated: a rainbow is visible *at* a place *from* a place, and that is the last word as to where it is.

The example of rainbows shows, I believe, that the physicalist theory of sounds is unmotivated. There is every reason to treat sounds as *audibilia*, in just the way that we treat rainbows as *visibilia*. In doing so we deny nothing that the physicalist affirms, other than a statement of identity that renders accidental all those features of sounds that we are normally disposed to treat as essential; features, in short, of *the way they sound*. By treating sounds as secondary objects we restore to them their true nature, as information-bearing events which are organized aurally.

Once we acknowledge the existence of events which are also secondary objects, the way is open to the 'pure event': the event which happens, even though it does not happen *to* anything, the event which cannot be reduced to changes undergone by reidentifiable particulars. This, I believe, is how we should think of sounds. They occur, but they stand alone, and can be identified without identifying any individual that emits them. Of course, our language for characterizing sounds tends to describe them in terms of their normal source—dripping, croaking, creaking, barking. But reference to a source is not essential to the identification of the sound, even when it is compelled by the attempt to describe it. It is in some sense an accident if we can attribute a sound to a particular—to say that it is the sound *of* this thing, caused by changes *in* that thing, and so on. It would be quite possible for us to be surrounded by sounds, like Ferdinand on Prospero's Isle, which we individuate, order and interpret without assigning to any of them a physical process as origin or cause. (See the example of the 'Music Room', discussed in Chapter 1 of *The Aesthetics of Music*.)

This gives me another reason to be dissatisfied with the physicalist view. For it seems to tie sounds too firmly to their sources. In particular, it seems to suggest that our ordinary way of identifying sounds, as self-dependent events which bear their nature in themselves, are mistaken. The physicalist view banishes to the margin those features of sound that make sound so important to us, not only epistemologically but also socially, morally and aesthetically. In particular it does not recognize the 'pure event' as a distinct ontological category, and one that introduces unique possibilities of communication.

Being unencumbered by objects, so to speak, sounds come to us with their nature fully revealed. We can recognize them as qualitatively the same simply from hearing them, and in dividing them into kinds we are conveying information which is not blurred, as in the case of ordinary events, by the multiplicity of changes on which it is based. This is what enables us to refer usefully to sound types, such as the sound of the clarinet, or Middle C, or the sound of a person falling downstairs. Our ability to do so, however, is contingent on the existence of sound tokens, from which the types are derived by a kind of abstraction.

It is here that we should return to the psychologist's investigations into auditory streaming. Our ears are presented at every moment with an enormous perceptual task, which is to group sounds together in such a way as to make sense of them—either by assigning them to their causes, or by discovering what they mean. This 'auditory scene analysis', as Albert Bregman describes it, is carried on continuously, and

operates by amalgamating auditory episodes into temporal *Gestalten*.[9]
In certain applications this search for the good *Gestalt* can be explained
as the evolutionary epistemologist would explain it, namely as a first
step towards tracing a sound to its cause. However, it differs in a crucial
respect from the search for the good *visual Gestalt*.

Suppose you are looking at a dot-picture, and unable to make out the
figure that the dots compose. And suppose that suddenly the figure
'dawns' on you, and there, before you, in the unseen lines that join the
dots together, is the outline of a face. The joined-up *Gestalt* is unified by
a shape, and the shape is one that you recognize. It is quite clear how
this ability to amalgamate bits of visual information into a whole will
assist us in recognizing objects. For the perceptual *Gestalt* shares
properties, such as shape, size and colour, with its object, and the
emergence of a visual *Gestalt* involves conceptualizing visual experience in terms that the object too would fit. In describing the order of the
Gestalt you are unavoidably referring to an order of objects.

Auditory scene analysis is quite unlike that. Streams are not described
or recognized through properties that could be exhibited by the
physical events that produce them. Sounds which succeed each other on
the pitch continuum seem to 'flow' along the continuum; tones an
octave apart are heard as parts of a single tone (as when a congregation
sings a hymn in what sounds like unison). It seems that we have an
inherent tendency to group sound events as 'auditory figures', without
making bridges to the physical world.[10] In short, sounds are grouped
and streamed in ways that are unique to the sound world, and which
have no equivalent in the world of their physical causes. Another way
of putting the point is through the contrast between the visual and the
auditory field. The physical objects that cause my visual perceptions are
represented within my visual field: any description of the intentional
object of my experience is also a partial description of *them*. The
physical events that cause my auditory perceptions are not represented
within my auditory field, so a description of the intentional object is not
a description of the physical events. The auditory field, unlike the visual
field, does not depict its cause.[11]

Some examples will help to clarify the way in which sounds, as pure
events, can be detached in our experience from their physical causes.
Consider the octave illusion studied by Diana Deutsch.[12] In this
experiment headphones are placed over the subject's ears, and the notes
of a descending scale and an ascending scale played in each ear, in the
patterns shown on lines 1 and 2 (Ex. 1). The two ears therefore receive,
respectively, the inputs shown on lines 3 and 4. What they hear,

From Diana Deutsch

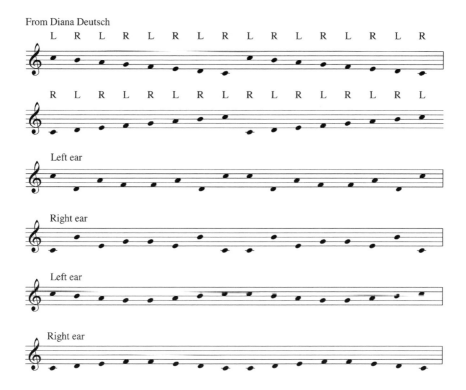

Example 1

however, are the two continuous sequences of lines 5 and 6. It is as though the sounds gravitate towards neighbours, where 'neighbourhood' is defined not by the physical proximity of the causative events, but by adjacent places on the pitch spectrum. Yet the sequences as heard are played into neither ear, and represent no causally unified process in the physical world. The auditory *Gestalt* is not merely incongruent with the physical events that produce it. It is organized according to principles that are intrinsic to the world of sounds, and which would be operative even if there were no physical events of the kind involved in sound-production.

Consider also the phenomenon of binaural beats. Beats occur when two tones of nearly equal frequency are sounded together, resulting in alternating increases and decreases in the amplitude of a sound-wave. They show a physical event clearly displayed in a sound event, and the temptation to describe the events as one and the same is perhaps never more strong than in such examples. The extraordinary fact, however, is that when the two tones are acoustically isolated from each other and sounded through headphones into separate ears, the subject still hears the beats.[13] Here is a sound event that can be traced to no physical cause that shares its salient feature, even though that feature has, in the normal case, a clear physical explanation.

The effect of such examples is not to cast doubt on the cognitive utility of the auditory *Gestalt*. Streaming is useful to us because, in the normal run of things, the streams that we hear correspond to causally unified processes. But the examples show that this correspondence is not *what* we hear, even when it *explains* what we hear. Moreover, they illustrate the way in which sounds are intrinsically ordered in our hearing, without reference to an order of physical objects and events.

The ability of pure events to stand in perceived relations to each other independent of any perceived relations between their causes is a deep presupposition of music, in which note follows note according to the internal logic of the musical line, giving rise to a virtual causality that has nothing to do with the process whereby the sounds are produced. That is not to say that the kind of 'streaming' that goes on in musical hearing is the same as the streaming of ordinary sound perception: in my view it is not, since it is shaped by spatial metaphors that are the product of a musical imagination.[14] Nevertheless, music is an extreme case of something that we witness throughout the sound world, which is the internal organization of sounds as pure events.

That is not to deny that auditory scene analysis is connected to the attempt to gather information about the physical events that cause us to hear sounds. It is rather to insist that sounds cannot be related easily to their causes by the perceiving ear, and are not imprinted, in the manner of visual images, with either the contours or the location of the things that produce them. If it is to make sense of the chaotic 'manifold' of impinging sound events, therefore, the ear must order them in ways that permit us to distinguish continuous processes from isolated events, simultaneous from complex sounds, and so on, without relying upon any observation of physical objects and their changes. That is precisely what is made possible, if sounds are pure events. For pure events contain within themselves the principles whereby they can be ordered—principles of aggregation and disaggregation, whereby events can be decomposed into smaller events, joined up into larger ones, and accorded precise relations in time, all by reference to the events themselves, and independently of any physical objects involved in producing them.

There is another matter that needs to be touched on in this

connection, which is the effect on hearing of the human voice. Aristotle makes the striking suggestion that the voice is distinct from all other objects of hearing since we hear it in another way.[15] First, he defines voice (*phonē*) as the kind of sound that is made by a creature with a *psuchē* – in other words, voice is the *sound of the soul*. Voice is also a 'kind of sound with meaning' (*semantikos . . . tis psophos estin hē phonē*)—voice is the *sound of meaning*. Aristotle's suggestive remarks gain some support from the following.

   (i) Unlike ambient sounds, vocal sounds are *addressed* to, and not merely heard by, others.

  (ii) They originate in, reveal and express a centre of consciousness—'a way the world seems'.

 (iii) They are, or include, language, and therefore exhibit grammatical order.

 (iv) Hence they convey information which is not (typically) information about their cause, but information about the world, encoded in their own symbolic structure.

All those features of vocal sounds make use, I believe, of their nature as secondary objects and pure events. It is because I order sounds according to intrinsic relations, to form longer sequences out of shorter, and separate streams out of a continuous babble, that I can hear sounds as addressed to me, ordered grammatically, and conveying a message from you to me about this or that. In hearing your voice I hear this kind of intrinsic sonic order, and attribute it not to the vocal chords or even to the body that contains them, but to you, as another subject. In an important way my grasp of your utterance by-passes the search for causes, on its way to a meaning that I can attribute directly to you. That is perhaps what Aristotle had in mind in saying that I hear the voice in another way: I hear it as detached from the natural order, so to speak, existing in a realm of pure communication. To put it in a more Hegelian idiom, speech sounds have been lifted from the world of objects into the world of subjects, and are intrinsically addressed from me to you and you to me. (Cf. Homer's metaphor of 'winged words'.) Hence the voice in the cinema calls the eye towards the person to whom it can be attached or, if there is no such person in view, to the perspective of an unseen observer.[16] The disembodied voice can *haunt* the cinematic image, so that it ceases to be a neutral scene awaiting action, and becomes somewhere 'seen by the unseen'.

Our way of hearing voices impinges elsewhere on our auditory experience. The experience of grammar inhabits our ears, so to speak, leading us to hear grammatical or quasi-grammatical order in all kinds of sequences that do not in fact exhibit it. The experience is particularly powerful in music, which often gives the impression of being addressed to us in something like the way in which speech is addressed to us, so that we turn to it with ears already attuned to meaning. This experience is an important motive for the view that music communicates states of mind by virtue of a quasi-semantic structure.

This brings me to the final reason for being dissatisfied with the physicalist theory of sounds, which is music. It seems to me that a theory of sounds ought to make sense not only of ordinary hearing, but also of all those special acts of attention of which sounds are the object. We hear sounds, just as animals hear them. We also listen to them, listen out for them, attend to them, and so on. All those mental acts could be accounted for, on the physicalist assumption, as acts directed towards physical vibrations. In the case of music, however, we hear an order which, while intrinsically auditory, is dependent on our ability to detach sounds entirely from their physical cause. This is the order granted by the acousmatic experience. Although this experience grows from and exploits the grouping, streaming and aggregating principles of ordinary hearing, it is also, I argue, shaped by an intentionality of its own. In conclusion I shall summarize views that I have argued for more completely in *The Aesthetics of Music*, by way of illustrating the way in which the peculiar metaphysical status of sounds endows them with the plasticity required by the musical experience.

The intentionality of perceptual experiences is determined by the concepts that inform them—either through perceptual beliefs or through acts of imagination. When listening to music we attend to sequences, simultaneities and complexes. But we hear distance, movement, space, closure. Those spatial concepts do not literally apply to the sounds that we hear. Rather they describe what we hear *in* sequential sounds, when we hear them as music. In other words the concepts that provide the fundamental framework for musical perception are applied figuratively, in the act of acousmatic attention.

In making sense of this imaginative transfer of concepts from the world of physical space to the world of tones we are obliged, I believe, to treat sounds as I have treated them: secondary objects which are also pure events. The sounds themselves form the ground in which we hear musical movement, in something like the way that the coloured patches on a canvas form the ground in which we see the face. This experience of movement is possible, however, only because sounds are heard to occupy places on the pitch spectrum. They map out distances and points on a one-dimensional continuum. They form recognizable auditory types, classified by timbre, pitch and duration. They define the boundaries of musical space, places where melodies begin and end, and so on.

Now the physicalist might say that, in describing those features of sounds I have merely described secondary qualities of physical vibrations. However, I believe that it is only because sounds are objects, all of whose properties lie in the realm of the audible, that they can be organized as tones. When so organized they serve to pin down the auditory space in something like the way in which physical objects pin down physical space, occupying places, moving between places and standing in spatial relations.

In hearing sounds as music we hear them as pure events that we can also reidentify—as when we recognize a melody sounding in another key, with another timbre, or at another pitch. And because we detach sounds in imagination from their physical causes they become individuals for us, with a life of their own. They can amalgamate with other such pure events to produce larger events; they can divide and fragment; they can occur in the background or the foreground, on top or underneath, augmented and diminished, half hidden, ornamented, varied and implied. In hearing sounds in this way we rely at every point upon our ability to deal with them as pure events, while neither reflecting on nor hypothesizing the background causality from which they arise.

Notes

1 An earlier version of this chapter was read by David Wiggins, Bob Grant, Barry Smith and Matthew Nudds, to all of whom I am grateful for criticisms and suggestions. The chapter is condensed from a much longer paper to be published in Casey O'Callaghan and Matthew Nudds, eds, *Sounds and Perception: New Philosophical Essays*, Oxford 2009.
2 Roberto Casati and Jérôme Dokic, *La philosophie du son*, Jacqueline Chambon, Nîmes 1994. Casey O'Callaghan, in *Sounds: A Philosophical Theory*, Oxford 2007, argues that sound-events are 'object-involving' though they do not strictly take place in the object, consisting as they do in a disturbance that occurs at the interface of a source and a medium.
3 R. Pasnau, 'What is sound?', *Philosophical Quarterly* 49 (1999), 309–24, and 'Sensible qualities: the case of sound', *Journal of the History of Philosophy* 38 (2000), 27–40. Locke's suggestion occurs at *Essay* II, viii.
4 Having a sound, however, is a property. For example, it is a property of a jar that it has a certain sound (when sounded). The relation between having a sound and emitting a sound when struck or otherwise disturbed is discussed by Aristotle in *De Anima*, 419b–421a.
5 See S. A. Gelfand, *Hearing: An Introduction to Psychological and Physiological Acoustics*, 3rd edn, New York 1998.
6 Albert S. Bregman, *Auditory Scene Analysis*, Cambridge, Mass. 1990, 1999, p. 138.

7 The use of the term 'acousmatic' in this context (borrowed from the Pythagoreans) is due to Pierre Schaeffer, *Traité des objects musicaux*, Paris 1966, and has been taken up e.g. by me in *The Aesthetics of Music*, Oxford 1997, and by Michel Chion, *La voix au cinéma*, Paris 1982, tr. Claudia Gorbman, *The Voice in Cinema*, New York 1999.

8 *Op. cit.* p. 179.

9 Albert S. Bregman, *Auditory Scene Analysis*, *op. cit.*

10 P. L. Divenyi and I. J. Hirsh, 'Some figural properties of auditory patterns', *Journal of the Acoustical Society of America*, 64 (1978), 1369–86; Bregman, *op. cit.*, p. 141.

11 The picture theory of the visual field, which derives from J. J. Gibson (e.g. 'The visual field and the visual world', *Psychological Review* 59 (1952), 149–51), reflects a basic truth about vision, which is that it is spatially organized, in the manner of visible things.

12 Diana Deutsch, 'Grouping mechanisms in music', in D. Deutsch, ed., *The Psychology of Music*, New York 1982.

13 See Gefland, *op. cit.*, p. 373, and sources cited therein.

14 See Chapter 4 below.

15 *De Anima* 420b.

16 See the illuminating discussion in Michel Chion, *The Voice in Cinema*, *op. cit.*

3

Wittgenstein on music

The philosophy of music is big business in the Anglophone academy, with books and articles on the subject emerging every month. But the later Wittgenstein is rarely mentioned in these publications. On the surface this is strange. For Wittgenstein was probably the most musical, and certainly the most musically educated, of all the great philosophers after Al-Fârâbî. He also wrote about music (in *The Lectures on Aesthetics* and here and there in *Philosophical Investigations*, *Remarks on the Philosophy of Psychology* and *Culture and Value*), and directly identified one of the problems in the philosophy of music that is not a general problem of aesthetics: the problem of musical understanding. True, his remarks about this are too fleeting to constitute an argument. But that doesn't distinguish them from his remarks about virtually everything else.

The failure to discuss these fleeting remarks seems less strange when we see Wittgenstein's contribution in its historical context. Analytical philosophy of music has grown around the question of musical meaning, which became articulated, during the twentieth century, in ways that were inimical to Wittgenstein's vision. It is true that Suzanne Langer's theory of musical meaning in *Philosophy in a New Key* is explicitly derived from Wittgenstein. But her source is the Wittgenstein of the *Tractatus*, whose theory of logical form she puts to stunning and outrageous use, in order to articulate a new version of the Croce-Collingwood theory of expression.

That instance apart, discussions of musical meaning have followed the path laid down by Hanslick and Gurney in the nineteenth century, debating whether music is capable of expressing, representing or in some other way conveying extra-musical emotions, and whether—if so—this is an important part of its value. Musical meaning has been seen, in other words, as a relation between music and something else. For Wittgenstein it is either not a relation at all, or at best an 'internal relation', in the idealist's sense: a relation that denies the separateness of the things it joins.

In his later philosophy Wittgenstein awakens to the true importance of Frege's insight, that we can speak of meaning only where we can also speak of understanding.[1] The meaning of a sentence is what we understand when we understand it. Constraints on understanding are therefore constraints on meaning. We cannot give a sign a meaning, merely by associating it with an object, event or property. The connection has to be made in the understanding of those who use the sign, and this understanding is part of a complex social process.

This observation applies to music too. If music has meaning, then that meaning must be understood by the one who understands the music. Hence the concept of musical understanding displaces that of musical meaning: we have no idea what musical meaning might be, until we have some grasp of the distinction between the one who hears with understanding and the one who merely hears. If understanding music were like understanding a language, then musical meaning would be given by a semantic interpretation. But the analogy with language is no more than an analogy. Linguistic signs are entirely conventional, and their semantic properties are governed by a generative grammar. Neither of those things is true of music, not even of serial music, composed according to what seems to be a rigid and quasi-grammatical convention.[2]

In many places where Wittgenstein raises the question of musical understanding he connects it with two other subjects that obsessed him: facial expressions, and the first-person case. His greatest contribution to philosophy, it seems to me, lies in his discussion of first-person ascriptions of mental states, and especially in his argument for the impossibility of a 'private language'. His tantalizing remarks on facial expressions have been less influential, although they too constitute an important contribution to philosophy. The following sections from *Culture and Value* show the way in which the three issues of musical understanding, facial expression and the first-person case get connected:

What does it consist in: following a musical phrase with understanding? Contemplating a face with a feeling for its expression (*mit dem Gefühl für seinen Ausdruck*)? Drinking in the expression on the face?

Think of the demeanour of someone drawing a face in a way that shows understanding for its expression. Think of the sketcher's face, his movements—what shows that every stroke he makes is dictated by the face, that nothing in his drawing is arbitrary, that he is a fine instrument?

Is that really an *experience* (*Erlebnis*)? What I mean is: can this be said to express an experience?

Once again: what is it to follow a musical phrase with understanding, or to play it with understanding? Don't look inside yourself. Consider rather what makes you say of someone else that this is what he is doing. And what prompts you to say that he is having a particular experience? For that matter, do we actually ever say this? Wouldn't I be more likely to say of someone else that he's having a whole host of experiences?

Perhaps I would say, "He is experiencing the theme intensely"; but consider how this is manifested.

Those sections connect directly with Wittgenstein's 'third-person' approach to philosophical psychology. The burden of the argument in *Philosophical Investigations* Part 1 is that neither the sense nor the reference of mental predicates can be specified from a consideration merely of the first-person case. We learn to apply mental predicates by connecting them to the expressions, gestures, behaviour and circumstances of people (and presumably other animals). While there is such a thing as a 'first-person perspective' on my own mental state, this does not reveal to me some private fact, hidden from the publicly observable world. It is a perspective on the very same thing that you observe, when you see that I am thinking, angry or in pain. I learn what this thing is by sharing in the public discourse, which enables me to recognize your states of mind and to give them a name.

Although there are no 'first-person' facts about the mind, there is certainly first-person knowledge, and this knowledge is irreducible to any knowledge that might be gained from the third-person perspective. First person knowledge is knowledge of 'what it is like'. This is not a species of knowing *that*, nor a species of knowing *how*: it is in fact entirely *sui generis*, and might be described as 'knowledge by acquaintance', in order to emphasize that it is not knowledge *of* a fact, but familiarity *with* it.

Wittgenstein's hostility to the Cartesian habit of 'looking inwards' in order to discover the meaning of a word, the reality of an experience, or the sense of a work of art, is revealed in the second section quoted above. In effect he is saying that we can never discover what we mean by musical understanding from our own case alone. We must look at the publicly observable facts which lead us to describe another as understanding what he hears. And Wittgenstein implies that musical understanding is importantly like understanding a facial expression, and is displayed in similar ways.

Wittgenstein's emphasis on the concept of musical understanding does not only reflect the influence of Frege. It is part of a complex response to musical modernism. Wittgenstein had been a modernist in

Example 1

architecture, following Loos in the bid to purify and decongest the lines of the classical style. But he was not a modernist in music. Many of his remarks suggest that he believed musical modernism (at least in its more austere varieties) to involve a mistake about the nature of listening. When I listen to a piece written in the idiom of twelve-tone serialism I may recognize that all the notes of the series have been exhausted except one—G sharp, say. I then know that G sharp *must* follow. And someone might be misled into thinking that this is just like the case of someone listening to a piece in the classical style, who hears it settle on a dominant seventh, and therefore is led to expect the tonic. Musical understanding is in each case a matter of grasping the way in which one musical event compels the next one. And satisfaction comes from perceiving order and discipline in what, from the acoustic perspective, is no more than a sequence of sounds.

In fact, however, the knowledge that G sharp must follow, in my hypothetical example, is no sign of musical understanding. I can have this knowledge, even if the passage makes no sense to me. And it can make sense to me, even though I have no knowledge that G sharp is required by the grammar. The grammar of twelve-tone music is not a musical grammar. If someone tells me that he does not understand, say, the opening theme of Schoenberg's Violin Concerto, it does not help to show how it is derived from the two hexachords of Schoenberg's series, by assigning the remaining notes to the lower strings. From the musical point of view this may sound entirely arbitrary. (And those chords on the lower strings *are* musically arbitrary, and weaken the impact of the melody. They are there to 'use up the series', and have nothing to say of their own. Ex. 1.)

The development of atonal and serial music brought out, for ordinary listeners, the difference between music that they don't understand, and music that they do. And no amount of theorizing, no number of self-imposed rules, conventions and constraints, will enable them to pass from one condition to the other. Musical understanding is not a form of theoretical understanding, and the kind of necessity that we hear in a musical phrase or sequence, when we hear that it *must* be so, is not the kind of necessity that we know from rule-following or mathematical proof.

So why do we speak of musical understanding, and what kind of knowledge is conveyed by it? This is the question at the back of Wittgenstein's mind in the passages quoted, and it is a question that is both immensely difficult and fundamental to musical aesthetics. We can agree with Wittgenstein that we are not going to find an answer to this question by looking inwards. But we may doubt that he has given us a clear alternative. At various points he remarks on the analogies between music and language—a phrase may sound like a question; a cadence may have the character of a semi-colon or a full stop, and so on. But, as he himself recognizes, these analogies refer to things that we 'hear in' the music, when we hear with understanding. They do not enable us to know what understanding music really is, since we need a theory of understanding to make proper sense of the analogy. 'Hearing in' is precisely the kind of experience that we are trying to explain.

Indeed, if we adopt the third-person perspective that Wittgenstein recommends, the differences between understanding music and understanding language become far more obvious than the similarities. A person demonstrates his understanding of a word by using it, according to syntactical and semantic rules. A person might similarly show his understanding of a piece of music by performing it, and to that extent the analogy with language holds. But most of us are not performers, and ours is a listening culture. It is in listening, not playing, that the average musical person exhibits understanding, and without listeners performance would lack its *raison d'être* (even if sometimes the only listeners are the performers).

Moreover, musical understanding is not revealed in performance in the way that linguistic understanding is revealed in speech. A person who speaks woodenly, unfeelingly, grotesquely, may nevertheless show that he has understood the words he utters. A person who performs woodenly, unfeelingly or grotesquely may make all the sounds prescribed by the score, but he will show nevertheless that he has understood nothing. Musical understanding is a form of aesthetic understanding: it is manifest in the conscious search for the right phrasing, the right dynamics, the right tempo. And the listener too distinguishes right from wrong ways of playing, even when acknowledging that no mistakes are being made.

But it is not only the performance that is being judged: there is the music itself. Wittgenstein asks 'What is it to follow a musical phrase with understanding, or to play it with understanding?' Doesn't it depend on the phrase? A corny, sentimental or insinuating passage can be performed naively by the one who identifies with its phony idiom; but another performer, who hears the pretence, will be unable to perform the passage naively. He will send it up, place discreet inverted commas around the most offensive phrases, give it the air of a joke, so as to turn bad taste to good in a spirit of satire. (Think of how you would play 'Angel of Music' from Lloyd Webber's *Phantom of the Opera*, for instance.) Which of these performers understands the music? Well, you might say, they understand it differently. But then the one who has seen through to its real meaning is precisely the one who cannot play it as it was intended: his performance is really a way of discounting the passage, as you might discount someone's words by instantly quoting them in a tone of irony.

The same happens with listening. Consider two people listening to a grossly sentimental song, one naively enjoying it, the other turning up his nose. The first says to the second: 'you just don't understand this music'. 'On the contrary,' the second replies, 'I do understand it. And that is why I hate it.' Do we say that they have both understood the music, but understood it differently? Or that one has misunderstood it, since he has not seen what it means?

Here we might have recourse to the other subject that Wittgenstein puts in play in the passages quoted: the subject of facial expressions. Wittgenstein wishes to say that understanding a passage of music is in some way like understanding a facial expression. And he suggests that someone could show this understanding in the way that he draws the face. He describes a person intent on drawing, becoming a 'fine instrument', attending to every detail of what he sees. But is that right? Surely you could be an expert at transcribing the observable features of a face, and yet miss the expression, and vice versa. (Picasso could capture an expression in a few lines and an eye; photographs capture everything, except the expression.) The problem here is that the account verges on circularity. The fine instrument is the one that transcribes *expressions*, not the one that notices everything *else*.

Nevertheless, the point bears on the problem of music. For it is certainly true that two people can understand a person's expression and yet react to it differently. The grim disaffection on the face of the teenage pop-star, for example, is understood equally by the one who identifies with its pseudo-defiant aura, and by the one who is repelled by it. It is not that they understand the expression differently; it is rather that they understand it in the same way, and react differently.

An expression is not understood by diagnosis. We do not grasp an expression by discovering something else (a mood, emotion or attitude) which is related to it as content to form. The expression is understood by a spontaneous act of recognition, which might be conveyed as well by an answering expression or gesture as by some appropriate description in words. The difference between the two people in my example *may* reside in a different diagnosis. One person sees the expression on the pop-star's face as a sign of *Weltschmerz*, the other sees it as a sign of belligerent narcissism. Equally, however, people can understand an expression differently, even when neither is disposed to identify a state of mind that the expression supposedly conveys.

We might say that the face has a *particular expression* which both observers recognize; and also that it is the expression of a *particular character or state of mind*, concerning which the two observers differ. The term 'expression' can therefore be used in two ways—on the one hand to denote a property or aspect of the face; on the other hand to denote a relation between the face and a mental state. Wittgenstein's remarks about expression, both here and in the *Lectures on Aesthetics*,[3] suggest that the first, non-relational, sense of the term is more important in aesthetics. He likens understanding music to grasping expression in this non-relational sense; and seems to be implying that we make a mistake if we think that we understand music by diagnosing what is expressed by it. When we speak of 'recognizing the expression' in a piece of music, or playing with expression, the term 'expression' is being used 'intransitively'.[4]

This point touches on another of Wittgenstein's interests: that in aspects. Facial expressions are not aspects; but they are like aspects in that they are perceivable only to beings like us, who can understand the world as replete with symbols and signs. Expressions can be ambiguous in something like the way that aspects can be ambiguous. And they are supervenient on the first-order properties of a face in just the way that aspects are supervenient on the first-order properties of a picture. To understand an expression is to grasp a *Gestalt*, and to attribute to that *Gestalt* a social currency. You fit the expression into the game of human faces, aligning it with this one, distancing it from that one. And each expression marks out a field of possible responses—it has a valency, so to speak, reaching out for the human response that will complete it.

To return to the example of the sentimental song. It seems to me that the naive performer and the stern critic may both, up to a point, understand it. Its musical personality comes across equally to both of them. But understanding does not, and should not, stop at this first stage of recognition. The case is similar to that of facial expressions. We do not merely recognize expressions. We look behind them to what they mean. We seek and find character, mood and emotion in faces, as we do in gestures and words. And if understanding music is like understanding facial expressions it too must admit of this search for a meaning beyond the immediate *Gestalt*.

For this reason, it seems to me, Wittgenstein's comparison of musical and physiognomic understanding does not have the implication that he seems to draw from it, which is that musical expression is confined to the intransitive idea. For Wittgenstein the crucial fact lies in the 'recognition of expression', rather than the perception of a state of mind that lies behind the expression, and which is revealed in it. Likewise in understanding music, the crucial fact, for Wittgenstein, lies in an act of recognition, comparable to grasping the expression on a face, rather than in any familiarity with the state of mind expressed.

But why does the 'recognition of expression' (in the intransitive sense) have such importance for us? Surely because it is the vital first move in understanding other people—in grasping what they think, feel or mean. Likewise in art, the act of recognition is the first stage in a process of imaginative involvement, the end point of which is familiarity with a character or a state of mind. If Wittgenstein appears in places to deny this, it is because of his severe attitude to the first-person case. In his anxiety to prevent us from 'looking inwards', he fails to see that you can be looking outwards and yet gaining first-person knowledge.

This happens with faces in the following way. When we understand the expression on a face it acquires, for us, an individuality, a personality, which readies us for the human encounter. Not understanding an expression means not seeing where it fits into our gallery of portraits, and therefore not knowing how to encounter the person whom it prefigures. But once we have understood we are drawn in: we preconsciously imitate the facial gestures. We come to 'know what it's like' to have a face like that. And this knowledge from within offers a first-person perspective on another's life. This experience is very like the 'dawning of an aspect' that Wittgenstein studies in *Philosophical Investigations* Part 2 section xi. In particular it is subject to the will. I can decide to enter into another's expression; or I can decide to remain outside it, so to speak, and to see it as a thing apart.

When we enter into another's physiognomy in this way we begin to imagine his states of mind. We don't necessarily have words for these states of mind, and our familiarity with them is purely a form of 'imagining what it's like'—the imaginative equivalent of first-person knowledge. But by focusing on the other's features and gestures we find these states of mind unfolding within us—not really felt, but entertained in imagination. This is why the face is so important to us: it is the window into another self. The recognition of expression is the first stage in the process whereby we recreate in ourselves the first-person viewpoint of another. We become familiar with states of mind that we cannot necessarily name, but which we know from within, as we know our own emotions. This, surely, is part of what makes a belligerent or contemptuous face so repulsive: not that we can name the emotions that speak from it, but that we are offered sudden glimpses of what it's like to respond to the world in that way.

Wittgenstein is surely right to think that there is a primary act of musical understanding comparable to the understanding of a facial expression. We hear the melody of 'Angel of Music' and it is at once a personality for us. It has the come-hitherishness of a baby in a loo-paper advert: 'only a world without embarrassments could contain a thing so sweet'. We can turn away from this, with a sarcastic performance that sets it at a distance. But we may also be seduced. And then we become the music, while the music lasts. Into our own first person perspective there creeps a phony state of mind that sits uncomfortably with our sense of who we are. It is surely one of the roles of taste or aesthetic judgement to discriminate between the expression with which we might identify, and the expression that invites us to sympathize with a state of mind that in our better moments we seek to shun. But this discrimination would be impossible if we did not advance, in our thinking, from the intransitive to the transitive idea of expression.

Wittgenstein was aware of this, as is shown by his unflattering remarks in *Culture and Value* about Mahler, whose music he dismissed as entirely worthless. It is hard for us to agree with those remarks, but not hard to see why Wittgenstein made them. Mahler himself was conscious of the problem, and even sought the help of Freud in overcoming it. Those sweet *Ländler* melodies and open horn chords, those distant trumpets and *faux-naïf* up-beats: do they not invite us to wallow in griefs and longings that lack the seriousness that griefs and longings should have? At least we can recognize that Mahler is, for us as for himself, a problem, and that this problem can be fully understood only if we allow ourselves a richer conception of musical understanding than Wittgenstein, in his more austere remarks, is prepared to offer. That richer conception requires us not to dismiss the first-person case, but to give a fuller account of it—to recognize that there is such a thing as first-person knowledge, even if the object of that knowledge must be described (should we wish to describe it) from the third-person perspective.

And that, I suggest, is why music criticism is so hard. As Wittgenstein rightly reminds us, we cannot find the meaning of a piece of music by looking inwards. Nevertheless, even if we are looking outwards, our ability to understand what we are looking at depends on what is happening within. To give a full account of musical understanding, therefore, we must go beyond Wittgenstein's laconic comparison with the recognition of facial expressions. We must see music as an act of communication, which crucially depends upon placing within the listener's first-person perspective a state of mind that is not his own.

Notes

1 The implications of this insight are spelled out by Michael Dummett, *Frege: Philosophy of Language*, Oxford 1971.
2 The attempt to give a generative syntax for tonal music has been made by Fred Lerdahl and Ray Jackendoff in *A Generative Theory of Tonal Music*, Cambridge, Mass. 1983; I criticize the attempt in *The Aesthetics of Music*, Oxford 1997, Chapter 7.
3 *Lectures and Conversations on Aesthetics, Freud and Religious Belief*, ed. Cyril Barrett, Oxford 1966.
4 Though it is true that Wittgenstein often attributes the ambiguity between a 'transitive' and 'intransitive' use to the term 'particular', in 'particular expression', as in *The Blue and Brown Books*, Oxford 1960, p. 162. See the argument in my article on 'Expression', in the *New Grove Dictionary of Music*, ed. Stanley Sadie, London 1982 *et seq.*

4

Movement

In *The Aesthetics of Music* I make the claim that musical movement (such as we hear in a melody) must be explained in spatial terms: the melody moves from one place to another in a one-dimensional continuum. I also claim that when melodies sound, nothing that we hear literally moves. For what we hear are pitched sounds, played successively, not sounds that can be identified as numerically the same, now at one pitch, now at another.

I reconcile those two claims by suggesting that the musical experience —like much aesthetic experience—has 'double intentionality'. You hear a succession of sounds, ordered in time, and this is something you believe to be occurring—something you 'literally hear'. And you hear *in* those sounds a melody that moves through the imaginary space of music. This is not something you believe to be occurring, but something you imagine: just as you imagine the face in the picture, while seeing that it is not literally there. Double intentionality, I suggest, is explained by our ability to organize a single *Gestalt* in two ways simultaneously—in one way as something literally present, in another way as something imagined. The literal perception and the imaginative perception can cohabit the same experience, since they do not compete. To clarify this further requires a theory of imagination, such as I tried to develop in *Art and Imagination*. But one way to understand the point is through the contrast between literal and figurative uses of a predicate. Your experience of the music involves the concept of movement, but it is a concept that is being metaphorically applied to what is literally a sequence. Explaining music this way, I claim, you can begin to grasp the distinction between sound and tone, the nature of harmony and counterpoint, and the gravitational force that is at work in the musical stave.

Malcolm Budd has mounted an interesting challenge to all that.[1] His argument seems to me to involve the following claims:

(a) The concept of 'double intentionality' stands in need of clarification.

(b) It is not clear what is meant by saying that an experience 'involves' a metaphor.

(c) It is not possible to hear a movement in musical space, since this would require us to hear one pitched sound as moving to another place on the pitch-continuum. But we can make no sense of that, since the sound cannot move to another pitch and still remain the same. It is as though C were to move to E flat, say, and still be C.

(d) Such spatial terms as we do apply to music—'high', 'low', 'dense', 'spaced', 'moving towards', 'away from', and so on—are not necessary to describing the features of music that we have in mind. Hence they (or their applications) are not 'part of the musical experience' as I claim.

(e) We can understand musical movement in another and better way, as a feature of a purely temporal *Gestalt*: it is a movement in time, with a beginning and end, which is not a movement in space.

Here, in briefest summary, is my response:

(a) It is true that 'double intentionality' stands in need of clarification. Single intentionality is hard enough! Those who have written about the problem have noted the phenomenon, given it a label, and then moved on. Wollheim, for example, in *Painting as an Art*, offers us the distinction between *seeing* and *seeing in*, but stops short of clarifying how these radically different mental acts can actually be united in a single experience.[2] I attempt to clarify the point in *Art and Imagination*, by arguing that the thoughts which identify the content of 'aspect perception' (my term for 'seeing in') are unasserted, whereas those in a normal perception are asserted. I still think there is mileage in this idea, since it connects with an important insight of Frege's concerning propositional content.

Imagination, I suggest, is the capacity, which all rational beings exhibit to some degree, to entertain thoughts without affirming or asserting them, and to create an order among those thoughts which makes each in some way answerable or appropriate to the others. It is a cognitive capacity which, unlike belief or desire, is directly subject to the will. ('Imagine that *p*!' is a sensible order; 'Believe that *p*!' is not.) It may or may not involve imagery, though not all imagery is an exercise of the imagination: dreams and hallucinations, for example, are 'impressions' that severely limit one's freedom to alter or dissent from them. ('See a dagger before your eyes!', 'Dream of Kitty!' are neither of them sensible orders.) Imagination, as I envisage it, is a response to the question 'what if . . . ?'. And it involves the construction of an imaginary world by unfolding a narrative, whether in literary form, as in a play or a novel, or in visual form, as in a painting. The relation of imagination to belief, I suggest, can best be understood in terms of two contrasts: that between unasserted and asserted sentences, and that between active and passive mental states—states which are, and states which are not, subject to the will. And Frege's proof that assertion is no part of the meaning of a sentence implies that when someone imagines that p, and when he believes that p, he is in one case imagining exactly what in the other case he is believing. Hence, what we learn from the imagination we might also apply in life.

Double intentionality arises when a mental state involves both belief and imagination: the first focused on realities, the second on what can be imagined in those realities. And because they belong to different orders of mental organization, beliefs and imaginings can co-exist, with a common focus, so that the one informs and controls the other: that, in short, is the origin of the 'double intentionality' that governs our experience of art.

(b) I admit that this does not give us any final grasp of what it is for an experience to 'involve' a metaphor. But here we are up against a kind of bedrock. Kant was probably the first philosopher to recognize that the empiricist account of experience is untenable, since experience has both a sensory and an intellectual component—there is the 'intuition', located in time, and the atemporal 'concept' that somehow informs it. But when it came to saying how the two are joined, Kant referred to a 'transcendental synthesis': a process that does not take place in time and which is therefore not a process. A better way of putting Kant's point is surely to say that the reference to the concept is presupposed in any attempt to identify the intuition, even though the concept can be identified independently, through thought alone.

So here is how I would explain the term 'involves': in just the way that seeing a dog as a dog involves the concept *dog*, so does seeing a dog in a picture involve the concept *dog*. In the first case, however, the concept is applied in a judgement, in the second it is applied in an 'unasserted thought', and therefore figuratively. The judgement that there is a dog before me informs the one experience in the same way that the unasserted thought of a dog before me informs the other. And in something like that way we apply the concept of movement in hearing a melody, but apply it to things (namely pitched sounds) which (as *we also hear*) do not and cannot exemplify it.

(c) Hence I agree with Budd's point (c), and regard it as a proof of my position. It doesn't make sense to say that C moves to E flat and thence to G. If the spatial metaphor were to imply that we hear pitched sounds as moving along the pitch-continuum then it would be setting our ears an impossible task. However, we must distinguish sound from tone. The first is a physical event, occurring in the ordinary three-dimensional space in which we too exist. The second is an intentional object, one that we hear in a sound, but which has properties that no sound can have: for example direction, energy, a kind of internal 'wanting', together with relations of attraction and repulsion towards other tones.

When we hear tones in the pitched sounds we may also hear a melody: the first subject of Beethoven's 3rd Piano Concerto, say, which starts on C, moves to E flat, and on to G, before going step-wise back to C. Our way of hearing melodies implies that we identify the pitches as places through which the music moves, not as items which are themselves in motion. Of course the melody doesn't *literally* move; and it isn't *literally* there. But we hear it all the same, by virtue of our capacity to hear metaphorically—in other words to organize our experience in terms of concepts that we do not literally apply.

(d) I hold on to that position partly because I profoundly disagree with Budd's suggestion that the spatial metaphor is dispensable, which is what is implied by his view that spatial metaphors do not feature in the experience of music at the 'foundational level'.[3] We *have* to hear up and down, towards and away, soaring, plunging, coincidence, distance, density, proximity, mirroring, inversion, forwards, backwards, same direction, and so on, if we are to make sense, not just of the classical tradition of harmony and counterpoint, but even of the basic phenomenon of melisma. The proof that this is so is not easy to give: but you could read *The Aesthetics of Music* as an attempt at proof. I try to show that, from this description of the intentional object of musical perception, you can derive an account of the nature, meaning and value of music. Maybe such an account can be derived without starting from the spatial metaphor. But it is a metaphor that gives us a head start in the attempt to understand how music works—how it works, in other words, on *us*.

(e) As to Budd's rival suggestion, I don't see it as a rival. For what exactly is meant by a 'merely temporal' movement? What is supposed to move, from where to where? If this is not a metaphor, I don't know what is. Indeed, I think it is the very same metaphor as the one that I am trying to explicate—the metaphor of movement, applied to a succession in which nothing literally moves. I don't doubt that there are ways of making sense of the merely temporal *Gestalt* that do not involve the concept of movement. At some pre-conceptual level experience is organized into temporal chunks, which could be broken down into their component parts but which are experienced as unified wholes. But this level, I believe, lies below the experience of music, in the world that we share with tone-deaf people and with animals. (On this point, see further Chapter 6 below.)

Suppose, however, that my account of metaphorical perception is false, and suppose that there is some other and maybe more literal way of construing the reference to musical movement. Does this undermine my claim, that the world of music is a virtual world, with spatial, causal and dynamic characteristics that are detached from things and causes in physical space? I think not, and it is worth saying why.

When we hear music, three things occur. There is a vibration in the air; by virtue of this vibration we hear a sound, which is a 'secondary object', heard as a pure event; and in this sound we hear an organization that is not reducible to any properties of the sound, nor to any properties of the vibration that causes it. As a result of hearing this organization we may also feel an urge to move in time to the music, to dance or sing along with it. Or we may, on the contrary, fall into a rapt silence, listening from a state of motionless attention. Hearing sound involves an exercise of the ear: it displays an *acoustic* capacity, and all that we hear when we hear sounds are the properties of sound events. Animals also hear these properties, and respond to sounds and to the information contained in sounds. But to hear music we need capacities that only rational beings have. We must be able to hear an order that contains no information about the physical world, which stands apart from the ordinary workings of cause and effect, and which is irreducible to any physical organization. At the same time, it contains a virtual causality of its own, which animates the elements that are joined by it. The first note of the melody brings the second into being, even though the first sound is produced by someone blowing on a horn at one end of the orchestra, the second by someone pulling a bow across a cello string at the other.

The reason for speaking of *movement* in musical space, is that both melodic and harmonic relations can be described in this way without ambiguity, while capturing the character of the changes in which they are involved. In Ex. 2, Chapter 1 (p. 16), I described the upper voice as moving *from* G *to* F sharp. And I suggested that the upper voice moves in this way because of the *gravitational pull* of the tonic. The resulting chord is full, without internal tension, whereas the first chord, treated as a sus chord in jazz, is hollow, with sharp edges, occupying musical space in a nervous, dissatisfied manner. Sure, those are all metaphors. But they fit together, endorse one another, give a continuous idiom in terms of which we can say all that we want to say about the *musical* potential of the elements that we hear. But suppose we discard the spatial metaphor, and find some other idiom. It will still be necessary, in that idiom, to capture the phenomena to which I have just referred if we are to describe the musical potential of the chords in Ex. 2. We would still need some way of characterizing the transition from G to F sharp which will capture the influence on that G of the dissonant A below it, and of the tonic sounded in the bass. Nothing that we can identify in the acoustic properties of sounds will enable us to capture what is going on here, since it will precisely leave out of account the fact that there is something *going on*, that one tone is *influencing* another, and that things are changing in obedience to fields of force that emanate from other musical objects. The world of sounds contains no such influences, no such changes, no such fields of force. Drop the spatial metaphor, if you like, but you still have the task of representing this strange world of virtual forces which opens to the musical ear, and which is forever inaccessible to the ear of an animal, since only a creature with imagination can hear it.

Notes

1 Malcolm Budd, 'Musical movement and aesthetic metaphors', *British Journal of Aesthetics*, 2003.
2 Richard Wollheim, *Painting as an Art*, London 1987.
3 *Op. cit.*, p. 222.

5

Expression

In a recent review the composer and critic Robin Holloway wrote thus of Schubert:

Schubert is at the very heart of music. More: definition of what he is, account of what he did, in music, are tantamount to a description of music itself in its most normative and widely shared sense—what it is, how it works, what it is *for.* No composer is less dispensable, more essential and intrinsic. 'Essential' meaning closest to the art's grammar, syntax, language, which he employs with extraordinary purity and exactness even while they undergo in his hands the most radical extensions ever made by one individual. Their purpose, of course, to expand, to deepen, intensify expression: to which the same superlative applies—no other single composer has added so largely to what music, in its innate nature, not foisted upon it, can *say.* This is just as essential and intrinsic as the linguistic usage. They can't be separated: the wider key-relationships, the major/minor ambiguity, the enharmonics, the enhanced dissonances, equally with the exploration of the most basic facts of diatonicism, and every motive, melodic, rhythmic, textural element; all this is in such perfect fusion with the affective ends that he has to be called Apollonian, whatsoever is being expressed—amiable/convivial, frenzied, doom-laden, *angstvoll*, erotic, pantheistic, radiant, desolate, God-forsaken, weary-unto-death, furious, frustrated, fragmented, nihilistic, nostalgic, or just *cold*! Many more words could thus be adduced, for Schubert covers a wider range of emotion than any other composer and most other artists in any medium; but they would be mere signs and ciphers apart from the way their every nuance within the comprehensive coverage is imprinted into the notes.[1]

The passage is written from the heart, and I doubt that there is a musical person who will not be disposed to agree with it. This *is* the genius of Schubert, that he is able to express the whole range of human emotions, and to do so by 'imprinting' those emotions 'into the notes'. But what exactly does that last phrase mean, and why is it important?

In *The Aesthetics of Music* I argued that a theory of musical expression must pass certain tests if it is to establish a real relation between music and our states of mind. There are four of these tests, which I summarized as follows:

(1) The 'semaphore test'. Musical meaning is not established by convention, assigning meanings to musical objects in the manner of a code of semaphore signals. The meaning of a work of music is given only in the aesthetic experience, and is not available simply by applying rules.

(2) The 'understanding test'. The meaning of a piece of music is what we understand when we understand it as music. (This parallels a well-known thought of Frege's concerning the meaning of a sentence.) Most existing accounts of expression fail to pass this test—or at least, fail to show that they can pass it. We just do not know what is proved by them, or whether anything important is being said—for instance by Peter Kivy, when he points to the way in which the shape of a musical phrase may 'resemble' the shape of an emotion.[2] As I pointed out in Chapter 3, it was Wittgenstein's important insight that the key concept in the philosophy of music is not that of expression or meaning, but that of understanding.

(3) The 'value test'. A piece of music expresses something only if it is *expressive*, and expressiveness is an aesthetic value. An empty piece of music (Vivaldi's C Major Mandolin Concerto, for example) is the worse for its emptiness; a piece of music that *expresses* emptiness (the Prelude to Act 3 of *Tristan und Isolde*, for example) is all the better for its expressive power. It succeeds in communicating something, while the merely empty piece communicates nothing.

(4) The 'structure test'. The expressive quality of a musical work is developed through the music, and the elaboration of the musical line is at the same time an elaboration of the content. Expression does not reside in some passing resemblance or aspect: it is brought into being through the musical line, and worked into the musical structure. (This is what Holloway means, in saying that every nuance of emotion in Schubert is 'imprinted into the notes'.)

The difficulties presented to a theory of expression by those tests are compounded by two further observations. First, it seems quite possible to understand an expressive piece of music and at the same time to deny that it is expressive—or at least, to deny that there is anything, besides itself, that the music means. The defence of music as an 'absolute' art, as one which achieves a pristine self-containment and objectivity, has been conducted by people like Hanslick and Stravinsky, who understood music as well as any of their opponents.

Secondly, and relatedly, we find it almost impossible, and in any case hardly necessary, to detach the meaning from the music and to give it a name. The meaning resides in the music, and—while we have a concept of the 'identity of expression'— it is only in very special circumstances that we are prepared to apply it, and to admit that two separate works of music might express the same thing. *Identifying* the content seems to have little or no role in the appreciation of music. This fact lies behind our frequent adoption of the 'intransitive' concept of expression which I discussed earlier in connection with Wittgenstein.

My contention is that, if we are to develop a concept of expression which passes those four stringent tests, and which also explains the two observations that I have appended to them, we must in the first instance remove our attention from the musical work and focus it instead on the response of the listener (who may also be a dancer or a performer). For it is here that understanding resides, and it is through 'taking up' a work of music in our own response to it that we show our grasp of its expressive power. That we should be able to describe what we hear is unimportant. We may feel not only that words are inadequate, but that the communication between music and audience is too immediate, too 'free from concepts', to warrant the attempt. This does not mean that the many musicians, critics and philosophers who have referred to music as an expressive art have been wrong. It means only that understanding and describing are two different activities—just as they are in human relations (of which our relation to music is after all only a special case).

It is a further consequence of this approach that we should not attempt to account for the expressiveness of music in terms of realistic truth-conditions. No useful theory of expression will result in a proposition of the form 'x is expressive of y if and only if x exhibits features $f, g, h \ldots$ '. For such a proposition misrepresents *what is being done* by people who describe the emotional content of musical works. Terms like 'expressive' are used to make connections, to evoke experiences, to show how one detail hangs together, emotionally speaking, with another. Giving their meaning is like giving the meaning of a metaphor: it involves continuing the very same associative process which the term itself embodies. I 'unpack' a metaphor by describing the experiences and thoughts that it brings to mind; and that is how I should explain any description of music in terms of its expressive power. This does not mean that such a description is merely 'subjective', or that there is no such thing as a justification to be offered, that will show it to be appropriate to what we hear. But it means that we justify the description of the music only by justifying a way of responding to it. The rightness of the description has to be *heard* in the notes.[3]

Moreover, certain features of the emotional life need to be borne in mind, if we are to capture the role of emotions in understanding music:

A. Emotions are intentional states. They are directed towards objects, and founded on thoughts, beliefs and comparisons in which those objects take a pivotal role.
B. Emotions are motives for action. You act *out of* love, fear or remorse, and the emotion is the vital link from a judgement to the action that expresses it.
C. Emotions can be justified—both theoretically, by justifying the judgements on which they are founded, and practically, by justifying the actions to which they lead.
D. Inter-personal emotions are, or involve, complex forms of social adjustment. We *experiment* with remorse, love, sympathy and anger—trying out our emotions towards others and adjusting them in the light of their reciprocal response.

That last feature implies that, in the realm of inter-personal emotion, our feelings have a double focus: on the other as object, and on the self as subject. Philosophers influenced by Fichte and Hegel go further, and argue that we *become what we are* through our inter-personal emotions, building our personality as freely acting subjects through the interaction with others, in which we shape and are shaped by our own emotional life. Emotion, on this view, is a fundamental part of the *Entäusserung* of the self, whereby subjective states of mind are transformed into rational responses to a public world, so that the subject comes to know himself as one subject among others, who is also an object in their eyes. If works of art are expressions of emotion, this would go some way towards explaining their importance: they could be seen as rehearsals for, and refinements of, the process of emotional interaction whereby we 'realize our freedom' as responsible members of a shared public order.

To put the point in another way: self-conscious subjects put themselves into their emotions, and express themselves through them. To a varying extent their emotions are artefacts, which grow through dialogue—through witnessing the effect on others and responding to their response. It is probably more nearly true of emotion than it is of any other aspect of human life, that it has the structure laid down as universal law by Hegel. According to Hegel our states of mind begin in unstructured immediacy, move into a realm of contest and collision, overcome that contest through mutuality and dialogue, and so emerge at last as fully articulate and self-conscious versions of themselves—versions *mediated* by reflective thought.

Hanslick regarded the intentionality of emotion as posing an insuperable objection to the expressive theory of music. Music could express an emotion, he thought, only if it could also depict the objects of emotion. But music is an abstract (i.e. non-representational) art-form, in which genuine depiction is impossible. As it stands Hanslick's objection is far from conclusive. When we respond to another's emotion we don't necessarily know anything about its object. The person in tears calls forth our sympathy even though we don't know what the tears are about. The person jumping for joy infects us with his emotion even though we have no idea why he is jumping. If our responses to music are forms of sympathy, then Hanslick's objection is without force: through sympathy we recognize and respond to emotion, even when we know nothing of its object.

Sympathetic responses are nevertheless critical of their object. In real life we don't have much sympathy to spare, and we don't want to waste it on the undeserving. It is also a precious asset, the cement of personal ties and the proof of our humanity. As Adam Smith plausibly argued, sympathy lies at the heart of our moral nature, and is our primary resource in the regulation of social life.[4] We are therefore alert to the corruptions of sympathy, such as sentimentality (which diverts sympathy from object to subject and establishes a regime of pretence) and coldness, of which sentimentality is a special case. Education of the sympathies is all-important to us, and this is one reason why we read stories to children and worry about what they are watching on TV.

When we respond sympathetically to another's feeling it is not, as a rule, because he gives an articulate account of it. We respond to the way he looks, the way he moves, the visible dynamic of his body and posture. And music exhibits something similar. If the argument of the last chapter is right, music moves—not literally, but figuratively. And we *move with* music, responding to accent and line, as in a dance. There is something primitive in this response and it has an intrinsic tendency to turn in an aesthetic direction. In 'dancing with' the music you are also conjuring an imaginary other with whom you move, and taking an interest in his movements, for their own sake, and for what they intrinsically mean.

Plato and Aristotle emphasized the character-forming nature of music partly because they thought of music as something in which we *join*. When we dance or march to music we move with it, just as we move with other people in a march or a dance. And although there are forms of dancing which break free from the bounds of aesthetic experience, there is a kind of dancing which parallels acting or singing, in being the product and the producer of an aesthetic response.

In responding to a piece of music we are being led through a series of gestures which we imagine as the gestures of the 'other' with whom we move. As with a dance, a kind of gravitational field is created, which shapes our sympathies as we fall within its influence. We move for a while along lines of force that we did not create, and our truncated movements are also acts of attention: we do what we do in response to the sounds that we hear, when we attend to them aesthetically and become aware of the virtual movement and virtual causal order that inhere in them. If this is what it is to hear the expressive content of a work of music, then hearing expression is inseparable from the aesthetic experience. A theory which accounted for the expressive character of music in these terms will therefore pass the first two of the tests outlined at the beginning of this chapter.

It will also explain the inseparability of form and content in music. The experience of musical form is an experience of movements and gestures, detached from the material world, and carried through to a purely *musical* completion. In hearing the expressive content of a piece of music, therefore, we are also hearing the form—the life that grows and fulfils itself in tones.

But why is the 'experience of expression' so important? Why is it that so many musical people deny the expressive character of music, and why is it that we find it difficult, and usually unnecessary in any case, to put the meaning of music into words—to move from the 'intransitive' to the transitive idea of expression?

Notice that I have given no analysis of the terms 'expression' and 'expressive'. I have been describing a certain *response* to expression in music. 'Moving with' expressive music is one form of the 'recognition of expression'. When this recognition occurs listeners may have no words for *what* they recognize. In describing the music as expressive they are giving voice to their response, as when they describe a work of music as moving, exciting or troubled.

The response to expression, as I have described it, is an aesthetic response, and one that finds intrinsic value in its object: to respond to the work in this way *is* to value it. A theory that begins in this way will in all probability pass the 'value test' given earlier. It will pass the 'structure test' too. When you move to music, the music takes charge of your response to it—you are being led by it, from gesture to gesture, and each new departure is dictated by the musical development. You are not merely noticing analogies between the movement of the music and some state of mind: you are entering into dialogue with it, fitting your own emotions to the rhythm that it conveys, as you might when experimenting with inter-personal sympathies, and coming to understand both self and other more completely. You are *in the hands* of the music; your sympathetic response moves in parallel to the musical development, and you may taste the same experience of 'exploration' and 'resolution' that attends the performance of a tragedy.

This explains something which many people have found puzzling: the attribution of moral virtues and vices to purely abstract music. The 'heroic' quality of Beethoven's Fifth, the 'sentimentality' of Tchaikovsky's Sixth, the 'narcissism' of Skryabin's 'Prometheus' Symphony—and so on: all such judgements take on definite sense if we see them as reflections of sympathetic responses to musical movement. For this movement is an 'invitation': it asks us to join in an extended dance, to identify ourselves with its movement, and to follow it even when it takes short cuts or lapses into banality and cliché. The invitation to sympathy that is uttered in the voice of pure music is one that we are eager to accept; but the slightest borrowing of some stock effect makes us doubt the voice's sincerity. We encounter the temptation to pretence, and to the community established by pretence—that complicitous humbug which is the goal of sentimentality. Even if that is how our *lives* must be, we can surely be spared such an experience in art. For we enter the realm of art of our own accord and precisely to understand what *might* have been, had we been free from the tyranny of habit. Art is the record of human ideals, and in abstract music those ideals concern the higher order of our feelings—the order that is free from pretence, which confronts hardship in the way that we hear Beethoven confronting hardship in the first movement of the Ninth Symphony; which gives itself completely as Mozart does in his instrumental works; or which wins from tragedy the consolations of tenderness that Schubert finds in the sublime C major Quintet.

In the second part of this book I hope to give some examples of what I have in mind. The point of this chapter is to indicate the direction in which a theory of expression must go if it is to meet the stringent tests which it seems to me are implied in our way of appreciating music. It is only through an exploration of sympathy in general, and sympathetic movement in particular, that we can hope to explain the meaning of music.

Notes

1 Robin Holloway, *Essays and Diversions II*, London 2007, pp. 77–8.
2 Peter Kivy, *The Corded Shell: Reflections on Musical Expression*, Princeton 1980.
3 This paragraph points towards an anti-realist theory of aesthetic judgement. This is what I try to give in *Art and Imagination, op. cit.* That anti-realism does not imply that moral or aesthetic judgements are merely 'subjective' is well demonstrated by Simon Blackburn in *Ruling Passions*, London 1997.
4 Adam Smith, *The Theory of Moral Sentiments*, 1759.

6

Rhythm

1. Perceptual information must be assembled into comprehensible units if it is to guide us around the world. This is as true of the ear as of the eye; hence *Gestalt* principles operate in the auditory as in the visual sphere, though applied to temporal rather than spatial configurations.[1] Some philosophers might wish to speak of a 'nonconceptual' or 'preconceptual' unity in the auditory *Gestalt*—even of a nonconceptual *content*.[2] For the unities and wholes that we hear are, in the first instance, presented under no description. When, for example, a regular sequence of scale steps is interrupted by noises that mask individual pitches, we hear a continuous sequence, interrupted by foreground noise, rather than discontinuous sections of a scale. This perception does not require us to conceptualize the sequence as a scale, as musical movement, or indeed as anything else. It requires only that we group together the sounds that precede the noise with those that follow it.

It is clear, therefore, that we could group sounds into coherent temporal figures without hearing them as music. Hence there is a real question as to what must be added to transform an experience of sound into an experience of music. To say that we must hear the sounds as *music* is either vacuous or false (false if it implies that we apply that very concept, a concept which many a singing, listening, dancing infant has yet to acquire). I argue elsewhere that sounds become music when organized rhythmically, melodically or harmonically—with the implication that each form of organization is sufficient to provide an experience of music. But I also suggest that these forms of organization pertain to the intentional rather than the material object of perception. Melody is something that we hear *in* a sequence of sounds, and is not something that would be mentioned in a description, however complete, of the sounds themselves, judged as items in the material world.[3]

2. Our ways of grouping and streaming individual sound events —both in everyday perception and in musical attention—reflect the peculiar metaphysical feature of sounds discussed in Chapter 2, namely that they are 'pure events'. A sound is not a change in something else.

It is a self-subsisting object. When a sound occurs we assume that there is some physical cause. But we do not need to identify that cause in order to identify the sound, and the sound is fully intelligible as sound without reference either to the cause or to any other spatio-temporal particular.

One consequence of this is that auditory streams can be organized internally, by reference to audible features of the sound events, and without invoking any order in the objects that produce them. An illustration is provided by the octave illusion studied by Diana Deutsch and discussed in Chapter 2.[4] The auditory *Gestalt* in Deutsch's experiment is not merely incongruous with the physical events that produce it. It is organized according to principles that are intrinsic to the world of sounds, and which would be operative even if there were no physical events that could be identified as the causes of the individual sounds.

The streaming that occurs in Deutsch's experiment is not yet musical streaming. This kind of grouping by pitch proximity and sequential 'flow' could occur even in the experience of the wholly unmusical person—perhaps even in the experience of an animal. Musical experience, I suggest, involves the importation of a spatial framework, and the organization of the auditory field in terms of position, movement and distance. Those spatial concepts do not literally apply to the sounds that we hear. Rather they describe what we hear *in* sequential sounds, when we hear them as music. In other words the concepts that provide the fundamental framework for musical perception exhibit the comprehensive metaphorical transfer that lies at the heart of musical experience. The relation between auditory 'streaming' and the perception of musical movement can be likened to the relation between the perception of shapes and the perception of their figurative content. In the second case you see something *in* the shape that in the first case you merely see *as* a shape. In like manner the musical experience arises when you hear movement *in* a stream that you might otherwise hear merely *as* a stream.[5] (The word 'stream' here is not a metaphor, but a primitive term denoting a continuous temporal *Gestalt*.)

The musical order emerges when we adopt the 'acousmatic' attitude to the world of sounds, attending to sounds without focusing on their material causes. There is a virtual causality that governs musical movement, as when one note in a melody 'causes' its successor, even though sounded on another instrument in another place, and this virtual causality organizes the acousmatic *Gestalt*. The acousmatic experience is associated with a certain kind of listening, in the concert hall or at home. But it occurs also when musicians play together and

Wagner: Prelude to *Parsifal*

Example 1

become united in the first-person plural of the band, the music flowing through them as though with a force of its own.[6] It occurs too when we dance to music, and match the movement of our body to the movement that we hear. Dancing is both a response to musical movement and a way of understanding it *as* movement. And it is partly through its connection with the movement of the body and its social meaning that music acquires its moral character, a point made in other terms by Plato.

3. My subject in what follows is rhythm, and the distinction between rhythms imposed by metre, and rhythms generated by musical movement. By metre I mean the measuring and parcelling out of the temporal sequence. Not all music has a metre, and not every metre is like the metres familiar in Western music, which govern the divisions and subdivisions that correspond to time-signature and bar-line. There are musical traditions that derive metrical patterns by adding note-values and not, as we do, by dividing larger units symmetrically. In classical Arab music, for example, rhythmic cycles are composed of time units added together to make often asymmetrical patterns, which do not permit whole-number division.[7] The metres (*tâlas*) classified by Sharngadeva, the thirteenth-century Indian theorist, and co-opted in our time by Messiaen, are likewise formed through addition rather than division, so that the rhythmic unit is assembled from note-values, rather than deduced by whole-number division within a bar.[8]

Metre is—as its name implies—a form of measurement, in which time-values are ordered into repeatable segments. Christopher Longuet-Higgins has argued that we understand metrical organization by a kind of 'generative grammar', through which smaller units are derived in a rule-governed way from larger.[9] Thus I hear the first note of *Parsifal* (Ex. 1) as the second of four crotchet values, and therefore locate it on a weak beat, after the strong but silent beat that begins the bar. The off-

Example 2

beat experience is intensified by the tie, which pushes the second note
on to the second quaver value of a further subdivision within the bar. I
do not carry out this calculation consciously. Nevertheless by unconsciously latching on to the generative hierarchy I am able to assign a
measure, a beat and a temporal value to the notes that I hear, and
thereby strain after the music as it flees my attempt to fix it to a
downbeat, catching up with it, so to speak, only at the beginning of the
third bar.

Whatever the plausibility of that account, we should recognize that it
applies only to the kind of metrical organization with which we are
familiar from our own tradition, founded on the division and subdivision of the bar. The oriental traditions referred to above introduce
metres that are generated by addition, not division, and which therefore
impose quite another order on the musical line—one in which syncopation cannot easily take root. Moreover, even if we confine ourselves to
works in our own tradition, we must acknowledge that metrical order
and rhythm are distinct. In grasping the rhythm of the opening phrase
of *Parsifal* I am distinguishing accented from unaccented beats; I am
responding to differences in stress, hearing certain notes as part of an
'upbeat', others as initiated by a downbeat, and grouping the tones into
separate rhythmical units, as in Ex. 2.[10] These other aspects of rhythm
belong not to number but to life: they are features of the virtual energy
that flows through the music, and which causes me to move with it in
sympathy.

The ancient musicologist and pupil of Aristotle, Aristoxenus of
Tarentum, argued, in this connection, that rhythm is a temporal order
imposed upon, though not inherent in, the sequence in which it is
heard.[11] The sequence is 'rhythmized' by the perceiver, by dividing it
into upbeat and downbeat, and assigning a variable duration to each
(the first always shorter than the second). It is clear from Aristoxenus's
account that he has dancing primarily in mind, upbeat and downbeat
being explicitly connected to the *arsis* and *thesis*—lifting and falling—of the foot; nevertheless, his discussion reminds us that rhythm is

a phenomenal, not a mathematical, property of a sequence, and that our capacity to perceive it is dependent upon our wider ability to respond to movement.

Often the metre is an *ad hoc* attempt to place bar-lines across an organism that has no such divisions, as in certain parts of the *Danse sacrale* from the *Rite of Spring* (which, incidentally, is measured out somewhat differently in the four-hand piano score and the orchestral score). Consider the opening theme of Bartók's *Music for Strings Percussion and Celesta* (Ex. 3). Here the bar-lines and time-signatures seem like a tentative analysis of stress patterns, rather than an authoritative division into beats. This impression is even more evident in the measures from *Le marteau sans maître* (Ex. 4), where time-values are established by addition and not division within the musical line. (A comparable example is given in Ex. 5, from *Le maître sans marteau* by Nabil Az-Zéloub, a poignant lament over the death of Jacques Derrida.) In such works the time-signature is like a piece of speculative commentary placed above the score, and identifies no feature of the musical process. An analysis of Boulez's rhythms, for example, would show them to be derived by the superposition of two or more metres, each formed by addition of time-values, rather than division of the bar. There is a real question as to whether we hear the result as a rhythm at all: paradoxically, the attempt to escape from metrical division has led, in *Le marteau*, to the cancellation of rhythm by metre, though a metre hidden behind the time-signatures that straddle the bars. Here the mathematical order seems to arrest the forward movement, rather than to guide it. Likewise with Az-Zéloub, who uses in this piece the *himar* metre of his native Algeria, transformed by successive augmentations which are then rearranged in a permutational sequence. The result is again entirely a-rhythmical.

In the classical tradition metrical divisions coincide with significant junctures in the rhythm. However, as I suggest below, this coincidence can occur in two quite distinct ways. In one kind of case the metre is laid across the movement like a grid. In another kind of case it *emerges* from the movement, as though 'precipitated out', in the way that the hexagonal cells of the honeycomb are precipitated out of the honey-making within them.

4. The musical phenomena that we group together under the rubric of rhythm have their counterparts in other areas of human activity. Stress and measure occur in dancing and also in the movements required by certain kinds of physical work, such as those remembered in sea-shanties, in the occupation songs of India, and in the Negro

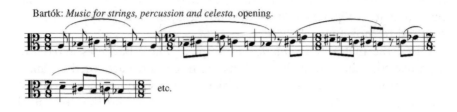

Bartók: *Music for strings, percussion and celesta*, opening.

Example 3

Boulez: *Le marteau sans maître*

Example 4

spirituals.[12] Stress, accent, metre and grouping all occur in speech, and speech-rhythms are both patterns and constraints when set to music. The rhythms of hymn tunes are classified according to their syllabic rather than their metrical structure since, from the liturgical point of view, it is more important to know what texts can be sung to them than to assign a time-signature to their musical line. And folk rhythms reflect syntactical features of the associated languages.[13] I suspect that there

Example 5

might be a useful contrast to be made between composers whose
rhythmic organization primarily reflects dance patterns, and those for
whom speech patterns are more important. Tchaikovsky, Dvořák,
Elgar and Stravinsky belong to the first kind; Musorgsky, Wagner,
Janáček, Puccini, Britten and Schoenberg to the second. (In Stravinsky's
Les Noces, for example, the composer uses nonsense syllables, precisely
in order to reconstitute speech-rhythms as dance-rhythms. In Stravinsky it is not words that give the meaning of the dance, but dance that
gives the meaning of the words.) A. H. Fox Strangways has argued that
classical Indian music uses time-value rather than accent to emphasize
a note because that is how you emphasize a syllable in Sanskrit. He
explains the complex Indian *tâlas* as derived from the verse metres of
Sanskrit liturgy and poetry, in the way that the metres danced by the
Greek chorus reflect the quantities exhibited in the verse.[14]

Elgar: Violin Sonata, 1st movement

Example 6

Music supporting movement and music supporting words will differ in measure, accent and stress. In dancing and marching small-scale repetitions are necessary, whereas in song the strophe overrides small-scale regularities and encourages their variation. If there were nothing to rhythm save measure each piece of music could be assigned a clear and unambiguous rhythmic character simply through tempo and metre. But this would be to ignore the effects, not only of grouping and stress, but also of melodic and harmonic organization which, in our tonal tradition, exert their own gravitational pull over the rhythmical movement. A very obvious instance of this is the device of suspension, in which a phrase is held back from its melodic or harmonic closure across a metrical closure, as in the straightforward example of repeated suspensions from Elgar in Ex. 6. The result is a tie across the barline—hence a form of syncopation—and also a clash of movements, as metrical closure anticipates the harmonic closure that follows. Atonal music, which (officially at least) does not admit suspensions, cannot generate this kind of rhythmic pulse. Nor can it reinforce rhythmical closure by creating melodic and harmonic closures that coincide with it.

The rhythmic effect of harmony is not confined to cases where the harmony is explicitly stated. It can be witnessed in an unaccompanied line, such as that from *Parsifal* in Ex. 1. Here the first seven notes (all off the beat) arpeggiate the triad of A flat, to which they add first the sixth and then the major seventh, creating an implied dissonance that is resolved on to the C minor triad, as G, C and E flat are sounded successively in an emphatic downbeat. The intense upbeat experience here is dependent on the cadence implied in the melodic line and could not be reproduced merely by reproducing the note values.

Example 7

5. The considerations raised in the previous section suggest a use (though not the only possible use) for the distinction between 'beat' and 'rhythm'. 'Beat' denotes a pattern of time-values and accents, while 'rhythm' denotes the movement that can be heard in that pattern, and which may be influenced by harmony and melody so as to reach across metrical closures and establish contrary motions of its own. A piece of music may have a strong beat but little or no rhythm, and some of the most rhythmical pieces in our tradition are characterized by a light beat and a refusal to emphasize the bar-line. Often a composer will present accompanying figures which shift the accent sideways through the music, as in the trio from Dvořák's *New World Symphony* (Ex. 7), where a rhythmical cell, replete with melodic and harmonic meaning, imposes its own micro-metre on the over-arching triple time. To see the point of this it is sufficient to imagine how uninteresting Ravel's *Bolero* would be, were it to consist only of the underlying beat, overlayed by a melody that exactly ran in its groove. The rhythm of this piece is generated within the never-ending syncopated melody, which plays against the beat like a squash-player against a wall. The beat is what makes the rhythm possible, but in itself it is without rhythmic interest.

In this connection we should draw a contrast between ostinato rhythm, in which a relentless beat subjects the music to a discipline that might have nothing much to do with its melodic and harmonic movement, and rhythm which adapts to and takes its accents from the musical movement. Stravinsky in *Oedipus Rex* sustains the chorus with an ostinato 6/8 beat, on G and B flat, and the result is rhythmical but static. The beat is like an external force, constraining the music from outside. It is the steady march of fate that can be deflected by nothing in the action.

This does not mean that ostinato is a substitute for, or denial of, rhythm, or that it can be understood without those other features —accent, stress and grouping—which I earlier mentioned as fundamental to the rhythmical order. On the contrary, even the simplest

Example 8

ostinato can be heard in competing ways, if accent and grouping are left
ambiguous by the melodic line. (Witness the sustained ostinato of the
last movement of Sibelius's Violin Concerto, a fragment of which is
given in Ex. 8.) Such examples show that measure is never sufficient in
itself to determine rhythm, even when made fully explicit to the ear.

    6. There is an extreme case of the ostinato phenomenon, in which
rhythm seems to become detached from harmonic and melodic organization, so as to be fired at them from outside, as it were. I refer to
rhythmic 'backing', as exemplified by a certain style of pop. This might
have a mechanical 'tic-toc' character, as in 'No Son of Mine' by the
group Genesis (from the appropriately named album, *We Can't Dance*);
or it may depend upon mixing, in which melody and harmony are
smeared together so as to become indistinct, leaving only percussive
ostinato to establish some kind of measure—as in 'Be Here Now' by the
group Oasis. Here rhythm has fallen away from the music altogether,
leaving a bare shell of melody and a harmonic progression without
cogent voice-leading, both overwhelmed by the percussive noise from
next door.[15]

    We encounter in the idiom adopted by Oasis a disaggregation of
music into beat and pitch, neither giving true support to the other. The
drum-kit has the role of marshalling the music to its stride, forbidding
all deviation, while adding nothing to the melodic or harmonic
development. (Contrast the Dvořák; here the lilting phrase that generates the rhythm is also replete with melodic and harmonic implications, which subsequently unfold through the melodic line.)

    The use made of the drum-kit in contemporary pop is to a great
extent an innovation. Classical jazz introduced the drum-kit as an
embellishment to a pre-existing rhythm, often sounded on the off-beat

and hidden, as it were, behind the strumming of the banjo. The rhythm
was generated by the syncopated voices of the instruments, each of
which played its part in breathing rhythmic life into the bar-lines. The
result resembles (in this respect at least) a Courante or Gigue by Bach.
Strictly speaking, New Orleans jazz has no need of percussion, which it
uses—if at all—purely ornamentally. In modern pop, percussion has a
constitutive rather than an ornamental use: without it, there would be
no music, since the beat—on which everything depends—would not
exist. (All that, it seems to me, is already implied in the word 'backing'.)

In the early days of rock you find a jazz-like use of the drum-kit—not
to impose a rhythm synthesized outside the melodic line, but to
emphasize and vary a rhythm generated within it. The *locus classicus* of
this is Elvis Presley, whose extraordinary voice, with its barely perceptible micro-rhythms and tremors, produces melody and rhythm together,
so that the one is inseparable from the other. In 'Heartbreak Hotel', for
example, the rhythm is compellingly announced by the solo voice, and
the bass and percussion seem merely to take it up and prolong it.[16]

Equally impressive in this respect is Eric Clapton, who uses the guitar
rather as Elvis uses his voice, to set the music in motion before the
drum-kit enters, so establishing the rhythmical identity of the piece as
an internal feature. ('Lay Down Sally' is an effective instance.) It is
interesting to note that Clapton, in his days as leader of Cream, was
criticized by Jimi Hendrix as rhythmically incompetent—a criticism
taken up by David Henderson in his biography of Hendrix.[17] Cream
was disbanded in 1969, and Clapton turned his back on Hard Rock, an
idiom which in any case destroys the need for rhythmic competence.
The guitarist that has emerged from this is surely one who has 'got
rhythm' in the sense that Gershwin intended.

7. The dance-forms adopted by Bach and Handel were attached to
elaborate rituals and courtesies, and required complicated steps and
formations from the dancers. In the ancient dances to which Debussy,
Ravel and Respighi looked back with such poignant emotions, partners
were assigned by courtesy and exchanged by rule, with people of all
ages participating without embarrassment in a dance which could at
any moment place them side by side and hand in hand with a stranger.
In a very real sense the dancers were generating the rhythm that
controlled them, and generating it together, by attentive gestures
governed by a ritual politeness. The experience of dancing as a 'dancing
with' (usually with a group, subsequently with a single partner)
survived right down to the days of rock 'n roll. This 'withness' of the

dance is captured by the baroque and classical idioms, in which rhythmic organization is not imposed but *extracted* by the metre, as song-like phrases weave around and embellish one another, moving to closures of their own.[18]

The human need for this kind of dancing is still with us, and explains the current craze for Salsa as well as the periodic revivals of ballroom dancing and Scottish reels. The 'withness' of the reel was noticed and commented upon by Schiller, who regarded what he called 'English' dancing as confirming the connection between beauty and gentility. His words are worth quoting:

The first law of gentility is: *have consideration for the freedom of others*, The second: *show your freedom*. The correct fulfilment of both is an infinitely difficult problem, but gentility always requires it relentlessly, and it alone makes the cosmopolitan person. I know of no more fitting image for the ideal of beautiful relations than the well danced and multiply convoluted English dance. The spectator in the gallery sees countless movements which cross each other colourfully and change their direction wilfully but *never collide*. Everything has been arranged so that the first has already made room for the second before he arrives, everything comes together so skilfully and yet so artlessly that both seem merely to be following their own mind while never impeding the other. This is the most fitting picture of a maintained personal freedom, which respects the freedom of others.[19]

It is undeniable that, for many if not most young people, the experience of 'withness' is absent from their dancing, which typically involves neither complicated steps nor formations. The normal dancing of the disco floor involves little or no contact with or recognition of a partner, and may occur with no partner at all. You dance to Heavy Metal by head-banging, slam-dancing or 'mashing' (pushing people around in the crowd). Such dancing is not really open to people of all ages, but confined to the young and the sexually available. Of course, there is nothing to forbid the old and the shrivelled from joining in: but the sight of their doing so is an embarrassment, all the greater when they themselves seem unaware of this.

The social impoverishment of disco has a rhythmical cause. The pulse of disco music sets the dance in motion and controls its beat, but it does little to suggest how or with whom you should move. The dance, like the rhythm, remains external to the music, a kind of generalized 'setting in motion' rather than a balletic commentary on the musical line. You see this at its most extreme in techno music, especially when embellished with strobe lights and similar psychedelic effects. Such dancing is like throwing oneself into a pool of collective emotion, to be swept away in its frenzy. There is nothing you can do, either to create or to embellish the rhythm. And communication with a partner is rendered impossible by the noise, the lights and the sheer formless press of the crowd to every side. Schiller saw 'English' dances as emblematic of personality, freedom and the civic community. If we were to view disco dancing through the same Kantian spectacles we should describe it as 'pathological'—an event in which freedom is displaced by empirical causality, personality by nature and will by desire. Sarabandes, galliards and reels were social dances in the very real sense of being society-forming dances. Modern rock is crowd-forming, rather than society-forming.

8. Dancing shapes the body rhythms and trains the ears of those who engage in it, and changes in the dance-culture will lead of their own accord to changes in the rhythmical organization of music—even the music of the concert hall. This is what we witnessed in the nineteenth century, when gipsy rhythms affected the music of Brahms (explicitly, in works like the G minor piano quartet, but implicitly in many of the other chamber works, songs and concerti), and when the waltz exerted a ubiquitous fascination that was to begin with Schubert's drawing-room waltzes for piano, and to culminate in Ravel's monumental *La Valse*.

This is one of the factors that must be borne in mind when we consider the relation between serious and popular music today. People have become used to the ostinato beat of pop, which throbs in the background of life and shapes the expectations of all of us, like it or not.

It is hard to attract modern audiences to music in which rhythm is either melodically generated or measured out in Messiaen's way, by addition rather than division of time-values; it is comparatively easy to attract them to music with an ostinato propulsion, regardless of its melodic or harmonic invention. Hence the popularity of John Adams, whose 'The Chairman Dances' (from *Nixon in China*) and 'Short Ride in a Fast Machine' typify a new kind of ostinato writing, with the melodic instruments assigned essentially percussive tasks, and with continual repetition of elemental rhythmical cells. For the pop-trained ear this music is easy to listen to, since its rhythmic structure does not have to be deciphered by following the melodic line but is imposed by a regular external emphasis. Composers used to be wary of 'the tyranny of the bar-line'; in Adams, however, the tyranny is accepted, as a benign dictatorship which gives us all what we want.

9. This bears on the controversy surrounding atonal music. Much music theory conceives tonality as a melodic and harmonic system, in which both harmony and melody are goal-directed. Chords in this system are not simultaneities, but nodes in a web, bound by functional relations to the chords that precede and follow them. Musical order is achieved when voices move together towards closures that are harmonically driven and melodically complete. Theories of tonality—such as that defended by Schenker—see these features as giving the essence of tonal music. Hence they have a tendency to leave rhythm out of the picture.[20] And those who propose atonality as a genuine alternative to the tonal tradition often describe it in similar terms, as replacing the horizontal and vertical relations of pitches with a new order based on the permutation of pitch-class sets. Rhythm is again left out of the picture, often with counter-intuitive results, since the experience of rhythm is an experience of grouping, and will therefore affect the segmentation of the musical surface on which the pitch-class structure depends.[21]

It seems to me, however, that we should see tonality as in part a rhythmical system, and recognize that the difficulties of atonal music are experienced as much at the rhythmical as at the melodic and harmonic level. The harmonic and melodic principles of tonal music arose out of the desire to make satisfying sequences, in which movement begins, continues and comes to a conclusion—not only on the large scale but also region by region and voice by voice. Rhythm is not an addition to this, but a part of it, both sustaining and sustained by the harmonic and melodic relations. Measure is useful not only because it corresponds to familiar movements of the body but also because tonality is founded in repetition, with the music constantly returning to identifiable places, and constantly departing on some new but related journey of its own. Take away the old tonal order, however, and rhythm has a tendency either to collapse entirely—since it is not driven by the forward movement of the musical line—or else to become external to the music, a frame supporting an inert display of musical fragments.

The atonal composer therefore has a serious dilemma. To suspend organized pitch-class sets on an ostinato frame is to take a big step backwards into banality. On the other hand, to reconstitute rhythm outside the expectations fostered by the tonal order—expectations of grouping, closure, accent and so on—is to lose the connection between rhythm and the life-phenomena that give sense to it. In response to this problem Milton Babbitt has produced 'serialized' rhythms in which the twelve pitch intervals are set in relation with twelve equal time intervals, and both subjected to systematic permutation. However, the very procedure shows that it is not rhythm, but measure, that is being reconstructed. Serialized rhythm is really serialized metre, and is as little part of the rhythmic surface of the music as is the drum-kit in synthetic pop. It seems to me that Messiaen's rhythmical experiments were prompted at least in part by an awareness of this problem. Messiaen sought to reinvent rhythm as an internal feature of the musical line, even when the melodic and harmonic language had abandoned all the old forms of closure.

Messiaen's experimental approach was taken further by Stockhausen, who attempts to reconstruct the rhythmic dimension of music by localizing movement in competing orchestral units. Stockhausen's large-scale music shifts great blocks of sound through musical space, often with an indifference to human life and bodily sensations that reminds one of a slave-minder building a pyramid. The result is a meticulous, though hidden, metrical order, which generates an entirely a-rythmical surface. If you were to introduce rhythmic motion into a piece like *Gruppen*, for example, it would have to be an external rhythm, like a pop-ostinato, laid on top of the musical structure but generated outside it. In itself the music has no enduring pulse; the emphasis generated within one episode does not survive to the next, and therefore cannot combine with it in a dance step. There is a curious parallel here, between Stockhausen and John Adams: both think of rhythm in ostinato terms, the one therefore rejecting it as an extra-musical device, the other accepting it as the sole organizing principle of a musical surface that in all other respects may be wholly monotonous.

10. Like his teacher Olivier Messiaen, Stockhausen uses metres formed by the addition rather than division of time-values. The result may be a-rhythmical, but it is meticulously measured. Messiaen's music, on the other hand, is not merely highly rhythmical but organized rhythmically, so that rhythm permeates the music with the same intensity as it permeates a symphonic movement by Beethoven. Messiaen has himself written of this subject,[22] emphasizing the way in which rhythm can be altered through 'added values' and 'non-retro-gradeable rhythms' so as to defy metrical symmetries, and compel the listener to cling to the musical movement, rather than the bar-line, in following the score.

Messiaen took the idea of additive metre from the *deçî-tâlas* of Sharngadeva (see above, section 3 p. 59), in which the notion of a beat is replaced by that of the shortest note-value (*mâtra*), and metres are

Example 9

Example 10

classified as repeatable sequences, of which Sharngadeva lists 120. Some of the *tâlas* are extremely long—no. 35, *simhanandana*, has 21 separate 'beats', comprising 62 *mâtras*—and could not, therefore, be heard as self-contained rhythmical units, on the model of the bars in Western music.[23] And Messiaen's use of them does not compel us to hear rhythmic groups in his music that correspond exactly to the metrical order: for example, in the *Turangalîla Symphony* at its most rhythmical, we tend to hear curtailed polyrhythms based on division of the bar, rather than the underlying additive order.

Messiaen's principal device is illustrated in Ex. 9, showing the method of 'added values'. The first sequence (Ex. 9 a, b and c) shows three bars in standard metre; the second (d, e and f) shows the transformation of these bars either by adding a rest or lengthening one of the notes by a fraction. Ex. 10 illustrates the method in practice: Messiaen's transformation of a Peruvian folk song, *Delirio* (Ex. 10a) in the second of the *Harawi* songs (Ex. 10b).[24]

In such examples time-signature is clearly of little importance. Ex 9f, for example, can be assigned a time-signature; indeed the performer will be helped, up to a point, if the bar is prefaced with the metrical sign

Example 11

13/16. But this measure misrepresents the rhythmical movement: the bar has six beats, each subdivided and one of them stretched. By recursively adding or subtracting note-values in this way, Messiaen attempts to build character into his motives, which develop over time by acquiring or losing note-values, while retaining the same number of 'syllables' overall. (Compare the way in which a face changes over time, as age first strengthens and then weakens the flesh, always retaining a certain recognizable outline.)

Ex. 11 illustrates the method of 'non-retrogradeable rhythms'. Here Group B is the retrograde of Group A, with the central five semi-quaver note shared between them. The whole sequence forms a rhythmic palindrome which is unchanged when played in retrograde, and hence 'non-retrogradeable'. Again this metre can be assigned a time-signature, but the result (19/16) is even less informative than in the previous examples. What we hear is a rhythm which seems to flow back into itself, constantly returning the energy that propels it to its source.

Messiaen's rhythms are completely emancipated from the bar-line, and the metrical markings of his scores say little or nothing either about the underlying additive metre, or about the movement that can be heard in it. The result owes its rhythmic vitality not to any regular beat that can be mapped onto bar-lines, but to the energy that flows from note to note and which is inseparable from accent and grouping, both enforced by the melodic line. A work like *Cantéyodjayâ* (Ex. 12) offers the supreme instance of an organization in which rhythmical order has been emancipated completely from measure, with accent and grouping becoming the unaided vehicles of the rhythmic movement. Certain commentators have described Messiaen's music of this period as conveying a new, or at any rate unconventional, experience of time: the forward-moving temporal order of the classical style, which leads to the relentless drive of a Beethoven symphony, has been replaced by a kind of circularity, in which everything returns into itself as though in a state of rapt contemplation.[25] One can see the point of such descriptions, whether or not one endorses the claim that it is time, rather than musical sequence, that is being experienced differently. What is said of

Messiaen: *Cantéyodjayâ*

Example 12

Messiaen's approach to time has been said not only of Indian music but also of the Benedictine plainchant, to which Messiaen frequently referred in his lectures, and in particular to the account of rhythm given by Dom André Mocquereau of the Abbé of Solesmes.[26]

However, a word of caution is in order. Messiaen, like Babbitt and Boulez, often uses metre in ways that make no contact with rhythm, as this is perceived by the listener. The metrical schemes deployed in *Chronochromie*, for example, involve permutations of *tâla*-like sequences, of a kind that cannot be followed by the ear, still less by the body.[27] If we hear rhythms in these permutations it is not because of the mathematical order but in spite of it. Fred Lerdahl has argued that musical understanding looks for elaboration rather than permutation in its object,[28] and therefore that serial organization will always be irrelevant to the organization that we actually hear in the musical surface. Even if not true of all musical phenomena, Lerdahl's observation is surely true of rhythm, which we understand through patterns, accents and repetitions, creating a movement in which we can join. The passage quoted from *Cantéyodjayâ* in Ex. 12 can be supplied with a full metrical analysis, in terms of fundamental sequences and their successive permutations. But the rhythm resides in the groupings of semiquavers, the pauses, and the accented notes, which shake us around as we try to fit them to patterns that cannot quite contain them. The

Bulgarian Christmas Carol

Example 13

experience of rhythm here cannot be captured by metre, and certainly not by the arcane metrication that preoccupied the composer.

11. Although Messiaen deserves credit for recognizing that melodic and harmonic innovation require new ways of grouping tones, and that this, in turn, requires new forms of rhythmic organization, we should recognize that the practice of adding value to notes has been widespread in folk-music, and is by no means confined to oriental traditions. Ex. 13 gives a Bulgarian Christmas carol, in which the lengthening of certain syllables has led to the stretching of a bar of four semi-quavers to 9/16 and even 10/16 time, while retaining the same basic rhythm of four beats to the bar.[29] Fox Strangways, in his closely observed study of Indian classical music as it was before the disease of Western harmony, persuasively argues that measure is prior to rhythm in the Indian raga because melodies originated as hymns in the Sanskrit language, which emphasizes a syllable by lengthening rather than stressing it.[30] Moreover the metaphysically conceived *tâla* system of Sharngadeva does not represent the rhythmic organization that we hear in Indian classical music, as will be evident to anyone who has swayed to Ravi Shankar. Most of the melodies written down by Fox Strangways can be divided into bars of equal length, with the stretching of syllables marked by a pause. Structurally speaking, it is true, additive measure dominates

Wagner: *Tristan und Isolde*, motive of the 'look'

Example 14

rhythmical division. But this can be accounted for not only by the peculiarities of the Sanskrit language, but also be the early emergence in India of a listening culture, with dancing as an art to be observed rather than an event to join in.

12. The need for rhythmical organization to change with the change in harmonic language was widely recognized in the wake of Messiaen's teaching. But it was not Messiaen who first observed the connection. Wagner was already aware that genuine melodic and harmonic innovation require a new approach to rhythm. If Wagner is not often thought of as a rhythmic innovator, this is because the ostinato conception of rhythm has to a great extent obscured the origins of rhythm in the grouping experience, and obscured the roots of that experience in speech, song and dance.

In fact the path-breaking character of *Tristan und Isolde* is shown as much in the rhythmic organization of the musical line as in melody and harmony. This is so in spite of the fact, and also because of the fact, that Wagner hardly ever uses percussion as a rhythm-generating device. The timpani play an enormous role in *Tristan*, but it is a melodic role, consisting largely of prolonged tremolandi which swell the melodic line and suggest reserves of unexplored emotion beneath it. And the other instruments of the orchestra are used melodically rather than percussively, even in the most frenetic passages such as the scene in which Tristan tears the bandages from his wound, and the music enters a kind of rhythmic catastrophe as it strives to keep pace with his delirium.

Wagner's motives in *Tristan* have pronounced rhythmical contours, but, unlike the motives in Beethoven say, their emphasis is rarely on the downbeat. Consider the motive sometimes known as the 'look' (Ex. 14), which sets the Prelude in motion, after the interrupted cadence on to F major. This establishes a complex rhythm in 6/8 time, with a fractured triplet followed by a crotchet+quaver sigh. The melodic line here, and the chromatic movement in the bass which lifts the harmony from F major to G major, endow the rhythmic pattern of this phrase with a kind of completeness. This is a rhythm that has been 'sung out', and which henceforth bears the memory of the phrases that sang it.

Wagner: elaboration of the 'look' motive.

Example 15

Wagner promptly repeats it, incorporating it into no less than five subsequent motives, which he draws together with the original 'look' to form a continuous sequence. (Ex. 15 illustrates the musical process.)

In the classical style the closures imposed by tonal melody and diatonic harmony are aligned with rhythmical closures reinforced by bar-lines. In *Tristan* all three forms of closure are minimized or avoided entirely: they are symbols of a law-governed order that passion has undermined. Hence the motives that take up the rhythmic organization of the 'look' involve ties across bar-lines, off-beat accents, and the ubiquitous fracture in the triplet, that together create a rhythmic profile that cannot be understood apart from the melodic pulse in which it originates. The prelude to *Tristan* is already moving in the direction of Messiaen, with the bar-line as the effect, rather than the cause, of the rhythmic organization, which deploys highly energized and repeatable cells, and in which accent and grouping are often at variance with those suggested by the metre.

13. Rhythm is a property of dancing and also of speech. As Aristotle pointed out, we hear speech differently from other sounds,[31] since speech is an expression of soul, and is organized semantically. The surface order of speech may be highly irregular and punctuated by silences, but it is heard as flowing from a single source. Its movement is the movement of meaning, and its pulse is the pulse of life. Speech is therefore a paradigm for us of a rhythmical organization generated not by measure and beat but by internal energy and the intrinsic mean-ingfulness of sound. Hence there is a great distinction to the ear between speech and chant, in which speech sounds are suspended at a single pitch and on a single pulse. A chanting voice sounds from another region, a place of unseen powers. The ostinato chant represents the inexorable order that controls us and which forces our words to move in time to its commands.

(One of the most remarkable developments within the sphere of pop is the 'rap' artist, who speaks toneless rhyming prose along the groove of a relentless percussive rhythm, so replacing speech-rhythms with chant-rhythms. This is an extreme form of the ostinato experience, in which not only harmony and melody but speech itself are annihilated by metre.)

Often Janáček is given credit for being the first composer to build speech-rhythms into his melodic line. It seems to me, however, that speech-rhythms have been part of phrasing in classical music at least since Monteverdi and the *stile rappresentativo*, and that the conscious attempt to give them musical form began with Wagner, not Janáček. Wagner himself discusses the matter in *Opera and Drama*, referring to the accents that are natural to the spoken language as underpinning the musical divisions within the bar.[32] His use of *Stabreim* arose directly from his search for a language that could be sung out without losing the inflections of natural speech. *Stabreim* derives from two musically important features of Germanic languages, namely their preference for accent over quantity as a form of emphasis, and their wealth of plosive consonants.

Schoenberg was heir to Wagner in this as in other things. Unlike so many of his successors on the path of atonality, Schoenberg recognized that atonal music would succeed only if it could emerge as a rhythmical system. His early atonalism was therefore as much a rhythmical as a harmonic experiment. Schoenberg did not wish to repudiate the connection between rhythm in music and rhythm in life. Instead he wished to replace dance-rhythm by speech-rhythm as the organizing principle of the musical line. The instrumentation and harmony of a work like *Pierrot Lunaire* are dictated in part by the desire to generate speech-like rhythms in all the instrumental voices. Tonal harmony compels voices to move together, to magnetize each other, to work towards the same points of closure and stasis—as in a dance. Hence in tonal music, even when speech-rhythm inspires the melodic line, a reminiscence of dance-rhythm will inhabit the harmony.

In order to free the music entirely from this dance-like togetherness, Schoenberg pulls the harmony apart, so that what we hear is a simultaneity of utterances rather than a sequence of harmonizing songs. The instruments speak to us, in rhythms that match the *Sprachgesang* of the voice. The later development of the serial technique likewise has a pronounced rhythmical meaning. The serialization of the pitch sequence permits a kind of polyrhythmic structure, in which accents in the various voices seldom coincide, and the unified chorus gives way to a conversation. (An interesting example is provided by the chorus of the Israelites wandering in the desert in *Moses and Aaron*—contrast the flat and ineffective dance-rhythms that accompany the worship of the Golden Calf.)

14. Rhythmic organization is fundamental to musical meaning and intimately connected with the moral character of music. The externalized rhythm of much contemporary pop invites people to move in crowd-like rather than conversation-like ways. You do not 'move with' rhythm of this kind; you surrender to it, are overwhelmed by it. You lose yourself in it, as in a drug. And that is a feature not only of the way pop is received, but also of the moral character that we hear in it. By contrast the ostinato rhythms in the Bartók piano sonata, for example, have no reality apart from the sharpened harmonies and emphatic melodic line that produce them. You do not lose yourself in these rhythms: rather you discover something *other* than yourself—an idealized form of human life, in touch with the soil and with the natural world.

The Darmstadt orthodoxy (as propagated by Stockhausen, Boulez and their immediate followers) effectively killed off rhythmical organization as an intrinsic feature of the musical line. Somehow the dancing musical line that Messiaen discovered through the *tâlas* disappeared from the music of his followers. The idea of additive metre became institutionalized and mathematized, and accents lost all connection with the body. People can listen to Stockhausen's *Gruppen* and move 'along with' it, even be moved by it. But the experience of rhythm is absent from Stockhausen's block-like sounds, as it is absent from the meticulously metrical music of Brian Fernyhough. In reaction, composers like John Adams have tried to address our need for rhythm by *adding* rhythm to melodic lines and harmonies that do not have the strength to generate rhythm out of their own inner movement. The rhythm is pumped in from outside, not breathed out by the melody. It seems to me that we are placed by this music in the vicinity of the 'crowd' experiences that dominate the world of pop. There are, by contrast, composers still writing who invite us to join in rhythms that are intrinsic to the melodic and harmonic life of their music: David Matthews, for example, in his string quartets and symphonies; John Borstlap in 'Psyche'; Michael Berkeley in his concertos; Oliver Knussen in his two operas on childhood themes, *Higgledy-Piggledy-Pop* and *Where the Wild Things Are*. And these works make systematic use of tonal relations, illustrating the thesis that tonality is a *rhythmical* system, arising when voices 'move with' each other, as in a dance. They illustrate both the depth and the importance of the controversy surrounding musical modernism. This is not a controversy about harmonic systems only; it is primarily a controversy about the nature of listening, about the role of music in the shaping of our emotions, and about the connection between music and life.

Notes

1 See Albert S. Bregman, *Auditory Scene Analysis*, Cambridge, Mass. 1990, and Stanley A. Gelfand, *Hearing: An Introduction to Psychological and Physiological Acoustics*, New York 1998.

2 See Christopher Peacocke, *Sense and Content: Experience, Thought and their Relations*, Oxford 1983, Chapter 3.

3 *The Aesthetics of Music*, Oxford 1997, Chapter 2.

4 Diana Deutsch, 'Grouping mechanisms in music', in D. Deutsch, ed., *The Psychology of Music*, New York 1982.

5 On the distinction between 'seeing in' and 'seeing as' see Richard Wollheim's account of 'representational seeing', in *Painting as an Art*, London 1987. For reasons given in Chapter 5 of *The Aesthetics of Music*, I do not regard 'hearing in' as sufficient foundation for musical representation, and in general prefer to discuss these phenomena as varieties of 'double intentionality', rather than 'representational perception'.

6 See Alfred Schutz, 'Making music together', in *Collected Papers*, vol. 2, The Hague 1964, pp. 159–78.

7 See the article by O. Wright, 'Arab music', sections 1–4, *The New Grove Dictionary*, ed. Stanley Sadie, London 1980.

8 See Joanny Grosset's article 'Histoire de la musique: Inde', in *Encyclopédie de la musique et dictionnaire du conservatoire*, ed. A. Lavignac, Paris, 1913–31, vol. 1, pt. 1, pp. 287–324, and the discussion of modern Indian *tâla* in A. H. Fox Strangways, *The Music of Hindostan*, Oxford 1914, pp. 191–224. See also Messiaen's eight-volume *Traité de rhythme, de couleur et d'ornithologie*, Paris, Leduc, 1996 onwards, bringing together Messiaen's previously unpublished lectures on the topics that concerned him as a musician and a theorist.

9 H. C. Longuet-Higgins, *Mental Processes: Studies in Cognitive Science*, Cambridge, Mass. 1987, pp. 150–68.

10 The term 'upbeat' is contentious, and can mean one of at least two things: the entire preparatory phrase that precedes some musical emphasis, or the short intake of breath that leads directly into it. The first use began with J. J. de Momigny and was elaborated into a theory by H. Riemann, *System der musikalischen Rythmik und Metrik*, Leipzig 1903, to be further adapted by Edward T. Cone, *Musical Form and Musical Performance*, New York 1968.

11 Aristoxenus, *Elementa Rhythmica*, surviving fragments of Book 2 translated in A. Barker, *Greek Musical Writings*, London 1989, vol. 2.

12 See Karl Bücher, *Arbeit und Rhythmus*, Leipzig 1909.

13 See Béla Bartók, tr. M. D. Calvocoressi, *Hungarian Folk Music*, London 1931.

14 See the illuminating discussion in M. L. West, *Ancient Greek Music*, Oxford 1992, pp. 129–59.

15 The prohibitive cost attached to the copyright of pop music prevents me from giving examples. I have been interested to discover that the worse the music, the more expensive it is to reproduce it.

16 Presley's vocal style—heavily influenced by both R&B and Gospel—is a subject in itself, addressed in part by Henry Pleasants, *The Great American Popular Singers*, New York 1974 pp. 270ff., and by Peter Guralnick, both in *Lost Highways: Journeys and Arrivals of American Musicians*, New York 1982, and in his liner notes to *Elvis Presley: The Sun Sessions CD* (BMG/RCA 6414-2-R, 1987).

17 David Henderson, *'Scuse me while I Kiss the Sky: The Life of Jimi Hendrix*, Toronto 1983, p. 133.

18 On the 'withness' of the dance see R. Scruton, *Perictione in Colophon*, South Bend, Ind. 2000, pp. 164–76.

19 Friedrich v. Schiller, 'Kallias or concerning beauty: Letters to Gottfried Keller', in J. M. Bernstein ed., *Classic and Romantic German Aesthetics*, Cambridge 2003, pp. 173–4. (I have slightly changed the translation.)

20 Heinrich Schenker, *Free Composition*, tr. Ernst Oser, London 1979; Felix Salzer, *Structural Hearing*, 2 vols, New York 1952–62.

21 See Nicholas Cook's devastating demolition of Allen Forte's set-theoretic analysis of Stravinsky's *Excentrique*, in *A Guide to Musical Analysis*, London 1987, pp. 138–51.
22 *Technique de mon langage musical*, Paris 1956. And see also the *Traité de rhythme, de couleur et d'ornithologie, op. cit.* Messiaen's theories and practice are lucidly presented by Robert Sherlaw Johnson, *Messiaen*, 2nd edn, London 1989, Chapter 4.
23 The *tâlas* are listed in Appendix 2 to Johnson, *op. cit.*
24 See Messiaen's discussion of this example in *Traité de rhythme, op. cit.*, vol. 3, p. 284.
25 See for example Audrey Ekdahl Davidson, *Olivier Messiaen and the Tristan Myth*, Westport, Conn. and London 2001.
26 *Le nombre musical grégorien*, available as *A Study of Gregorian Musical Rhythm*, from the Church Musical Association of America, Richmond, Virginia 2007.
27 See the table of permutations set out in Johnson, *op. cit.*, p. 177.
28 Fred Lerdahl, 'Cognitive constraints on compositional systems', in John A. Sloboda, ed., *Generative Processes in Music*, Oxford 1988.
29 Harmonized by Raina Katzarova, and quoted in Béla Bartók, 'The so-called Bulgarian rhythm', in *Essays*, selected and edited by Benjamin Suchoff, London 1976, p. 48.
30 A. H. Fox Strangways, *op. cit.*
31 *De Anima*, 420b. (Discussed above, Chapter 2.)
32 *Oper und Drama, dritter Theil: Dichtkunst und Tonkunst.*

Part II: Criticism

7

My Mozart

I discovered Mozart at the same time that I discovered music: indeed, during those early days of wonder at this thing which had been unaccountably missing from my life for the first thirteen years, music and Mozart were virtually indistinguishable. Those were the days of 78 rpm gramophone records; we had just acquired a gramophone, and almost simultaneously a piano had come into the house—an old upright inherited when my grandmother died, the very same upright which had been purchased on the never-never for the parlour of the Victorian slum in Upper Cyrus Street, Ancoats, Manchester, when my father was a boy. The record that acquainted me with Mozart was *Eine Kleine Nachtmusik*. I forget who was playing, though I do remember that it was one of the cheerful inauthentic performances then in vogue, with a full string orchestra. The upper parts bobbed along like a flotilla of brightly coloured boats on the deep swell from the double basses. The violins soared in scintillating unisons, and the violas had that peculiar mahogany sheen that they so often have in Mozart symphonies. I listened to it again and again in rapture, putting the record on the gramophone as soon as I came home from school.

I was not the first person to fall in love with *Eine Kleine Nachtmusik* nor the last. You cannot love this music without also sympathizing with the life that produced it, and knowing that life from within. Its freshness and simplicity speak to us of another and somehow cleaner world than the one that surrounds us. Straightforward emotions, exquisite manners, a gay but serious acceptance of life and death all resound from its unhesitating syntax. The voice is unmistakeable from the very first bars. But what are those bars? Just the two broken chords of the key: a G major arpeggio going upwards; a D major seventh going down. (Ex. 1.) Anybody could have written such a thing! And yet, nobody but Mozart could have written it.

I started lessons on the piano, and inevitably worked my way towards that simple sonata in C major—so simple that no pianist has ever felt confident that he has mastered it. But there it is again, that opening melody: just the two chords of the key. Up the triad of C major,

Example 1

Example 2

down to the leading note and the seventh chord on G, and then straight back to the tonic! (Ex. 2.) Anybody could have done it. Nobody else could have done it. Which do we choose?

There is a mystery here, and in the years since then I have often tried to make sense of it. But I have never got closer to understanding it than such random thoughts as these:

First, Mozart was not an innovator in the same sense that Wagner was, say, or even J. C. Bach, Mozart's mentor. He inherited the idiom in which he worked from the surrounding musical culture, and although he studied the works of Handel and J. S. Bach, and absorbed from them a wonderful competence in counterpoint and sinuous melody, he did not break free from, nor did he really stretch, the syntactical conventions of his day.

Secondly, the comparison with J. C. Bach tells us something about Mozart. The young Bach was an original. He took the harmonic language of his father and rolled it up into chords, as you might roll up a pastry. Then he baked those chords into blocks. He showed how to construct whole paragraphs of music by pounding away on a single harmony, and how to use chord sequences to create a tight musical logic, even when there was little or no counterpoint guiding the individual voices. This style was, of course, not entirely JCB's invention. Others were working on it at the time, and it is sometimes known as the 'galant' style, as opposed to the 'learned' style of Johann Christian's father. JCB made this galant style into a live musical language, and this was the language that Mozart learned. Yet, set beside the most callow work of Mozart the entire oeuvre of JCB is dispensable. For all its

Example 3

felicities and triumphs of musical organization, it would not really matter if it were forever lost. What did Mozart add to it? Melody, of course, a mastery of structure and form. But there is something else, something that seems to elude the musicologist, something for which the most obvious word is 'soul'.

Thirdly, we should never forget that Mozart's simplicity, when it is there, is there for a reason. The simplicity in the two examples I gave is not just a simplicity of syntax. It is a simplicity of message. It is the simplicity of a perfectly unaffected and at the same time perfectly graceful person—a person who makes a gift of his feelings, for the reason that they are honest, transparent and good. That is the simplicity that you hear in Mozart. Not a simplicity of syntax only, but an echo in music of a virtuous simplicity of soul.

I have used the word 'soul' twice, and this leads me to the fourth observation I want to make, which is that the soul of Mozart was not simple at all. He knew how to convey simplicity, and to show it for what it is worth, as one of our highest values. But his was a universal intellect, like Shakespeare's. His music explores every mood, every character, every turn of the human spirit. He is one of the greatest dramatists who has ever lived, capable of using the classical idiom that he absorbed from the air of Salzburg and Vienna to convey any kind and any degree of passion.

For Mozart was unlike JCB in that the classical style had become, in his hands, entirely plastic. He could bend it to any shape, any mood, any musical need. He was capable of working miracles of counterpoint, such as the last movement of the Jupiter symphony, without departing from the syntactical conventions of classical harmony. He was equally capable of producing a sublime melody from a plain arpeggiated chord—as though he had peered into a chord as into a clear pool and suddenly pulled a gleaming mermaid from its depths. Consider Susanna's aria in the garden, in *Le nozze di Figaro* (Ex. 3), in which arpeggiated chords are stapled together with scalar passages, to produce a melody that again anybody might have written, and also nobody but Mozart could have written.

What do I mean by that? Well, first that there is an exquisite taste

Example 4

revealed in Mozart's musical line. You could go up and down an arpeggio to your heart's content, making sweet sounds and thinking they were music: it was what I did when I first sat at the piano, intoxicated by *Eine Kleine Nachtmusik*, and amazed at the simple effects of natural harmony. But the result is normally tasteless and overindulgent. That really *is* the sort of thing that anybody could do. In Mozart, by contrast, we constantly meet the little obstacles, the graceful steppings to one side, that prevent the chord from entirely taking over and which turn it with the gentlest of pressures in another direction—rather as a skilled dancer turns his partner. And, like a dancer, Mozart introduces little skips into the rhythm, so that the common chord of the key comes across as something infinitely rich in possibilities. (Ex. 4.)

Furthermore Mozart's melody is being led onwards by a feeling—a state of mind that he is perfectly dramatizing, which is that of a girl reaching through all the sordid machinations into which she has against her will become involved, to the pure and innocent desire that she hopes soon to consummate. This is an invocation of erotic sentiment which is also a triumph over evil. Mozart leads us to hear this in the musical line in a hundred subtle ways: for example, by taking us (as in the fragment just quoted) both to the top and then to the bottom of the soprano register, spanning, as it were, the feminine psyche, telling us that this is the whole woman and not some girlish part of her.

And again, the arpeggio is constantly lifted up from its falling motion by the rhythm, so that you feel yourself breathing with it, breathing the intoxicating summer air in which Suzanna is standing, conjuring connubial love. This is not just craftsmanship, it is inspiration.

Mozart was that rare thing: a master of opera, who was also a master of instrumental music. His string quartets show the influence of Haydn, but not so much as Haydn's late quartets show the influence of Mozart. And the Mozart quartets, like all his chamber music, are entirely rooted in the medium. His melodic writing for voice is nowhere replicated in his string quartets; and the studied weaving together of parts that you find in those masterpieces is nowhere to be discerned in the operas, where all is paced by the drama. Yet it is impossible to hear either the quartets or the operas and not to hear in them the soul of Mozart, that versatile, meditative sympathizer with the human condition, whose voice touches the truth in us all.

It is difficult to say anything about this kind of genius that has not been said before. So let me turn instead to the piano concerto, K. 450. Mozart was the inventor of the piano concerto. Of course there had been keyboard concertos before, including some magnificent examples from J. S. Bach. But Mozart was the first composer to put the piano at the head of things. As in the quartets, he achieves a perfect match between the instruments and the musical material, giving to the piano what is the piano's by nature, and to the orchestra what only an orchestra can do. This means that in many of the concerti there are themes, passages and episodes which are given uniquely to one or other of the partners; it also means that Mozart doesn't think in the standard symphonic way, with a first movement containing first and second subjects, exposition and development, and recapitulation at the end. There is an ease and freedom about these works which stems, not from a self-conscious attempt to be original but, on the contrary, from a humble retreat before the medium. Mozart is allowing the instruments to speak for themselves. It is precisely his refusal to be original, his modesty in the face of an instrument and its potential, that enabled Mozart to invent the piano concerto—one of the great possessions of our musical culture. He did for the piano what he also did at the end of his brief life for the clarinet: he gave it the context in which it could sing out from the many-timbred orchestra, and display the individuality of its voice.

The concerto begins with a little chromatic motive, followed by the arpeggiated chord of the tonic arriving, as expected, on the dominant, at which the motive is repeated. (Every eighteenth-century concerto opens with a figure based harmonically on the common chord, followed by an answering figure on the dominant.[1]) (Ex. 5). But notice the subtle change: the motive has slipped back by a quaver, so that the accent now comes on the fourth note and not on the third. (Tovey considers this change of accent to exhibit the irrepressible naughtiness of Mozart, who pleases and teases by turns.[2]) To accommodate this, Mozart must extend the flourish that introduces the arpeggio, and he effortlessly achieves it: Ex. 6.

It all sounds so simple and natural; yet it is something that only

Example 5

Example 6

someone living and breathing the classical syntax, so that his life as it were moves along with it, could achieve with such grace and ease of manner. The next step is—as always—the most important one for Mozart. Having laid out, in whatever form, the chords first of the tonic and then of the dominant, he normally takes off with an answering and energetic phrase, which pushes the music forward towards the dominant as its next tonal area. Instead, however, we are given a catchy little phrase that stays alternating tonic and dominant harmony in the manner of a chorus of hunting horns. (Ex. 7.) This phrase contains the essence of the movement. But it is also thinking forward to the dialogue that is to ensue between orchestra and piano. It is the kind of thing that sparkles on the piano, and which will permit endless repetition and elaboration. It is a phrase that will come again and again, but henceforth always on the piano, as the orchestra hums along in the background. It leads, however, to a characteristic bravura theme that, in any other context, would be taken to be the main subject of this movement, still in the home key of B flat. (Ex. 8.)

Again the theme is entirely composed of the arpeggiated chords of the

Example 7

Example 8

tonic and dominant: how often can you do this and produce something striking? Mozart is saying—forever! But this theme, which returns to mark every tutti of the orchestra, is never given to the piano: it is disdained by the soloist, as though too pompous and remote for his concerns. When the piano finally enters, after the orchestra has meditated on another and softer theme, still in the home key, and again a theme that is never wholly given to the piano, the soloist comes in, with a scalar passage that makes use of none of the material that we have heard, coming round to the opening motive (Ex. 5) only after twelve cadenza-like bars. And then, having stated that motive in ornamented form, and enjoyed for a while the horn-chord sequel (Ex. 7), the piano brings in a completely different melody, in G minor—and this is the first real change of key in the whole movement! (Ex. 9.)

This is one of those reflective themes with which Mozart's sonatas for piano abound—composed of delicate turns of phrase joined by scalar passages. It is never given to the orchestra and reappears only once in a variant form in C minor after the next orchestral tutti. The piano drops this exquisite melody almost at once, and goes off playfully in search of another. And again, instead of returning to the opening material of the movement, it lights on something wholly new, this time

Example 9

Example 10

Example 11

in the key of F major—the first time that the dominant has asserted its
rights as the alternative to the home key. (Ex. 10.)

This playful tune is again reserved for the piano. As the soloist goes
on to elaborate on it in a series of bravura arpeggios, the orchestra
answers with a theme of its own, related, but decidedly not the same, as
though it wanted to show that it, too, is capable of joy, though
somehow a joy less personal and less intimate than the one heard from
the piano. (Ex. 11.) The piano then takes off with a paragraph of
counterpoint and suspensions in the learned style, entirely blotting out
the innocent melody in F major.

And so it goes on, the piano being itself, the orchestra being itself,

Example 12

neither picking up the other's material, but each nevertheless listening
intently to what the other is doing, and responding in character.
Everything produced by the one seems a fit answer to the other. And
because of Mozart's incomparable melodic gift, each new theme seizes
our attention so that we unconsciously sing along with it, receive it as
natural, inevitable even, and entirely forget to ask ourselves what is the
form of the work or whether it has a form at all. I suppose the correct
description of the movement would be sonata-rondo, but the movement obeys very few of the rules of either sonata-form or rondo. Those
classifications of musical form are in any case *ad hoc*—records of things
regularly done and conventions easily followed, which neither command nor forbid what composers themselves are minded to do. In the
case of Mozart's piano concertos we see a new art-form emerging, from
a composer who has listened to the piano as he has listened to the
human voice, so as to discover the soul within.

Before concluding let me just say one other thing about this
particular concerto. The first movement goes from idea to idea and
melody to melody with an innocent joy, each melody new and
surprising, and yet each of them, without exception, based on the
simple device of a triad, followed by the triad of its dominant. You
might think at the end of this: well, how very clever, but is that all he
can do? Which is why you should listen carefully to the melody of the
slow movement, constructed in a completely different way, without
reference to the consonant intervals of the triad, and harmonized
chromatically, so as to venture constantly into neighbouring keys. (Ex.
12.) Haydn was able to do this kind of thing, so too were Schubert and
Chopin: but you won't find many competitors.

I have spent rather a long time on one work, and only on one movement of that work. But what about my Mozart as a whole? It is difficult to say anything new about Mozart's genius, but let me try, in a couple of paragraphs, to summarize what Mozart means to me and to those like me, who see Western classical music as part of an extended attempt to cast light on the human condition.

Mozart is a symbol of the Enlightenment. He belongs to an age when people thought seriously not just about our human intellectual capacities, but about our moral capacities too.[3] In his operas this is very obvious. He is at every point sifting the true from the false, the virtuous from the vicious, the lasting from the fleeting — leading us to see that life matters in ways that we, with our pampered habits, are too ready to ignore. He is a great comic, but in the higher style. Even when prompting us to laughter, as in *Figaro*, Mozart's purpose is deeply serious, leading us by the hand to come face to face with the depth and lastingness of our commitments.

We live a long way downstream from that Enlightenment vision, and our popular culture today is bent on exalting the trivial, the indecent, the sarcastic, over the deep, the committed and the virtuous. It is difficult for us to envisage that Mozart's music, in its day, was part of *popular* culture, that people in Vienna flocked to hear these concertos and that — although he had difficulties too, since audiences are fickle and fashions change — there was no barrier between Mozart's music and the society in which he moved. His seriousness came across each Sunday in liturgical music that must surely have stirred hearts yet more in those days of common piety than it does today. And it is this very same seriousness, lightened but not spoiled by his gaiety of manner and endless humour, that makes such a lasting impression in the piano concertos.

What I would emphasize, since it has been borne in on me in my own life and through my encounters with his music, is that there is, in Mozart, a purity which is at once musical and spiritual. No musical pollution, and no spiritual pollution, sounds through his music. It is angelic in the true sense of the word: a visitation from another and higher sphere, and we listen to it exactly as though it had a message of eternal validity. This music is not of mortal provenance: nor, it says, are we.

Notes

1 See Arthur Hutchings, *A Companion to Mozart's Piano Concertos*, Oxford 1948, p. 91.
2 Donald Francis Tovey, *Essays in Musical Analysis*, vol. III, Concertos, Oxford 1936, p. 31.
3 See Nicholas Till, *Mozart and the Enlightenment*, London 1992.

8

Beethoven's Ninth Symphony

Beethoven's Ninth is simultaneously the best known and least understood of all his works, the only classical symphony with a tune that
everybody, even the most unmusical, can quote, and at the same time a
symphony to which critics, composers and musicologists return again
and again in wonder and puzzlement, baffled by its power and at a loss
to say whence it comes or what it means. In this chapter I cannot hope
to resume all that has been said or thought about this work.[1] But I
should like to explain its importance, to smooth some of its harder
edges, and to justify its status as one of the great achievements of our
civilization.

It is useful to begin with a list of difficulties. The most obvious is that
presented by the choral finale. Why does the symphony suddenly burst
into song, discarding all the conventions of the concert hall and
introducing forces that radically change the whole character of the
symphony and our way of listening? Is it—as Wagner said (by way of
promoting himself as the true heir of Beethoven)—that the composer
has taken instrumental music to the limit of its expressive power, so that
now the human voice must emerge from behind it? Or is the finale (as
Beethoven himself said on one occasion) a mistake, like the Grosse
Fuge, op. 133, that was originally intended as the last movement of the
String Quartet in B flat op. 130, but then wisely set apart, as a piece too
angular and monumental to serve as the conclusion to an intimate
chamber work? Or is the symphony simply the first example of a new
musical form, exhibited also by the many subsequent symphonies, in
which the human voice and the setting of pregnant words are integrated
into the overall tonal and dramatic structure?

The second problem lies in the performance. Beethoven's instrumentation presents difficulties of balance, some of them due to the
orchestral forces available to him, others perhaps due to his deafness.
Should we rescore the symphony so as to remove these difficulties, or
should we on the contrary revere them, as integral parts of a work of art
too holy to be defiled by our adjustments? In a finely argued and
uncharacteristically modest essay, Wagner argued that many of the

oddities derive from the limitations of Beethoven's orchestra, and that most of them can be overcome by doubling, or by using the extended range of the valve horns that have replaced the natural horns for which the symphony was written.[2] There thus arose the tradition, in the nineteenth century, of rescoring the symphony, using triple winds, modern horns and valve trumpets, thereby so amplifying the sound that the work comes across as a great storm of noise like the 1812 overture or like Beethoven's own bombastic celebration of the victory at Waterloo. In reaction modern orchestras often follow the example set by Roger Norrington, using only authentic instruments and scaling down to the level that would have been normal in Beethoven's day. And there is much to be said for this practice. For modern audiences don't often understand that the effect of colossal size and relentless energy conveyed by Beethoven's first movement is achieved with what, by modern standards, are relatively meagre forces—only double wood-wind, for example, and no trombones. And it is arguable that, the more you augment the forces, the less colossal the sound. The vastness and strength of Beethoven's conception are due in part to the strain that he is putting on the players. Just as you lose the effect of the Grosse Fuge when you transcribe it for string orchestra, or that of Bach's famous Chaconne for solo violin when you add (as Schumann did) an accompaniment for piano[3], so do you lose the sense of superhuman tension that Beethoven achieves in his first movement, when you relieve the woodwind players of the need to do the utmost to make themselves heard in the climaxes, or when you relieve the horns of the strain involved, and the nuances achieved, when they must reach non-harmonic notes by stopping rather than by pressing a valve.[4]

A related difficulty is presented by Beethoven's tempi. Everything seems to be marked at breakneck speed and while there are those— Roger Norrington, for example—who believe that we must accept Beethoven's metronome marks as authoritative, and as a result change the mood of the Adagio from tender reverence to perky flirtatiousness, the consensus today is that the metronome marks are not a guide to tempo, and that the performance tradition is our best indication of what is appropriate. Although I doubt that Beethoven's deafness is to blame for the difficulties in his instrumentation—which stem rather from the originality and grandeur of his conception than from any deficiency in his mind's after all highly practised inner ear—I do believe that deafness affects the ability to judge the speed of a work. Silent reading always anticipates, and it would be intolerable to read in your head at the speed with which you read aloud. Likewise, if your

Example 1

experience of music comes from reading and imagining the notes, rather than from hearing them aloud, you inevitably pace things faster than they sound.

To those difficulties we should add the many difficulties of interpretation. These difficulties begin with the very first bars—perhaps the most influential bars of any symphony, more influential even than the choral finale in their impact on subsequent symphonic form. Instead of launching into the main theme of the movement, Beethoven sets the whole orchestra in tremulous motion on an open fifth on A, emphasizing the fifth with fragmentary horizontal statements, and leaving you guessing as to whether this is the ghost of a minor or of a major triad, whether it is the tonic or the dominant of the key, and whether these melodic fragments have anything to do with the theme or are merely preparing the way for it. And then, without resolving any of those questions, Beethoven brings in a D on bassoons and horns while replacing the open fifth with an octave on A. In other words the open fifth of the dominant gives way to that of the tonic, without, however, clarifying their relation or persuading you that this strange intrusive note really is, after all, the tonic. Only now, with the air full of unresolved questions, does the main theme enter—a colossal downward thrusting arpeggio of D minor, which seems to be knocking us to the ground in a series of hammer blows. (Ex. 1.)

How should we interpret those opening bars: are they an introduction to the theme that follows, or a part of it? Are they to be played as atmosphere, as accompaniment, or as the thing itself? And what do we do with that strange obtrusive D, which is like a messenger sent in advance of the theme, whose presence is not yet fully accepted? Should

Example 2

we emphasize it, or on the contrary slide it in unnoticed? In a striking image, Tovey compared these opening bars to a nebula, a concentrated mass of as yet formless energy, from which great constellations will in time condense. Yet, in striving to realize that image, conductors are sure to inflate, to magnify, to Brucknerize, in a way that detracts from the formal purity, the Mozartian simplicity, that attended Beethoven in this as in all his works.

Similar problems of interpretation present themselves throughout the work. For example the Scherzo (second movement) opens with an eight-bar tattoo, four bars of which are silent, and one bar of which is played only by the timpani. (Ex. 2.) How do we play those silent bars: as rests or as part of the theme? Is the bar for the timpani a joke, and if so is the humour black or white? Is this whole tattoo merely an introduction, or is it the true theme of the movement? To some extent these questions are resolved when we see that these first eight bars of the Scherzo present another downward-moving and hammered-home D minor arpeggio—in other words that they are a variation of the main theme of the first movement. And the joke consists in showing just what that theme would have been, without the mysterious mutterings that precede it. It is as though the suffering flesh has been stripped away, to reveal the grinning skeleton beneath. The tattoo stands alone, however. The two bar rest with which it ends is followed by a lively fugue whose subject incorporates only one bar of that initial passage, leaving the whole statement peculiarly isolated, like a disciplinarian's barking orders, followed by a playful dance that makes a mockery of his words.

There are other examples of these strange passages that stand out from the score, while seeming to be both outside and inside the musical argument. Famous are the two bars that open the third movement—the Adagio—beginning with an off-beat quaver on the bassoon. The effect here is like a curtain being drawn away from a holy icon, followed by an awed stillness as the vision is revealed. The melody that follows is

Example 3

one of those characteristically Beethovenian creations, like the earlier
theme of the slow movement of the Emperor Concerto, the result of
reworking, pruning and dividing, in which melodic cadences are echoed
on the woodwind. The echoes extract from the melody its most
poignant turns of phrase, and reflect them back as though agreeing
from another standpoint. (Ex. 3.) Only when you grasp the full
meaning of the echo—as a voice from outside—do you understand the
melody, and therefore the unveiling phrase that precedes it. This is a
melody without edges—a melody whose impact depends on the phrases
by which it is framed. These phrases give the edges and corners, which
compel the theme to take a definite shape.

Yet more famous, of course, is the long introduction to the final
movement. The Adagio ends in its home key of B flat major. And
immediately the orchestra takes up that final B flat and inserts it into the
middle of a D minor chord, making an atrocious dissonance that
introduces a huge *Schreckensfanfare*—horror fanfare—as Wagner
called it. This fanfare gives way to the strangest answering phrase of
all—an unaccompanied passage for cello and bass, marked by Beethoven as 'in the manner of a recitative'. The *Schreckensfanfare* and
recitative continue to alternate, with fragments of the other three
movements as though summoned forward to answer to their interrogation. All this leads at last to a statement of the well-known melody,
at first unaccompanied, and then varied three times and elaborated
until interrupted yet again by the *Schreckensfanfare* – opening this time
with the most atrocious dissonance Beethoven ever wrote, a first
inversion D minor triad slotted into a diminished seventh on C sharp,
to create a chord containing all the notes of the D minor harmonic
scale. When this too is answered with a recitative, it is in the sound of
a human voice.

This introduction to the last movement has been more criticized than
any other passage in the symphony. To some it is just a ragbag of
rhetorical devices, all presented by way of fudging the transition from

orchestral symphony to choral fantasia, and from abstract meditation to the explicit message of Schiller's 'Ode to Joy'—a message that is today barely believable in any case, and seemingly at variance with the sublime acceptance expressed by the Adagio. To the Wagnerians it was a kind of seismic upheaval, as the human voice rises up from beneath the music, casting the orchestra aside and finally standing bare and unaccompanied, a lonely premonition of the artwork of the future. To Martin Cooper, in his study of the composer's last decade, it is 'the kind of miscalculation that may endear rather than alienate', so typical is it of Beethoven's idiosyncratic mixture of musical sophistication and human naivety. To Verdi it was merely repugnant.

There is some help to be obtained, however, if we look back for a moment at a work from Beethoven's middle period, also, like the Ninth Symphony, in D minor—the Piano Sonata op. 31 no. 2. In the first movement of this work we see in embryo many of the curious effects that are spelled out at length in the symphony. The movement begins with two slow introductory bars on the dominant—not an open fifth, this time, but nevertheless something (from the point of view of the classical style) just as anomalous, namely a first inversion triad—a triad familiar from recitatives, to which it lends an unstable but forward-going character. The recitative-like nature of this chord is echoed in the upper voice, and emphasized when, after a busy passage, the music returns to an Adagio, and then repeats the opening two bars in the distant key of C major. The busy passage resumes, and eventually turns into a proper dominant, preparing the way for the main theme of the movement, which begins with a D minor arpeggio in the bass, answered by a turn on the dominant in the treble. When the slow introduction returns later, at the recapitulation, its recitative-like character is fully elaborated in a poignant quasi-vocal line reminiscent of the evangelist in Bach's St Matthew Passion, a line that is extended into a passage of rapid modulations that effectively prevent the first theme from returning as it should.

In the first movement of this sonata you see how Beethoven attempts to stretch the framework of the classical sonata, in order to incorporate elements of an imaginary drama. (The sonata, incidentally, is sometimes known as 'The Tempest', following Beethoven's cryptic reference, when questioned about it, to Shakespeare's play.) Beethoven's style remains strictly within the confines of the classical syntax; principal sonata-movement themes tend to be constructed by arpeggiating common chords; harmonic progressions are taken from the standard repertoire; key relations are—if not always orthodox—nevertheless arrived at by accepted modulations, and departures are achieved by bringing into the music from outside, as it were, the foreign resonances of the human voice.

All those features reappear in the Ninth Symphony. Beethoven prepares the way for the human voice using the device explored in the earlier sonata, namely poignant and highly articulated passages of recitative, in which meaning lies just below the surface, striving for words. When at last the voice becomes human the transition crosses the very narrowest of divides. He opens the first movement of the work with a dominant chord, preparing the way for the theme, but also building up tension, allowing a questioning atmosphere to permeate the music. And the theme, when it comes, is constructed on classical principles, by arpeggiating the common chord of the tonic, as in the sonata—though this time downwards instead of upwards, and with a movement, a rhythm and an emphasis that are entirely original and without parallel in earlier music. (The first idea for this theme, noted down in Beethoven's sketchbooks, has been described truthfully by Martin Cooper, as 'an eighteenth century idea that would not be remarkable in a symphony by Haydn or Mozart'.[5] The final version would be unthinkable in such a context.) There is another resemblance worth noticing between the sonata and the symphony, which is that in both works the slow movement is not in F, the relative major, as would be normal in the classical style, but in B flat major—the key of the sub-mediant, which also acts as a kind of secondary dominant in the first movement of the Ninth.

Such comparisons bring home to us that Beethoven was not, in the Ninth Symphony, embarking upon any new and uncharted course, but on the contrary refining and pushing to new limits the expressive devices that he had developed in earlier works. Moreover, he was working throughout within the constraints of the classical style. If you look in the symphony for new harmonies, new modulations, new relations between keys, new melodic shapes of the kind that soon became common in romantic symphonies, you will look in vain. The atrocious discord that introduces the last appearance of the *Schreckensfanfare*, for example, is not a new harmony in the manner of the first chord of *Tristan und Isolde* or the first chord of *Pelléas et Mélisande*. Romantic harmony, of the kind that reached a crisis in Wagner,[6] demands a new kind of syntax, a new way of building and resolving dissonance, a new sense of the relation between a chord and a key. Beethoven's dissonance is, by contrast, a mere interruption: not a new chord at all but the rude imposition of one chord from the classical repertoire upon another. The resulting clash is not resolved but cast aside, as the music returns to its original obsession with the D minor triad.

Likewise the melodic inspiration of the Ninth Symphony is entirely within the parameters of the classical style. A few years later Berlioz would be presenting as the motto theme of his *Symphonie fantastique* a melody that leaps to all parts of the octave, proceeding sometimes by consonant, sometimes by dissonant intervals, and modulating as it goes. In the Ninth Symphony, by contrast, Beethoven presents themes which are recognizably classical—whether shaped from the broken chord of the key, as in the first and second movements, or whether derived from the scale of the key, over a tonic-dominant harmonic scheme, as in the second subjects of the first and second movements or the great *Ode to Joy* of the finale. True, the first theme of the Adagio sounds, at first hearing, to belong to another sphere, outside the chord and scale-governed melodies of the classical tradition. In fact, however, the effect of sublime stillness is intimately connected with the way in which the classical language is here put to use. The melody is a sequence of cadences, which one by one spell out the resting places along the scale, either with a dominant to tonic, or a tonic to dominant progression. To say as much is not to deny either the originality or the beauty of the melody. It is simply to note that it is true of this great theme, as it is of the entire symphony, that it derives from a profound immersion in the classical language, which enables Beethoven to bend it to his expressive purpose without ever breaching its rules.

I believe it is necessary to bear this deeply committed classicism in mind if we are to understand the symphony for what it is. In no way should it be seen as repudiating the formal constraints and the ideals of musical closure inherent in the classical style of Mozart and Haydn. It is true that the Adagio is not strictly classical in form, being a set of double variations in which the second subject is never truly varied, and the first subject is constantly preserved in the beautiful echo from above. And it is undeniable that the last movement represents a break with convention of the most striking kind. Nevertheless, the detail of the musical argument is in every particular classical. Keys are always firmly established, clearly related, and properly prepared: even the surprising changes of key (such as that from E flat to C flat at bar 91 of the Adagio, or that from A major to B flat major at bars 330–331 of the finale) are prepared—but prepared as surprises. There are no surprise changes of key in Debussy, and few in Wagner, for the very reason that, in the language of those composers, any key can be reached in a jiffy from any other. Beethoven's surprises are huge, arresting and pregnant with significance, precisely because of the force and authority with which he embeds his music in a given key.

Likewise, Beethoven develops his material in a strictly classical way, building it up from motives that can be reassembled in novel permutations, prolonging ideas through amplification and development, and deploying strict counterpoint whenever the opportunity occurs. Indeed the Ninth Symphony is remarkable for the number of fugues that it contains: double and triple fugues, all carefully constructed, and arising with the utmost naturalness from the surrounding musical order. It is equally remarkable for its constant use of variation form, not the least in the Finale, in which the variations are overlaid by a large-scale symphonic scheme: Introduction and Allegro, followed by grotesque Scherzo, followed by an Andante Maestoso, and then a final Allegro — a scheme that replicates the structure of the symphony as a whole.

To appreciate this classical discipline, and what it brings to Beethoven's symphony by way of force and conviction, it is worth looking at the first movement's main subject, and Beethoven's way of extracting from it every ounce of meaning. (Ex. 1.) The theme has six clearly distinguishable parts — and this is perhaps what is most distinctive of Beethoven: his ability to produce themes which develop of their own accord, throwing off new and detachable motives that can grow independently like spores from a single organism. The parts I have in mind are these: the downward crashing arpeggio of D minor (1); the sequence that follows, landing on the tonic (2); the four rising chords that take us to the key of G minor (3); the sudden and striking phrase that follows, which begins by converting G minor to E flat major — the flattened supertonic — and then takes us back to the dominant (4); the march-like sequence that follows, with a dotted rhythm on drums and trumpets answered by a melodic motive in thirds on the woodwind (5); and finally the prolongation of this by the whole orchestra with chords tied across bar-lines, leading to the final emptying of energy, as the first violins rush down to the tonic, tension subsides, and we find ourselves back where we started, with a tremolando open fifth, though this time on the tonic rather than the dominant of the key (6).

Each of those elements follows on with exemplary logic from its predecessors; each forms part of a careful tonal argument, setting out the key relations that will be important in the movement as a whole, and each continues the emphatic gesture that sets them all in motion. And yet each is capable of independent development, through which to attain another and contrasting character. I will consider just the first

Example 4

two elements. At various points (measures 198 and 427, e.g.), Beethoven takes motive (1), and places it over the softest cushion of horns, strings and pizzicato bass, to create, from this fierce gesture of defiance, two distinct yearning melodies, which develop without using any other material. Such passages show the restraint of the original exposition, in which Beethoven denied himself the most beautiful of melodic and harmonic effects in order to wrap together motive (1) with all the other material that he would need. They also create an astonishing expressive effect, in which humble tenderness is shown united with heroic defiance, thereby enacting in musical form the human ideal that inspired their creator.

Motive (2) is developed in a yet more fascinating way. Beethoven soon splits it in two, developing each half independently. He then ingeniously joins the second half to itself with a tie across a bar-line, so depriving the motive of the emphatic down-beat and closure with which it first appeared and refiguring it as a link in a potentially endless chain. He then builds from the resulting free radical a spectacular double fugue (Bar 217 ff.), with the second half of motive (2) as the sinew that ties the great limbs together, and also sets them in motion. (Ex. 4.) Yet, when the movement seems at last to have exhausted its message of tragic defiance, there, at the start of the coda, is this same motive, appearing in the major key in a duet for two horns, like a sudden smile on a face schooled in suffering. This endearing episode is precious in just the way that smiles are precious in those who rarely afford them: it is the proof of a warm and vulnerable humanity, of a deep-down likeness to ourselves, which makes even the harshest of their humours bearable. And, having made motive (2) smile in this winning way, Beethoven brings it back at the end, to give the final grim, unanswerable and unharmonized crash on to the tonic.

Each of the six motives that compose the first subject is given its own elaboration and development in the texture of the first movement, yet when we look back at the subject's first appearance it retains its character as a single, classically composed statement, based on the D minor triad. In resisting the sublime melody that begins at measure 198, Beethoven is resisting a temptation to which Berlioz or Schumann would surely have yielded: the temptation to place lyrical expression before the building-block logic of the classical style. Again it is Tovey who saw most clearly what Beethoven achieved in this magnificent theme, whose 'gigantic proportions', as he put it, 'are only the more wonderful from the fact that the forms are still the purest outcome of the sonata style'.[7] Somehow Beethoven was able to concentrate six independently significant motives into a theme that moves energetically across them, establishing the key of D minor with maximum authority, by striding from D minor to E flat major and back again.

I have spoken only of the first subject of the movement, and only of two motives within it. But there is a second subject, and this too is composed of organically connected but independently developing parts. The whole movement grows from these tiny cells with a logic that is utterly compelling, since there is not a note that cannot be traced to the tightly compacted material from which it all begins. At the same time the movement presents an air of rock-like solidity. Keys are stated and maintained with a firmness that has hardly ever been matched, with unison tuttis climbing up and down the tonic chord for bar after bar, as at measures 150–159, in which B flat is drummed into you with relentless force, only to slip back to the open fifth on A with which the symphony began. This tonal solidity is achieved, however, without sacrificing the immense flexibility of the elements from which it is built, which are small enough, interesting enough, and sufficiently imbued with their own tonal logic, to admit of independent development. Tovey wrote that 'One of the reasons why the first movement of the Ninth Symphony dwarfs every other first movement, long or short, that has been written before or since, is that, more evidently than in other compositions, it shows that no member of its organization is so large as to lose freedom in its function as part of a larger whole.'[8] But we should not think that this kind of achievement is merely formal, like some intricate mathematical proof. Of course, it is very clear that Beethoven —whose conversation books show him to have been a supremely incompetent mathematician—had something of the mathematician's ability to see as far as possible into the logical consequences of every musical idea. But his genius would have been of far less significance to us, indeed of an order no greater than the genius of Vivaldi or Hindemith, were it not for his added ability to instil both the whole symphonic movement, and the elements from which it is constructed,

Example 5

with the noblest of human emotions. We may not be able to put these emotions into words—certainly not into words that match the concreteness and resonance of the music—but we have no difficulty in recognizing them. Our fist clenches, our heart melts, our body sways as the music courses through us, and these bodily tremors are the sign of an inner commotion, as the music draws us into sympathy with the heroic ideas that stirred the heart of its composer. We are not being told a story about these heroic ideas: we are being made to enact them. In doing so, however, we are being enrolled in the same relentless classical discipline that controls every note of the score.

Before moving on there are two other features of the first movement to which I wish to draw attention. The first is its remarkable conclusion. Having allowed motive (2) to take its course, leading to a descending scale passage from the second subject, and then reappearing in a plaintive form in the home key of D minor, Beethoven suddenly brings in a kind of funeral march, with a walking chromatic bass on tremolando strings, and an entirely new melody on horns and woodwind. (Ex. 5.) This passage—immensely effective in its air of resignation—shows Beethoven's fertile imagination at its most sublime. When all material has been exhausted and its emotional significance laid bare, he can suddenly step aside and, as it were, look on what has happened from outside, presenting his new and contemplative vision with a magnificent melody that remains in the mind forever afterwards, and which he gives us here for free.

The second feature that is worth attending to is the use of trumpets and drums, which throughout the symphony tend to sound together or antiphonally, like the distant echo of a military band. I doubt that there is any symphony, with the possible exception of Mahler's Sixth and Nielsen's Fourth, in which the timpani have so prominent a part, throbbing and crashing in all the tuttis, and accompanying even the tenderest passages with a pulsing commentary. No doubt Beethoven's deafness had a role to play in the attention that he paid to this kind of detail—for deaf people respond to vibrations even when they do not hear them as sounds. However, this is by no means the most important influence. Beethoven lived in the wake of a striking musical phenomenon which is now largely forgotten, but which had a formative influence on the style and intention of the choral finale. I refer to the official and semi-official music of post-revolutionary France.

Two composers in particular stand out among those who belonged to this musical movement, its immensely prolific founder, the Dutch-born François Joseph Gossec, and Étienne Méhul, whom Beethoven admired, and who was one of the best-loved opera composers of the Napoleonic era. Gossec had composed a vast choral *Hymn to the Supreme Being* for Robespierre's Fête de l'Être Suprême which took place in June 1794, and composed many works introducing martial effects and the muffled sounds of distant triumphs. Beethoven, through his friendship with Count Bernadotte, the French ambassador to Vienna, was well acquainted with the attempts to conscript the art of music to the French revolutionary cause, and—his subsequent disillusion with Napoleon notwithstanding—was deeply stirred by the effects of massed choirs and patriotic sentiment, which characterized the official art of the new republic. Both Gossec and Méhul were exponents of the classical style, the first being a follower of J. C. Bach and Stamitz who had begun his long life in Paris as a pupil of Rameau. It is to Gossec and Méhul that the trumpets and drums of the Ninth Symphony are most indebted, and it is in part because of their influence that the choral finale takes the exultant and overwhelming form that Beethoven conceived. The fifth motive in the opening theme of the first movement—dotted rhythms on trumpets and drums punctuating a marchlike melody in thirds on the woodwind—is straight from the repertoire of the French open-air triumph, and anticipates Berlioz only because Berlioz, like Beethoven, is down-stream from Gossec.

Of course, Beethoven was never a slavish copier. The influence of the French festivals was transmitted to him more by the cultural atmosphere that they generated than by any individual work of music. His use of the timpani is also marked by his entirely original creative genius, which saw their potential as melodic as well as rhythmic instruments. Thus, in the scherzo, he has them both tuned to F, the mediant of D minor, though an octave apart, in order to pass the initial theme to them and to allow them to play it without any accompaniment. This effect caused enormous excitement at the first performance, and does so still. Moreover, it creates a huge strategic problem for the composer, since he can no longer use the timpani to stress either the tonic or the dominant of the key, or to slip suggestively from one to the other by way of pressing the harmonic movement forward. Not the least of Beethoven's achievements is to have built the Scherzo—to my mind the greatest scherzo ever composed and a masterpiece of contrapuntal ingenuity —around those seriously disabled timpani, which win all the prizes not in spite of but because of their handicap.

However, I propose to pass over the middle two movements in order to address the well-known problems presented by the finale. We know that Beethoven had wished to compose a choral setting of Schiller's 'Ode to Joy' for twenty years before he finally got round to it. Moreover the notebooks suggest that he originally had a purely instrumental finale in mind for the Ninth Symphony. We also know that he worked long and hard on the first theme of the last movement, and that he had already made a trial run at it in the Choral Fantasia. It seems to me that we should begin by taking seriously Beethoven's ingenious way of introducing the human voice, by first imitating it on cellos and basses. The music of the French festivals had brought home to him a critical fact, which is that the classical language, which is the shared musical idiom of Enlightenment Europe, could be used to mobilize public as well as private sentiments. And it could be used to set vocal anthems that gained a new kind of authority from the firm tonal logic of the symphonic tradition. He therefore conceived the finale of the Ninth Symphony as an answer to the private and inward-directed emotions of the initial three movements, an answer which would turn the spirit once again outwards—not to a narrow community conceived, as the French revolutionaries had conceived it, in nationalist terms, but to the universal community of mankind.

The *Schreckensfanfare* offers a glimpse into hell: the deep well of despair into which we all can fall at any time and from which Beethoven, stricken by deafness and by chronic digestive disorders, raised himself only by Herculean efforts of will. Privately, and thrown back on our own resources, we have three ways out of this despair: the posture of tragic defiance; the attempt to laugh it off and gild its comic edges; and the serene and accepting surrender to God's love. The first three movements present incomparable images of those three con-trasted standpoints, and that is why Beethoven interrupts the fanfare with quotations from them. Do not forget, he is telling us, that you have it within yourself to master your fate—that even the greatest loneliness will not destroy you. Yet the recitative persists with its question—is it then merely for each individual to win through to a merely private consolation? Is there no help from outside, other than the help that God provides when, broken at last, we kneel in prayer? Notice here the brevity of the quotation from the third movement. Its work is not yet fully done, and its message will return in another and transmuted form, as the Ode runs its course. The *Schrekensfanfare* returns, reminding us that nothing that we achieve alone is really stable, that without some outside endorsement our joys and consolations are threatened by the inner darkness. When the bass voice enters to banish the fanfare for good, it is therefore in order to announce the true source of joy, which is the love of our fellow human beings. The choral theme has already been announced, and taken through three variations. Music, which is the voice of inner longing, calls of its own accord for the community that completes it.

So what of the theme? First, we should put it in historical context, which is the context of the national anthem. It is doubtful that there was such a thing as a national anthem before the eighteenth century. Maybe the Spartans had such a thing, since they were in the habit of assembling to sing the patriotic ode of Tyrtaeus before going into battle. And doubtless we can find, here and there, anticipations of the modern practice of singing collectively as an expression of national loyalty and civic obedience. Before the Enlightenment, patriotic songs existed, and often achieved an emblematic significance, like Purcell's setting of Dryden's 'Fairest Isle'. But they were not collective anthems, designed to arouse and consolidate feelings of national loyalty. The first genuinely popular example of such an anthem in modern times—the English National Anthem, to the words 'God Save the King'—began life as one among many popular responses to the 'knavish tricks' of the Jacobites, and acquired its status as a ceremonial anthem only by dint of customary usage. Meanwhile, with the emergence of national loyalties under the impact of Enlightenment conceptions of the state, the need was felt elsewhere for some similar communal song, whereby the populace could rehearse its obedience and its collective will to endure. The tune of 'God Save the King' was adopted by the Prussians under Frederick the Great, in order to proclaim the legitimacy of the Prussian monarchy. Meanwhile Haydn, during his visits to London, had conceived a great envy of the English for the anthem with which they could constantly refresh their obedience. In response he composed his famous 'Gott erhalte Franz der Kaiser', later to form the theme of the slow movement variations in the Emperor Quartet op. 76 no. 3, and to be stolen by the Germans for their national anthem, to the words 'Deutschland über alles'.

'God Save the King' and 'Gott erhalte Franz der Kaiser' are Christian hymns, and at the same time tributes to a monarch and affirmations

Example 6

of allegiance by his subjects. They belong to a pre-Enlightenment
conception of the state, and even if used as anthems, are not strictly
national anthems: indeed, both celebrate monarchs who ruled over
empires. Perhaps the first anthem to breathe the new spirit of nationalism and popular sovereignty was that composed in a fit of inspiration
by Rouget de Lisle, a captain of engineers, in 1792. It was this song, *La
Marseillaise*, that was sung by the band of volunteers who marched
from Marseilles in the summer of that year to launch the attack on the
Tuileries. This, the most rousing of all national anthems, was subsequently harmonized and arranged by Gossec, to provide one of the
main inputs into the festival music whose ripples reached Beethoven as
he was reflecting on his own anthem to the words of Schiller's Ode.

However, it was not the *Marseillaise* but Haydn's hymn that was in
the back of Beethoven's mind as he began work on the finale of the
Ninth. This hymn was Haydn's favourite among his works, and
towards the end of his life he would play it at the piano with great
emotion. And we all know it, of course, because it has entered the
English hymnal. It is a melody that moves through neighbouring notes,
while smoothly leading the harmony from tonic to dominant and back
again. And many of its phrases resemble or anticipate the phrases that
we find in the Ode to Joy. (Ex. 6.) At the back of Beethoven's mind was
surely the recognition that melodies like Haydn's are not just catchy
tunes, but cunning works of art, in which the most serious sentiments
are led by irresistible melodic and harmonic progressions, so as to
conquer all resistance in singer and listener alike. Haydn's is a melody
to stir the heart of everyone, while remaining open to the kind of
elaborate musical treatment that the classical style delights in. As it
happens, Haydn's variations in the Quartet are as simple and engaging
as the theme—more ornamentations than variations, in fact, like the
variations of the Adagio theme in Beethoven's Ninth.

If we turn to Beethoven's theme, and the first two variations, we see that, without disturbing the simple tonic-dominant harmony, Beethoven weaves an elaborate counterpoint, with suggestions of a countermelody from the bassoon, and a wonderfully mellifluous way of wrapping the melody in its own thematic fragments. He is revisiting Haydn's original inspiration, and drawing upon it, as he had drawn upon the recitative in the cello and bass, to remind his listeners of the human voice and its uses. Before you have heard the voice in this symphony you find yourself with an almost irresistible urge to sing along. You are already in the realm of the anthem, though an anthem raised to heights of sublimity not before attained.

After the third variation has run its course in a jubilant tutti, with brass and timpani on full martial display, the orchestra picks up the theme and runs with it, taking motives and fragments in the inspired manner of the first movement, and breaking the melody down into the slabs and sections that will be used to build the great edifice that is to come. Before another variation can begin, however, the flow is interrupted by the *Schreckensfanfare*. The message is clear: the consolation so far wrought and offered has been incomplete, and true joy can come only with the human community. It seems to me that the way the Ode is introduced at this point is a sublime stroke of musical rhetoric. We already know the theme, and its fragmentation has enabled Beethoven to provide four irresistible bars of introduction, in which the choir can make its presence known, while allowing the baritone nevertheless to convey the message that is soon to receive its musical illustration.

The message is not that of a national anthem, but of an anthem that transcends all national boundaries. The Enlightenment has found its voice, and it is one that denies the division between the nations and tribes of human kind. With a tune as catchy as this, and words as exultant, Beethoven is undeniably treading dangerous ground, as Gossec did in his now forgotten triumphs. Peaceful communities can turn without warning into dangerous crowds, and exultant dances into aggressive swarms. We may want to dance, but there is all the difference in the world between dancing around the Golden Calf, and dancing before the tablets of the law. We are suspicious of mass emotions and shrink from public celebration for fear that the wrong side of us will be nourished by it. In response I will try to show why the finale of the Ninth is a wholly innocent celebration of our shared humanity, and why we should receive this great movement in the spirit of jubilation with which it was intended.

Example 7

Once the voices have entered, and the choir has taken up the melody, the movement continues as before, adding three more ravishing variations of the theme in the home key of D major, and linked by a bridging phrase that Beethoven has managed to extract without our noticing it from his kitten-like games with the melody: Ex. 7 (bars 293–297). These variations are of the kind attached to his original anthem by Haydn: they alter neither the underlying harmony nor the implied melodic contour, but merely embellish both with exquisite decorative patterns. These are not variations in the mould of Bach's Goldberg Variations or Beethoven's Diabelli Variations, in which the theme is repeatedly lost to view, as the music meditates on its deeper and more occult forms of order. They are melodic embellishments, reminding the listeners that they too can join in, that nothing is required of them, save an instinctive wish to move in spirit with the music. Some regard this use of purely ornamental variations as an artistic failing, an implied recognition that there is nothing more to the theme than a catchy melody. Suppose, however, that Beethoven had composed in the manner of his own Diabelli Variations, changing key, tempo, harmony and melodic line, in order to meditate—as a composer of his genius most assuredly could meditate—on all the many musical questions and answers that could be extracted from his material. It is surely evident that the finale would promptly lose its character as a strophic ode, would leave the world of community and celebration, and re-enter those intensely private and often agonizing domains that Beethoven had explored in the preceding movements. In following Haydn's example in the Emperor Quartet, Beethoven shows his understanding of what an anthem should be, while at the same time inviting us into the only possible answer to the questions raised by the preceding movements.

However, that is not all there is to the form of the choral finale. Imposed upon the sequence of variations is another and grander structure, a division into sections which has a meaning quite different from that of naive jubilation. After the three vocal variations have run their course, ending on the line

Und der Cherub steht vor Gott (and the seraph stands before God)

Example 8

Beethoven repeats the line with a statuesque theme on minims for the choir, which is also a counter-melody to the charming bridging passage mentioned earlier. He then detaches the last two words 'vor Gott', and repeats them twice in a dramatic change of key to B flat. God's name, thus dramatized, is followed by a strange silence, bringing home the crucial idea to which Beethoven is to return just as soon as Schiller's verse allows him—the idea of God's fatherly love, as the cause of every genuine celebration.

The next variation is purely instrumental, however: a march in 6/8 time accompanied by a Turkish percussion band, a kind of grotesque parody of the French revolutionary triumphs. This introduces another variation for tenor, in which the chorus joins in, invoking the course of the sun, as it runs with God's will, and the human desire to run along with it. This desire is promptly turned into magnificent music, as Beethoven rounds off the variation with a skilful double fugue for full orchestra, one theme of which is derived by prolonging the catchy phrase with which the previous variation had begun. (Ex. 8.) This extended passage enables Beethoven to break free from the tonic-dominant harmony that had prevailed until this point. The music tears away from B flat major, knocking down key after key until arriving at B major, which is also knocked over to leave only a bare F sharp octave on the horns. Beethoven tickles this bare octave to life with the opening two bars of the original melody, first in B major, then in B minor, and finally, in a thunderous burst of joy from the whole orchestra and chorus, in D major, repeating the first verse of Schiller's Ode in a final ornamentation.

Thus ends what some have called the 'scherzo' section of the finale. It has brought us to the crux of the movement, a section marked Andante maestoso in which a new theme in G major, with a cathedral-like majesty, introduces another meditation on God's love:

Seid umschlungen, Millionen!
Diesen Küss der ganzen Welt!
Brüder, überm Sternenzelt
Muß ein lieber Vater wohnen.

(Be embraced, you millions, here is a kiss for the whole world! Brothers, above the starry firmament, a loving father must dwell.)

Beethoven did not lead a devout life, though he died in the arms of the Catholic Church. However, he was a profoundly religious man, whose notebooks testify to the deep faith exhibited also in his later music. Like Schiller, he believed that there could be true brotherly love only where there is a common father, and that to invoke joy and fellowship, without acknowledging the God who is the sole originating cause of them, is to give way to a kind of idolatry. Beethoven's theme, with its firm pillars of sound, embellished by strings that flutter around it like the wings of angels, banishes all thought of the Golden Calf. We are returned to the true object of adoration, the God who had been quietly acknowledged in the still, small voice of the slow movement, and who is now revealed in all his majesty and splendour. The theme is developed in a most sublime way, reaching ever upwards as though aspiring to the vault of some great cathedral, to reach a sustained and ethereal dominant minor ninth in the home key of D, thus ending the embryonic slow movement within the finale, and returning us to the original verses of the Ode to Joy in a new variation.

The original melody now appears in 6/4 time, with the theme of the Andante sounding along with it in perfect harmony—another example of Beethoven's amazing serendipity, which also treats us to a triple fugue of great brilliance. (Ex. 9.) The fugue exhausts itself and the verses and mood of the Andante return in a solemn acknowledgement of God's majesty. Thereafter, in an extended coda, the music runs on in joyous excitement, still mixing the original strophe with the verses that remind us of God's love, condensing everything into an idiom in which it is hardly possible to distinguish one variation from the next, and using all the melodic fragments so far accumulated to whip up an ecstatic riot of jubilation. The coda culminates in a Dionysiac presto, the last variation, which rushes to a conclusion with a phrase that, as Tovey points out, could have been yet another symphonic theme—further proof of the enormous generosity of inspiration exemplified in this work, a generosity that is the emblem of the joy that it expresses.

What should we make of this movement now? Some people find the Enlightenment vision of humanity hard to swallow, now that human

Example 9

beings have offered such devastating proof of their capacity for hatred. Others object to the frenzy with which it ends—which seems more like a loss of reason than a celebration of it, and a sign of an underlying lack of balance in Beethoven's vision. Others still find in this abstract invocation of brotherly love an echo of Beethoven's own inability (conveyed by the very title of his song-cycle *An die ferne Geliebte*) to love a real, present and imperfect human being. And the underlying naivety of the social and religious vision is seen by many not as innocent simplicity but as culpable indifference to real human failings. Thus Richard Taruskin writes:

Kerman calls the theme 'half folk-like, blinding in its demagogic innocence'. Is this the Elysium to which our noble guest has delivered us, the realm glimpsed mistily through visionary modulations amid the crags and ravines of earlier movements? And who are all this riffraff, with their beery Männerchöre and sauerkraut bands? Our brothers? And the juxtaposition of all this with the disclosure of God's presence 'above the stars'. No, it is all too much!⁹

And of course, a melody so often hummed, whistled and variously mutilated is not likely to be without its critics. Matters have not been helped by the EU, which has made the Ode to Joy into its official anthem, carefully excising, however, all reference to God, since the one thing that the EU is determined, in its official pronouncements, to deny, is the religion that created Europe.

Let me then say, in conclusion, that I think the finale of the Ninth Symphony is a genuine triumph, both musically and emotionally, and that it wants only a sympathetic attention to the musical language for this to become absolutely clear. The last movement is an anthem in the tradition of Haydn's: an invocation of community that is also a hymn to God. By using Haydn's musical language, Beethoven is also gently suggesting what his finale is not: it is not a *national* anthem, nor is it a prayer on behalf of some particular people or their monarch. It is emphatically not the kind of belligerent assertion of national pride that we find in the French revolutionary festivals or in *La Marseillaise*. On the contrary, it sounds a warning against all such frenetic celebrations of merely political power. It is devoted to an ideal of human community, one without barriers or frontiers, not because it is international or multicultural but because it is rescued from space and time, and restored to its place among things eternally hoped for. The quiet prayer of the slow movement is answered at last, with a vision of joy that belongs in the same transcendental sphere as the God there prayed to. The ideal community, Beethoven reveals, is never to be confounded with an actual community of people: it is a light that guides us, an Idea of Reason as Kant would describe it, visible only if we keep our eyes on God, who is the true source and object of the love that we seek in each other.

Notes

1 I record my debt here, however, to the illuminating, if characteristically exasperated, study by Heinrich Schenker, *Beethoven's Ninth Symphony*, tr. John Rothgeb, Yale 1992.
2 'Zum Vortrag der neunten Symphonie Beethoven's', in *Gesammelte Schriften und Dichtungen*, zweite Auflage, Leipzig 1888, vol. 9, pp. 231–57.
3 But not when you transcribe the work, as Brahms did, for piano left-hand, thereby retaining the sense of strain.
4 Note, however, that the C flat major scale in the Adagio, next to impossible on the natural horn, is given by Beethoven to the fourth horn. It has recently been ascertained that the fourth horn-player in Beethoven's orchestra had acquired an instrument with two valves.
5 *Beethoven: The Last Decade, 1817–1827*, London 1970, p. 281.
6 On this point see Ernst Kurth's still pertinent argument in *Romantische Harmonik und ihre Krise in Wagners "Tristan"*, Berne 1920.
7 Sir Donald Tovey, *Essays in Musical Analysis*, vol. II, London 1935, p. 6.
8 *Ibid.*, p. 20.
9 'Resisting the Ninth', in *Text and Act*, Oxford 1995, p. 249.

The trial of Richard Wagner

Wagner's mature operas concern heroes who move in a mythic realm, and who are prompted by emotions which have been lifted free of ordinary human contingencies and endowed with a cosmic significance and force. In works like *The Ring*, *Tristan* and *Parsifal*, the human condition is idealized, as it might be in the narratives and liturgy of a religion. To take these operas seriously is to be drawn into a peculiar modern project, which is that of remaking the gods out of human material. This project, it seems to me, identifies both the artistic triumph of Wagner, and the hostility with which that triumph is so often greeted.

Wagner tried to create a new musical public, one that would see the point of idealizing the human condition. This attempt was already doomed when Wagner first conceived it; since then, it has acquired its own tragic pathos, as modern producers, embarrassed by dramas that make a mockery of their way of life, decide in their turn to make a mockery of the dramas. Of course, even today, musicians and singers, responding as they must to the urgency and sincerity of the music, do their best to produce the sounds that Wagner intended. But the action is invariably caricatured, wrapped in inverted commas, and reduced to the dimensions of a TV sitcom. Sarcasm and satire run riot on the stage, as in Richard Jones's recent Covent Garden production of *The Ring*, not because they have anything to prove or to say in the shadow of this noble music, but because nobility has become intolerable. The producer strives to distract the audience from Wagner's message, and to mock every heroic gesture, lest the point of the drama should finally come home. As Michael Tanner has argued, in his succinct and penetrating defence of the composer, modern productions attempt to 'domesticate' Wagner, to bring his dramas down from the exalted sphere in which the music places them, to the world of human trivia, usually in order to make a 'political statement' which, being both blatant and banal, succeeds only in cancelling the rich ambiguities of the drama.[1]

In their attempts to rationalize their distaste, the critics of Wagner have approached his art with a no-holds-barred antagonism that has few parallels outside the chronicles of religious censorship. Nietzsche led the way, in writings that are penetrating in just the way that religious inquisitions are penetrating, seeking the proof of damnation in the smallest gesture. The interrogations have continued unabated, with critics freely exploiting the facts of Wagner's life, his writings, his powers of self-advertisement, and the corruptions of his worst admirers in order to place a massive moral question-mark over his works.

The recent assault on Wagner's anti-semitism owes much to Adorno.[2] But Adorno's reservations were also critical, and he tried, in his tortured and tortuous way, to discover corruption in the melodic and harmonic structure of Wagner's music, regardless of the composer's unpleasant opinions. Other critics have been less scrupulous, and seen the agitated anti-semitism of the man as a sufficient condemnation of the work, without troubling to ask themselves where, and how, the anti-semitism finds endorsement in the music.[3] Even a critic as thoughtful and alert to the musical argument as Barry Millington can write as though anti-semitism were somewhere near the top of Wagner's musical and intellectual agenda and as though it should therefore be constantly borne in mind as we study his works.[4] To a great extent, this obsessive distraction from the real questions surrounding Wagner's art and philosophy has been laid to rest by Brian Magee, in his account of Wagner's intellectual background.[5] Nevertheless, something needs to be added to Magee's defence, if we are to understand the root of the hostility to Wagner.

In the second half of the twentieth century, 'racism' became the first among political crimes, and one so broadly defined that even the most innocent remark may be taken as proof of it—for example, the remark that I have just made in this sentence. Racism has also been associated (at least by those on the Left) with the political and social beliefs of the 'Right', and especially with the defence of traditional order, social hierarchy and the inheritance of Western culture. Furthermore, crimes committed by the political Right are not forgiven by modern intellectuals, whereas those committed by the political Left, if noticed at all, are usually dismissed as errors, or justified in terms of their long-term effects.

Wagner was for much of his life a revolutionary, and one who distinguished himself in the liberal-socialist cause. But it cannot be denied that the philosophy that is most easily gleaned from his later works is in sharp conflict with the egalitarian project. Moreover, his celebration of the German idea, and of the folk-culture in which it is embedded, has made him far more useful to nationalists, traditionalists and reactionaries than he could ever be to socialists or liberals. Nor has Wagner's reputation been helped by Hans Sachs's appeal to the German nation in *Die Meistersinger*, or by the extraordinary restatement of Christian mysticism in *Parsifal*. Subsequent history has only confirmed the suspicions of left-wing critics, and as a result the crimes of Hitler are read back into the operas of Wagner, as though they originated in that source.

In his striking recent biography of the composer, Joachim Köhler associates Wagner with the German nationalist movement, in which the building of Bayreuth and the works performed there played an undeniable role.[6] He believes it to be no accident that Hitler's love of Wagnerian symbols fuelled the Nazi frenzy or that the anti-semitism so vehemently expressed in the composer's prose writings should later have re-emerged in Germany as a call to genocide. And Köhler's antagonistic reading of Wagner's personality percolates into his reading of the works. The Dutchman is Ahasuerus, the Wandering Jew; Alberich is the insidious money-grubbing Jew who pollutes the moral order from a place beneath it; Beckmesser is the Jewish interloper who undermines the honour and public spirit of the city. *Parsifal* is an affirmation of the divine light of Jesus — the light bestowed by mortal sacrifice — against the dark tyranny of the God of Israel. *Die Meistersinger* is not the innocent comedy proclaimed by its author, but a sinister avatar of German racism, so that Hans Sachs's interruption of the rejoicing at the opera's end to warn against the enemies of German art betrays, for Köhler, the real underlying tendency of the drama. And so on.

My response to this reading (which has been a commonplace of Wagner criticism since Adorno) is to ask: what if Wagner had never written his notorious pamphlet on Jewishness in music? What if he had never uttered an anti-semitic remark but merely greeted all reference to the Jewish race with an enigmatic smile? Would we then be inclined to read anti-semitism into the works that allegedly contain it? My response is: surely not. To someone who says 'Just look at Mime, the falsely humble, snivelling, wheedling, power-hungry schemer — isn't this the very caricature of the Jew?' I would reply simply: 'Who is the anti-semite?' Moreover, if the Dutchman is really the Wandering Jew, what a vindication of the Jewish race that Wagner should project on to it his own longing for redemption! If Veit Beckmesser is a Jew, what a great advertisement is *Die Meistersinger* for racial integration, that this vain little man should be so fully absorbed into the life of the city as to occupy the public office of Marker, that he should be accepted by everyone as a legitimate contender for the hand of Ewa, and that he should be judged at last only by his musical and poetical performance and not by his race!

But of course Beckmesser is not a Jew, Wagner's spite against the half-Jewish Hanslick notwithstanding. Nor is the warning that Hans Sachs pronounces at the end of the work an invocation of *nationalist* sentiments. Wagner hesitated on artistic grounds to include this passage, succumbing perhaps to Cosima's pressure but also aware of the artistic need, at this juncture, to hold up the flow of jubilation and to remind the *real* interloper, Walther von Stolzing, that he cannot simply back away from the community whose old order he has challenged. Sachs's intention is to enfold Walther within a common loyalty and common moral and artistic inheritance. He therefore reminds the company of what has really been at stake throughout the opera, namely the equal need in both art and life for 'tradition and the individual talent', to quote from another great artist who has been tarred with the anti-semitic brush.

Anybody who thinks of *Die Meistersinger* as a celebration of German nationalism as we know it has surely lost the plot. The drama is an invocation of the self-governing city. It presents us not with the new Germany of the nation state but with the old and lovable Germany of the Burg, the Germany celebrated by Hegel as 'bürgerliche Gesellschaft', in which autonomous corporations maintain order and meaning without depending on the state, in which local ties are sustained by religion, family and the 'little platoons' of civil society, and whose peace is symbolized in the serene F major melody of the Nightwatchman, as he obstinately disregards the dissonant G flat of his own policeman's horn.

True, this society needs to be renewed from time to time, and that is what the drama is all about—as are all comedies if we are to follow Christopher Booker in his brilliant summary of story-telling, *The Seven Basic Plots*. But it is not the state, still less the unified national state created by Bismarck, that Wagner summons to the aid of this community whose corporate feelings have staled. It is erotic love, shaped by the project of marriage, flowing through the channels of custom, and renewing family and civil society, along with the musical tradition that has the endorsement of these things as its true moral goal.

Wagner was in the business of creating legends, not dramas only. He therefore draws extensively on the archetypes of folk tales. As in so many 'rags to riches' children's stories, his heroes tend to be orphans, or else to arrive, like Walther, from an inexplicable 'elsewhere'. They are on the surface antagonistic to the existing social order: but their antagonism is gradually overcome, often by some wise father-figure like

Sachs or Gurnemanz, who is able to understand and forgive. Köhler is a modern German in this, that he prefers the revolutionary philosophy of Wagner's Dresden years to the later endorsement of the bourgeois order and the ethic of Christian renunciation. But that endorsement, made explicit in *Die Meistersinger* and *Parsifal*, is the true tendency of all the mature dramas, and is evinced in a final reconciliation between youthful adventure and aged restraint. The outward form of this reconciliation is presented in the last act of *Die Meistersinger*, and its inner price is the theme of *Parsifal*.

None of that will serve to rescue Wagner from his left-wing critics. Guilt by association is the fate of any artist who can be seen as a fellow traveller of the political Right; recent victims include Joseph Conrad, T. S. Eliot, Ezra Pound, W. B. Yeats, Ernst Junger, Hans Pfitzner and Igor Stravinsky. Such treatment rarely awaits the intellectual of the Left, and even those who have justified and encouraged crime on the highest scale—Sartre, for example, Aragon, Brecht, Hanns Eisler—are often forgiven by their intellectual judges, who assume the right in such matters to speak for all mankind.

Having pondered this asymmetry of blame for many years, I have drawn the following tentative conclusions. Crime, on however large a scale, arouses little or no revulsion among left-wing intellectuals, provided that the goal is social equality—the pulling down of those on top, or the raising up of those below. Sometimes those below are the victims: this is usually seen as an 'error'. If the victims are those on top, however, the measures tend to be perceived as expedient and justified. At the same time, crime committed in the cause of inequality—in order to maintain social hierarchy, ancestral privileges, or control over discontented elements—always arouses great revulsion, however economical it may be in victims.

Thus the 'Peterloo' Massacre, in which eleven people were killed in a cause generally endorsed by left-wing intellectuals, stands far higher in the list of recognized crimes than Katyn, where tens of thousands died, and certainly higher than the mass murders of priests by the Spanish Republicans, of 'right-wing' partisans by the Soviet 'liberators' or of just about everybody by the French Revolutionaries. Anybody who has noticed these remarkable facts will ponder, too, the comparison between the collective crime of the Nazis and that of the Soviet communists, and recognize the ease with which the first has been exalted into the greatest crime in history, and the equal ease with which the second has been dismissed as irrelevant to any rational assessment of Marxist philosophy.

Here, I believe, lies the root of the hostility to Wagner. His art is dedicated to human distinction. He did not believe that human beings are equal in any of the respects which make life worthwhile. His ideal hero could not possibly be taken as a model by socialists, liberals, urban intellectuals or anybody attached to the idea of human equality. Moreover, the dramatic context makes it all too easy to suppose that the composer's anti-semitism is of a piece with his hero-worship, and that both are founded in an ideology of racial supremacy. It is true that Shaw saw Siegfried as a portrait of the revolutionary anarchist Bakunin, with whom Wagner had been friendly in his revolutionary years. But the identification is wildly implausible, and proof, at best, that Bakunin would not have lasted long in his own utopia.

Nietzsche was less bothered by the anti-semitism than by the hero-worship. And this not for the reasons that trouble modern critics, who cannot abide romantic heroes in any form, but because, in Nietzsche's view, the heroic in Wagner is a sham. Rather than accept Wagner's characters in the terms suggested by the drama—terms in which Wagner himself, as a disciple of Feuerbach, did not believe—we should, Nietzsche advises, translate them 'into reality, into the modern—let us be even crueller—into the bourgeois!' And what then? We find ourselves among the 'metropolitan' problems of Parisian decadents—'always five steps from the hospital'.[7]

Whether or not we accept Nietzsche's strictures, we should recognize that they are genuine criticism. Nietzsche does not condemn the art by finding fault with the man. He purports to discern a profound artistic failing in the works themselves, a failing that undermines their clamorous appeal for our attention. And if he is right in this, then we should all treat Wagner with reserve—a reserve that would be fatal to the artistic intention. Nietzsche is asking us to see through Wagner's characters, with their vast fields of heroic action, to the repertoire of real emotions from which their deeds derive. What we then find, Nietzsche believes, is not heroic fortitude, generous love, or world-redeeming renunciation, but attention-seeking neurosis and a life-denying inability to accept the world as it is.

Nietzsche is inviting us to see Wagner's characters as one-dimensional people lifted free from the bourgeois reality of cost and benefit, to enjoy a spurious sovereignty over their fate in fairyland. But Wagner's dramas are not fairy tales. Nothing is more impressive in them than the grim realism with which wholly intelligible motives are carried through to their crisis. At the same time, these motives are placed in a pre-historical, mythical or medieval setting. Wagner's purpose was not to fill the stage with fantasies, but to create the kind of distance between audience and drama that would endow the drama with a universal significance. Hence his preoccupation with myths and legends—i.e. stories which depart from realism only in order to convey universal truths about the human condition.

When Wagner applied himself to the study of the surviving literature of the early Germanic tribes, and to the poetry of medieval Germany, it was not to identify exemplary people and historical events but to acquaint himself with a culture in which the real had been through and through penetrated by the ideal: a culture in which people did not merely do things, but also lived up to things. He discovered myth not as a collection of fables and beliefs, nor as a primitive religion, but as a distinct category of human thought, as open to us, Wagner thought, in a world of scientific scepticism as it was open to the inhabitants of ancient Greece or Iceland. Myth dawned on Wagner as a form of social hope. It was a way of thinking that could restore to modern man the lost sense of the ideal, without which human life is worthless.

Wagner's discovery of myth is not merely a matter of one person's moral and artistic credo. It is also one of the great intellectual advances of modern times, the ancestor and inspiration of comparative anthropology, symbolist poetry, psychoanalysis and many aesthetic and theological doctrines that are now common currency. Wagner is given credit for this by Claude Lévi-Strauss (who acknowledges the composer as the main inspiration behind his 'structuralist' method),[8] by the anthropologist and medievalist Jessie L. Weston, and by Weston's disciple, T. S. Eliot, in The Waste Land. The idea of myth as a dramatization of deep and hidden truths about the human psyche entered common currency with Freud's theory of the unconscious. However, the accumulation of myth-analysing, myth-dramatizing and myth-making that has ensued in the wake of Wagner has made it all the more necessary for us to revisit Wagner's own approach, and to study the freshness and vitality with which he transformed ancient myth and legend into quintessentially modern art.

A myth, for Wagner, is not a fable or a religious doctrine but a vehicle for human knowledge. The myth acquaints us with ourselves and our condition, using symbols and characters that give objective form to our inner compulsions. Myths are set in the hazy past, in a vanished world of chthonic forces and magniloquent deeds. But this obligatory 'pastness' is a heuristic device. It places the myth and its characters before recorded time, and therefore in an era that is purged of history. It lifts the story out of the stream of human life, and endows it with a meaning that is timeless.

Wagner's original impulse, therefore, which was to discover in the ancient legends of the Germanic people the living record of the time of heroes, led him back to his starting point in the modern world. The time of heroes was a mythical time—and mythical time is *now*. Myths do not speak of what was but of what is eternally. They are magical-realist summaries of the actual world, in which the moral possibilities are personified and made flesh. Hence *The Ring*, Wagner's incomparable synthesis of the Germanic and Icelandic myths as they were reflected in the dark mirror of early Germanic literature, became the most determinedly modern of his works, the one which more than any other provides a commentary on modern life and on the hopes and fears that thrive in it. Yet, planted within the bitter and often cynical drama, like a seed that survives in the desert and which suddenly flowers at the first drop of rain, is the heroic ideal—the ideal that Wagner had searched for as a past reality, but which he discovered to be a myth, and therefore all the more real for us, being written not in the past tense but in the eternal present.

The heroic ideal, enshrined in the love of Siegfried and Brünnhilde, was not refuted but vindicated, for Wagner, by its mythical setting. Of course, Wagner did not see the legends that he wove into dramas as we would see them. But he responded to their hidden fund of religious feeling, and this endows the Wagnerian music dramas with their distinctive spiritual glow. All the subtle emendations and elisions, whereby Wagner extracted from his sources a cogent and supremely logical foil for character and passion, were designed to reveal the sacred—indeed sacramental—character of our deepest emotions, and to isolate the moments of sacrifice in which ideals become real. The love-death theme that is made explicit in *Tristan und Isolde* propels also the inner psychic movement of *The Ring*, and is only superficially hidden by the veil of religious renunciation drawn across it in *Parsifal*. We are being constantly reminded that love, treated as a summons to sacrifice, becomes a sacred and redeeming force. All else is compromise.

In pursuing this theme Wagner created an array of unforgettable characters and a series of brilliant plots. He also invoked an eerie world without love—the world of Nibelheim, which we revisit again and again in *The Ring*, not as a physical but as a psychical realm, from which the tormented souls of Mime, Alberich and Hagen can never escape, since they are incapable of the one thing—renunciation—which would give them the power to do so. Wagner contrasted this loveless realm not with a *kingdom* of love—for there is no such thing, as the story of Walhalla reveals—but with moments of sacrifice and renunciation, in which love suddenly irradiates the human psyche and irresistibly persuades us that our mortal life is worthwhile, and worthwhile because mortal.

In *Parsifal* the moment of sacrifice achieves Christian form. But the Christianity is grafted on to a more pagan conception of sacrifice—a conception that comes vividly to mind in the two immolations of Brünnhilde and in the death of Siegfried. The connection between Siegfried's death and the pagan stories of victims sacrificed and sanctified so that the world might be renewed was noticed by Thomas Mann, in a vivid passage that deserves quotation:

The overpowering accents of the music that accompanies Siegfried's funeral cortège no longer tell of the woodland boy who set out to learn the meaning of fear; they speak to our emotions of what is *really* passing away behind the lowering veils of mist: it is the sun-hero himself who lies upon the bier, slain by the pallid forces of darkness—and there are hints in the text to support what we *feel* in the music: 'A wild boar's fury,' it says, and: 'Behold the cursed boar,' says Gunther, pointing to Hagen, 'who slew this noble flesh.' The words take us back at a stroke to the very earliest picture-dreams of mankind. Tammuz and Adonis, slain by the boar, Osiris and Dionysus, torn asunder to come again as the Crucified One, whose flank must be ripped open by a Roman spear in order that the world might know Him—all things that ever were and ever shall be, the whole world of beauty sacrificed and murdered by wintry wrath, all is contained within this single glimpse of myth.[9]

In *Opera and Drama* Wagner compared the role of the orchestra to that of the chorus in the Greek tragedy. Although this very imperfectly describes his own use of the orchestra in subsequent works, it perfectly fits the technique that the composer uses in order to set a frame around Siegfried as he is led forward to the slaughter. The orchestra is the supremely sympathetic observer of its own sacrificial victim, following his narrative in a kind of subdued awe, leading him on with gentle gestures as the sacred bull was led to the altar, encouraging him to give the sign of acceptance that will summon the sacrificial blow. It is precisely because his musical technique brought these undercurrents of religious emotion so infallibly to the surface that Wagner was able to iconize and idealize the passions of his characters, and to make it not just plausible but also right that they should sacrifice everything for what would otherwise be the transient nothingness of love.

In my view it is only if we understand the religious nature of Wagner's dramas that we will really be able to account for their appeal to modern people, and for the hostility as well as the devotion that they inspire. For Wagner, as for the Greeks, a myth was not a decorative fairy tale, but the elaboration of a secret, a way of both hiding and revealing mysteries that can be understood only in religious terms, through the ideas of sanctity, holiness and redemption. These are ideas that we all of us need, Wagner believed, and, although the common people perceive them through the veil of religious doctrine, they come alive in the great examples of love and renunciation, and find articulate form in art.[10] Wagner's own words best explain his stance: 'It is reserved to art to salvage the kernel of religion, inasmuch as the mythical images which religion would wish to be believed as true are apprehended in art for their symbolic value, and through ideal representation of those symbols art reveals the concealed deep truth within them.'[11]

Wagner's works are therefore more than mere dramas: they are revelations, attempts to penetrate to the mysterious core of human existence. They are not unique in this: Aeschylus and Shakespeare (to both of whom Wagner was hugely indebted) also present dramas that are shaped as religious epiphanies. But Wagner worked in another medium, which enabled him to present the conscious and individual passions of his characters simultaneously with their universal and unconscious archetypes. The orchestra does not merely accompany Wagner's singers, nor are they merely singers. The orchestra fills in the space beneath the revealed emotions with all the ancestral longings of our species, irresistibly transforming these individual passions into symbols of a common destiny that can be sensed but not told. Wagner acquaints us with our lot, and makes available to an age without religious *belief* the core religious *experience*—an experience that we need, but which we also flee from, since it demands from us even more than it gives.

To the religious mind nature lies beyond human control, though not beyond human damage. The natural world must therefore be approached with awe and piety, but also with a bold sense that we belong in it, and can abuse our position of trust. Moreover, for the religious person nature is governed by the very same forces that order the inner life, and is therefore, in the words of Baudelaire's sonnet, 'a forest of symbols'. This way of reading nature belongs with those 'very earliest picture-dreams of mankind' to which Mann refers. It is not only in children's stories that birds speak and trees have faces. This is our primal experience of the world—an experience of territory that we share with other species, governed by forces that we must appease through prayer and sacrifice, and which we must strive to get on our side.

Wagner perceived that the drama of *The Ring*, whose characters inhabit the landscape of the hunter-gatherer, required him to reinvent such a natural world. The forests and rivers, the fires and storms, the dragons and mermaids, the voices of the woods and the birds—all these are recreated in *The Ring*, with a freshness and poetry that owe everything to music, but with a directness that recalls the rich tradition of German children's literature. (All children have been brought up on this literature, even those who have never read a word of it, since it is the literature that created childhood. Christmas is only one of its many by-products.) The god-haunted, dream-enchanted landscape of *The Ring* is the first thing that modern producers hasten to air-brush from the story. For it creates the context in which religious awe is inescapable.

Looked at in that way, we can see Wagner's *Ring* cycle as a bridge between two far more humble productions: Grimm's fairy tales and the *Lord of the Rings*. Grimm influenced Wagner and Wagner made Tolkien possible. Indeed the emotions that are stirred by the cinematic realization of Tolkien's rambling story are a faint echo of what would be felt, were *The Ring* to be performed as Wagner intended, with every single stage direction realistically obeyed. This would be the film to end all films, the *Götterdämmerung* of our modern era, in which Wagner's moral would be apparent even to the unmusical. And almost certainly it would be banned.

Tolkien's passion for the medieval world arose, like Wagner's, from a lifelong religious quest. Unlike Wagner, however, Tolkien did not have the ability to remake the religious experience through art. He remained a 'good sad Christian at heart', but with a talent for pagan fairy tales. His novel has smatterings of the great conflict between good and evil, and an abundance of mysteries. But it does not re-create the experience that Wagner has always in mind in the tetralogy, which is the experience of the sacred. *The Ring* is not merely the greatest invocation of primeval Nature and the hunter-gatherer world in modern art. It also abounds in moments of genuine religious awe: Brünnhilde's announcement to Siegmund of his impending death; Sieglinde's blessing of Brünnhilde; Wotan's farewell; Siegfried's first encounter with Brünnhilde—and so on. Virtually all the turning points of the drama are conceived in sacramental terms; they are occasions of awe, piety and transition, in which a victim is offered and a promise of redemption received.

But a peculiar Wagnerian twist is given to each of these moments. While the sacred has in the past been interpreted as man's avenue to God, for Wagner it is God's avenue to man. It is the gods, not mankind, that need redemption, and redemption can come through love. But love, for Wagner, is possible only between mortals—it is a relation between dying things, who embrace their own death as they yield to it. This Brünnhilde recognizes during her great dialogue with Siegmund, resolving in her heart, but as yet not fully conscious that this is what she is doing, to relinquish her immortality for the sake of a human love.

But what, on this view, are the gods? Mere figments, as Feuerbach had argued? Or something more deeply implanted in the scheme of things, something that precedes and survives us? Wagner's answer is not easily explained in words, although it is transparently obvious in music. And it is an answer that makes him supremely relevant to us. For, despite our attempts to live without formal religion, we are no more free than people ever have been or ever will be from the religious need. Wagner accepted Feuerbach's view of the gods as human creations. But human creations include some very real and lasting things, like St Paul's Cathedral. Gods come and go; but they last as long as we make room for them, and we make room for them through sacrifice. The gods come about because we idealize our passions, and we do this not by sentimentalizing them but, on the contrary, by sacrificing ourselves to the vision on which they depend. And it is by accepting the need for sacrifice that we begin to live under divine jurisdiction, surrounded by sacred things, and finding meaning through love. Seeing things that way we recognize that we are not condemned to mortality but consecrated to it.

Properly produced, the Wagner music-dramas compel their audience to see things in that way, which is why they are no longer properly produced. The sacred prompts the desire for desecration, and—in those who have turned away from religion—this desire is irresistible.

Notes

1 Michael Tanner, *Wagner*, Princeton 1996.
2 Theodor Adorno, *In Search of Wagner*, Berlin 1952, tr. R. Livingstone, London 1981.
3 See Marc A. Wiener, *Richard Wagner and the Anti-Semitic Imagination*, Lincoln, Nebraska and London 1995, which verges on the insidious accusation that, if you don't see (hear?) the anti-semitism in Wagner, then that just proves you are an anti-semite. (See, for example, p. 30.)
4 Barry Millington, *Wagner*, London 1984.
5 Bryan Magee, *Wagner and Philosophy*, London 2001.
6 Joachim Köhler, *Richard Wagner, Last of the Titans*, tr. Stewart Spencer, New Haven and London 2004.
7 Friedrich Nietzsche, *The Case of Wagner*, section 9, in *The Birth of Tragedy* and *The Case of Wagner*, tr. Walter Kaufmann, New York 1967.
8 See the 'Overture' to *Le Cru et le cuit*, Paris 1964, tr. J. and D. Weightman, *The Raw and the Cooked*, London 1978. Lévi-Strauss refers to Wagner as '*ce Dieu, Richard Wagner*', quoting from Mallarmé's sonnet.

9 'The sorrows and grandeur of Richard Wagner', in Thomas Mann, *Pro and Contra Wagner*, tr. Allan Blunden, Introduction by Erich Heller, London 1985, p. 100.

10 See especially *Über Staat und Religion* in *Gesammelte Schriften und Dichtungen*, 2nd edn, Leipzig 1888, vol. viii, pp. 3–29.

11 *Die Religion und die Kunst*, in *Gesammelte Schriften und Dichtungen*, *op. cit.*, vol. x, p. 211.

10

A *first shot at* The Ring.

The Ring, nobody will deny, is a work full of meaning. Indeed it is super-saturated with meaning. We have but to plant the tiniest seed of interpretation and the whole drama crystallizes around it, an inter-locking structure of mutually reinforcing symbols. Invariably, however, the structure seems flawed or incomplete. And the ease with which, from another seed, a wholly conflicting precipitation is instantly obtainable, leads to a peculiar sense of enigma. The superabundance of meaning hides the meaning. And this too is part of what it means.

The Ring should be understood on four levels: mythic, dramatic, political and spiritual. The music brings the four levels together, and many of those who belittle Wagner's achievement do so because they do not understand the music as the primary vehicle through which the action is accomplished. The composer's remarkable gift of synthesis is of course already displayed in the libretto, which tells a rich and exciting story with remarkable economy. Although the narrative is punctuated by paradox, this lies in the nature of myths, which are attempts to see the temporal world from a point of view outside it, and which therefore abut at every point upon the inexplicable. At the same time the music is able to overcome the paradoxes, to propel us through them, while not relinquishing the thread of emotional logic binding scene to scene and character to character in a drama which presses on relentlessly to its end, which is the end of everything.

In *The Perfect Wagnerite* George Bernard Shaw famously dismissed the story of Siegfried and its culmination in *Götterdämmerung* as 'grand opera', in other words, as a derogation from the story of the gold, its theft, and the world's enslavement. This is largely because he could not see how to integrate the individual psychic process which is played out in *Siegfried* with the mythic and political message of *Das Rheingold* and its sequel, to which he gave a Marxist interpretation. Like many commentators before and since, Shaw backed up his interpretation with little musical analysis. Once we turn our attention to the music, however, it is obvious even from the beginning of *Das Rheingold* that the political and the personal are one and the same.

At the time when he completed the text of the cycle, Wagner was a follower of Ludwig Feuerbach, the Young Hegelian whose debunking of Christianity (*The Essence of Christianity*, 1841) had such a profound effect on Marx. Feuerbach's central thesis was that divinities are projections of human virtues, which we worship in order to set our own perfection at a distance from us, so excusing our moral indolence. Wagner did not endorse that thesis entirely: his gods are far lower in the scale of perfection than the humans whom they exploit. Nevertheless, the Feuerbachian ontology is fundamental to the mythic structure of *The Ring*. The gods and Nibelungs are projections—images formed from the raw material of human emotion, and representing forces which are realized in us, and which need us for their realization. These forces are of three kinds. Some belong to our pre-personal and pre-political nature (our 'species-being' in Feuerbach's idiom). These, represented in the Rhinedaughters and the Norns, in Erda and Loge and the woodbird, shroud the world and its origins in mystery. They also intrude into the flow of events, setting inscrutable limits to what can be done or hoped for, and impressing on us the image of a more innocent, more organic, and less conscious mode of being than the one to which the protagonists are fatally drawn.

The second kind of force is represented by the gods—beings who have freed themselves from the natural order sufficiently to take charge of it, and who enjoy the sovereignty which enables them both to satisfy their needs and to live in the civilized leisure of Walhalla. Although the inspiration for Wotan and Fricka lies in the Greeks, and ultimately in Homer, they are also distinctly modern creations. Wotan represents the aspiration for personal power—that is, for the freedom and sovereignty of the self. And there is embodied in his character and wanderings all that pertains to the search for self-realization: freedom, intention, guilt, anxiety, the need for personal satisfaction and inter-personal love, and the things which make all these possible and also constrain them: law, and the categorical imperative that plants law deep in the soul.

To understand Wotan in his full psychological meaning, we should look not to Feuerbach but to his master, Hegel. The Hegelian theory of consciousness tries to show how *Geist* or spirit realizes itself as an individual—i.e. as a self-conscious person. *Selbstbestimmung*—a term from Fichte which means self-consciousness, self-determination, self-certainty, self-realization and self-delimitation all at once—occurs in two spheres: that of 'objective spirit' and that of 'subjective spirit'. Spirit becomes determinate both in the world of institutions and laws, and in the free individual. That which exists objectively as sovereignty and law, exists subjectively as self-knowledge and will. Hence Wotan has both these aspects, and the spear on which all oaths are inscribed is both the rule of law which upholds them, and the will that intends them. This will shapes the individual, and sets him apart from nature. But since no being, not even a god, can be wholly apart from nature, law and will are subject to mutation. (Hence Loge flickers at the point of Wotan's spear, burning away the runes inscribed there.) The force of law and the force of personal existence are both projected in the character of Wotan. And both involve a defiance of the species, a hubris, from which punishment must follow. At first Wotan does not understand this. But gradually, as the gods become incarnate in the mortals whose dreams they are and whose suffering they have required, they are filled with knowledge and released from the burden of existence.

The third kind of force is represented by Nibelheim: the perversion of selfhood that comes through seeking power without law. The separation of spirit from nature can either acknowledge others, as Wotan does, or work like Alberich to enslave them. Alberich must renounce love, and with it the conception of the other as an end in himself. His world therefore involves a loss of inner freedom, a self-enslavement, and this self-enslavement is the objective reality of sin. Projected in the characters of Alberich and Mime are the forces which tempt us from the realm of nature in pursuit of power, and which lead to our spiritual destruction—the destruction portrayed in the preludes to *Siegfried* Act 1, and *Götterdämmerung* Act 2.

Just as the political order pulls the world from its primeval timelessness and places it in the flow of history, so does the individual will pull us from the changeless realm of natural needs—the realm of the species—and set us upon the path of self-realization. It is this dual departure from the natural order that is placed before us by *Rheingold*, and which is the true subject-matter of *The Ring*. The prelude to *Rheingold* is familiar to every musicologist, as the longest deliberation on a single major triad before Philip Glass deprived such things of their interest. It evokes a primeval world, lying outside time and change, the Ur-matter of existence, which has yet to be shaped by will. It is the musical equivalent of the 'state of nature', which does not precede history but lies, as it were, beneath it, the unseen depth of an innocence forever lost, because never truly possessed, and yet always imagined and endlessly longed for.

This world beyond history is filled with currents and eddies which might at any moment break through the mould of changelessness and shape themselves as will. We hear this happening; beneath the unbroken surface of the E flat major triad the horns move in counterpoint, each entering some space as another leaves it. To the undiscerning ear, all is changeless and still, a single chord, spread out over musical space, held constant in root position. But voice-leading and instrumentation ensure that the unisons in this chord are not real unisons; they are points where musical movements coincide, as they hurry on to distant destinations. Beneath its superficial calm the music is beginning to wrestle and break free. Of its own accord the triad becomes animated, pushing against the fragile seam of E flat, B flat and G, until finally bursting forth in an A flat major arpeggio, and incarnating itself as a voice.

The classical economists remarked on a strange paradox—namely, that those things which have greatest value in use, such as air, water and corn, tend to have little or no value in exchange, and this not because they are necessarily abundant or always easy to obtain. Conversely, things with great exchange-value—such as gold and gems—tend to have little or no value in use. And money is the supreme instance of this paradox: it is an object all of whose value is concentrated in its power of exchange, and which has no other use whatsoever.

Ricardo and Marx tried to explain the paradox in terms of the labour theory of value; but the true explanation has to do neither with labour nor with scarcity, but with the innate structure of desire. For those things which satisfy a natural and recurring need our desire is quickly satisfied; beyond a certain quantity we are surfeited. Such things have a rapidly diminishing 'marginal utility'—water and air being obvious instances. As for money, however, its very volatility, its ability to transform itself into any shape, so as to gratify now this desire and now another, means that its marginal utility hardly diminishes as its quantity grows. And precisely for this reason does it exert its terrible psychological power: the means to all ends, whose hold is endless.

The prelude to *Rheingold* shows three primal elements: water, and through that water the air and light which, mingling with its surface, are in due course to create the insubstantial vision which is the gold of the Rhine. The prelude continues to the point of saturation and beyond, so as restlessly to turn away from the surfeit. It is the pure expression in music of the dwindling marginal utility which pertains to our natural elements, and to the natural use we make of them. Adumbrated in this musical episode, therefore, are the premises of the four levels of meaning: the myth of nature; the dramatic temptation to break free from nature; the political transition from use to exchange; and the awakening of the individual from the species, as he sets forth on the journey towards personality, freedom and power. Already we sense, in the purely musical movement concealed within the E flat triad, that these four levels are merely different levels of a single process, and that this process is us.

At the political level, the theft of the fantasm that glitters on the water's surface represents the original usurpation by which nature becomes property and power. The subsequent forging of the ring represents the transformation of use-value into exchange-value (or, in more modern idiom, the conversion of value into price). That is Alberich's route to power; but the original usurpation, we discover, comes in other forms. Wotan too is a usurper, but his usurpation is so deeply hidden that only little by little during the course of the drama do we discover it, and always with a measure of admiration for the god who could have projected his will so deeply into the heart of things. The ring is not money, but all that money means to us—the concentration of power that results when our labour is devoted to exchange and accumulation. Need is now transferable, volatile, and unassuaged. As such, money is a symbol. It stands for the tendency of human beings to accept one thing in lieu of another, to exchange one thing for another, to situate each object in its class of substitutes. This tendency is the first temptation, the original sin. Transfer it to the human world, and the sin becomes the denial of love. This is because the object of love is the individual in his individuality, the incarnate self for which there is no substitute since he can be wanted and cherished only for the particular thing that he is. That is why those who choose this route to social power—the route of exchange and accumulation—must in their deep-est being forswear love, as Alberich did.[1]

That thought is put in play from the outset. The gold of the Rhine appears to Alberich at the very moment when his attempts to obtain love have been frustrated: and the gold appears as a substitute for love, which can be seized only if love is forsworn. Until seized, however, the gold is merely another aspect of the unspoiled natural order—it is the light that glitters in the primeval world, and which those who play in that world would never think of capturing or owning. They are guarding it only as nature guards her resources, with an innocent unconcern for rational plans. The original innocence that attaches to the gold is apparent from the theme which introduces it: an arpeggiated chord of G major beneath oscillating strings. (These oscillating strings will reappear as the voice of nature in Siegfried's ear.) (Ex. 1.) The theme is transparent, radiant, yet empty—a smile on the face of nature. It is followed by the Rhinedaughters' greeting (Ex. 2), which expresses

Example 1

Example 2   *Example 3*   *Example 4*

a joy without concupiscence, a delight without the desire to possess or exchange.

As *The Ring* unfolds it is this two-chord motive which suffers the greatest transformation, becoming gradually poisoned by greed, resentment, anger, and grief, and amalgamating at last with two other motives: Alberich's cry of woe (Ex. 3), and the motive of the curse, to form Ex. 4. (The curse is contained in the first chord—see below.) The subtle musical transformation here, from a V-I cadence to a keyless shift from a Tristan chord on to a dominant seventh, conveys the vast distance in emotion, between joy in the gold, and the hate-filled need to repossess it after many thefts. Yet the thing itself, the music implies, is the unaltered object of these mutating desires.[2] Ex. 4 is the symbol, or rather the musical enactment, of where we have got to since Alberich's original transgression—a transgression on which we all depend, just as the gods depend upon Alberich's theft to pay for their own usurpation. Ex. 4 has this meaning on account of its musical history. A continuous symphonic development has enfolded this cadence, sucked out its innocent life, and filled it with poison.

The Ring becomes a symbol, not merely of money and accumulation, but of an outlook on the world which disregards the personality of people, and looks upon them as we look on objects. Wagner shows us that this outlook exists at both the personal and the political level, portraying in his evocation of Nibelheim a world which has been voided of love and personality in both their inner and their outer meaning. Commentators influenced by Shaw like to see in this political

aspect a foreshadowing of the Marxist critique of capitalist society—and the interpretation seems all the more plausible when set in the
context of Wagner's involvement with the 1848 revolutionaries. My
own view, however, is that Wagner was too great an artist, and too
subtle a thinker, to be entirely taken in by Young Hegelian socialism,
and that, like Schopenhauer, he was instinctively averse to optimism,
whether in private life or in politics. The political vision of *The Ring* is
through and through tempered by the thought that the political and the
spiritual are one. It is composed of glimpses into the inner, phenomeno-
logical reality of power. Hence the need for myth, which shows
decisions and passions to be larger, less explicable and more lost in their
causes than the schemes of rational economic man.

For us, late witnesses to the calamity which *The Ring* foretells,
Nibelheim is a glimpse into the world of totalitarian government, in
which human beings are treated not as subjects but as objects, in which
the paramount concern is survival, and in which the moral life is
therefore eclipsed by calculation. Personal government, by contrast,
respects the freedom of its subjects, and is accountable for what it does.
It is mediated by law, which binds the ruler as well as the ruled. All
actions, whether of individuals or groups, are justiciable, and the state
itself wears the aspect of a person—not merely in the legal sense of
being liable for its actions, but in the moral sense, of being an object of
loyalty, praise and blame. Personal government respects the distinction
between the public and the private, and is reluctant to intrude on the
sovereign rights of subjects.

In *The Ring* the nearest approximation to personal government lies
in the sovereignty of Wotan: the spear which both confers authority and
also qualifies it, by subjecting it to law. This law is natural law,
enshrined in the maxim that *pacta sunt servanda*: treaties must be
honoured. We should not be surprised to find such jurisprudential ideas
evoked in *The Ring*. From *Tannhäuser* onwards, the Wagner operas
show a growing interest in law, as a social force which also shapes the
inner life of those who honour it. In Nibelheim we witness power
without law. Here, in this lower realm, the mask of personality, which
mediates between people and moralizes their dealings, has been
stripped away, leaving force and trickery exposed. Wagner saw clearly
what this means, both politically and personally. All people in this
nether world are objects, and even Alberich's victims lose the capacity
to relate to each other as persons. (Mime recounts to Wotan how the
Nibelungs had lived before Alberich's usurpation, and gives a touching
portrait of a people bound to each other by natural law. Since then, he

implies, all natural relations have broken down, giving way to craft, cunning and the war of all against all.) In Nibelheim power comes not through law but through spells—mysterious devices which can never be traced to any source, and which confer invisibility and impunity on the one who has mastered them. The Tarnhelm is an instance of this, and recalls the panopticon of the police state: wherever you are and whatever you do in that impersonal world, 'they' are invisibly watching you, and can strike you down at any time. You have no defences, no rights, no freedoms, but only whatever temporary barriers you are able to construct through caution and subterfuge.

Moreover, power can afflict you in a thousand forms: 'they' are ubiquitous and protean, changing shape with every attempt to confront or avoid them. All institutions in the totalitarian state are forms which the ruling Party takes in order to achieve its implacable and inscrutable purposes. Those corporate persons—schools, churches, universities, clubs and teams—which form the stuff of social life under personal government are not persons at all. They take no responsibility for their actions, and in any case make no decisions of their own. Under impersonal government there is only one institution—power itself, which penetrates all relations, all hopes and fears, reminding each subject that he is utterly dispensable and can be 'vaporized' at any time.

Nibelheim is perhaps the first premonition in Western art of Orwell's *Nineteen Eighty-Four*. And it is all the more prophetic in portraying the evil as simultaneously political and personal: Nibelheim remains in the soul of those who escape from it, for it is the objective form of an inner privation—the privation of love which will not acknowledge the personality of the other, or confront him as one free being confronts his equal. All this is conveyed inimitably in the Prelude to Act 1 of *Siegfried*, in which the obsessive mind of Mime is given musical expression. And the music of Alberich, of Mime and of Hagen persuades us that this world of pure power is also one of inner misery and moral destitution. Perhaps no modern work of art portrays as profoundly as *The Ring* the psychological force which created the modern world—the force that Nietzsche called *ressentiment* and which, in my view, is the force that takes over when religion dies.

Here we should pause to consider two of the puzzles that have occupied students of the leitmotive. The first concerns Ex. 5. Nineteenth-century Wagnerians called this the *Entsagungsmotif*—the motive of renunciation—because it is first sung by one of the Rhinedaughters to the words: 'Nur wer der Minne Macht entsagt'—only he who

Example 5

forswears love can acquire the magic that will forge the Ring—thus launching Alberich on his bid for world-domination. Later appearances of the motive, however, belie this description. It appears, in the original key of C minor, to the words 'Heiligster Minne hochste Noth'—the highest need of most holy love—as Siegmund pulls the sword Nothung from the ash tree. It appears as Wotan kisses away Brünnhilde's divinity, and lays her to sleep on the rock, without the faintest suggestion on Wotan's part that Frau Minne has anything to do with what is going on. (Though deep down, Brünnhilde's 'mortalization' is Minne's work.)

What this shows is not that Wagner is inconsistent, but that the old habit of assigning a meaning to leitmotives from the context of their first occurrence is based on a misunderstanding. Leitmotives do not have meaning as words do—by convention. Otherwise Debussy's mocking complaint against 'visiting cards' would have some force. Leitmotives acquire their meaning during the course of the drama; they acquire it not only from what is happening on the stage, but also—and crucially—from what is happening in the pit. In an illuminating study[3] William Mann catalogues all occurrences of Ex. 5 and writes as follows:

[Ex. 5] is about heterosexual attraction, about the relation between love and material power, about the ring which was forged as a consequence of the curse, about true and false remedies for the crisis. If you can find one summary label that fits all these meanings, you are cleverer than I am. I know what it means—and if you have traced the connection in all these references, you also know—but to name that connection was never intended by Wagner, which is why he wrote *The Ring* as music drama.

To put the point in another way: the leitmotive is not describing things but subjecting them to a process of musical development. If, in retrospect, we can summarize this process in a word or a phrase, all well and good. However the knowledge enshrined in the motive is not 'knowledge by description', but 'knowledge by acquaintance'. Wagner expressly compares the orchestra to the chorus in a Greek tragedy: it is not merely accompanying the action, but responding to it.[4] Hence it forges a connection between episodes, by responding to them in a

Example 6

Example 7

Example 8

similar way. We too enter into the orchestra's ubiquitous sympathy, and feel in ourselves the deep-down relation between the things that the music connects. In all the occurrences of Ex. 5 there is a common core of feeling: these are the points in the drama where world and spirit coincide, and the world is changed through an action which is both choice and destiny. The music recuperates moments which foreshadowed the present one, and amalgamates them in the listener's response. This is how we should understand the second problematic motive: Ex. 6b. The nineteenth-century Wagnerians described this as the 'flight' motive, since it first appears appended to Freia's theme (Ex. 6a), accompanying her flight from the giants. Deryck Cooke has famously exploded this piece of nonsense.[5] The theme, derived from a four-note cell which occurs so widely in Wagner (for example in the grail theme from Lohengrin, Ex. 7) that Ernest Newman has described it as a Wagnerian tic,[6] is associated almost everywhere else in the cycle with love and the suffering of love. It is the leading device of *Die Walküre* Act 1, where it persuasively sympathizes with what is, from the standpoint of traditional morality, the most criminal of all sexual unions. (See Ex. 8.) The theme is noteworthy not only for its poignant beauty, but also for its harmonic versatility. It can effortlessly modulate from C sharp minor to C minor in the space of a bar (Ex. 9); it can go on falling for bar after bar, or even, though rarely, find completion in a

Example 9

Example 10

Example 11   *Example 12*

great rising arch, as at Ex. 10. In all this it conveys some of the abandon of erotic love, and also the acceptance of suffering that comes through love.

But there is one place where the occurrence of this theme has seemed mysterious—which is in the descent into Nibelheim, where Wagner first evokes the bondage which has entered the world with the forging of the Ring. The theme does not merely occur here: it binds everything together, first in an agitated diminished form (Ex. 11), which anticipates the hammers of the factory below, and then, introduced by the Rhinegold motive (Ex. 1), in an augmented version (Ex. 12) which takes us in trepidation down to Nibelheim. All this occurs before the theme has acquired its subsequent identity, as a theme of love and the suffering of love. Until now we have heard it only in association with Freia, who represents not love but, so to speak, the plastic material from which love is moulded. However, nothing could be more gripping or dramatically right than this descent into Nibelheim, and when, in *Die Walküre*, the passage is recalled in quite another context, that too sounds right. Why is this?

The answer goes to the heart of the drama. Love, in *The Ring*, means two different things: the need implanted by the species—that natural force which spreads its fickle attentions far and wide—and the longing which is also an existential choice, a meeting of self and other and an assumption of responsibility for another life.[7] Personal love grows from the invisible root of sexual need, and the pre-personal voice of the species sounds through this, our most free and individual endeavour. Alberich is susceptible to the first kind of love—the need which flits from object to object, as he flits from one Rhinedaughter to another in his vain efforts to seduce them. But he cannot attain to love of the second kind, the love which wins the heart of an individual and overcomes the baseness of desire. Therefore he renounces it, and with it every hope of personal fulfilment: now there is nothing for him to strive for, save power. Hence, for Alberich, even love of the first kind is a cause of suffering, and launches him on the loveless path which he thereafter follows.

Freia's charms and youth belong with love of the first kind; hence Ex. 6a is a 'nature' theme in *The Ring*, sounding always with the voice of the species. It is ethereal, impersonal, conveying the primordial delight of sensual love. But when Freia first appears she has been precipitated into another and more passionate love—that of Fasolt, before which she trembles. A force greater than Freia's divinity threatens to overwhelm her, and the motive flees before this force in terror. In other words the two parts of Freia's original theme point in two quite different directions. The first is eternal, immutable, the Ur-principle of carnal love. The second is agitated, variable, pursued and fulfilled by circumstance: in other words, it has a history. Hence the character of this second motive is acquired historically, so that, by the end of the cycle, it bears an enormous accumulation of meaning. By then it is overborne by personal tragedy and by the catastrophe of erotic love—a catastrophe which cannot be avoided, since the attempt to avoid it, as Alberich shows, is simply catastrophe of another kind.

Freia's double theme captures a metaphysical truth about the erotic: that it is a mysterious synthesis of a primeval, pre-personal force with that which is most intensely personal and most deeply compromised by time, history and circumstance. While the first is always pure delight, the second, which grows from it, is fraught with shame and fear and tragedy. Hence the first part of Freia's theme innocently soars, while the second part sinks constantly lower, borne up from time to time by a forlorn yet renewing hope, but ineluctably sinking nevertheless under the weight of its own tragic message. When Ex. 6b reappears during the descent into Nibelheim, the context is again one of suffering, the ultimate cause of which is the first kind of love—Alberich's desire for the Rhinedaughters. The suffering is amplified by Alberich's inability to transcend the first kind of love, and by his forswearing of the attempt.

Example 13

The music consequently curses love and its suffering, takes hold of the motive and hammers at it in order to annihilate its power. Ex. 11 is, as it were, beaten flat by the relentless 9/8 rhythm, losing all trace of organic emotion and transforming itself at last into the mechanical smithing theme of Nibelheim (Ex. 13). Only then does the augmented version—Ex. 12—sound through the orchestra, now in tones of helpless lamentation for a world deprived of love in its personal form.

Return now to the motive as it appears in *Die Walküre*. Here it conveys not lamentation but a kind of grieving gentleness. Love has passed from the general to the particular; two individuals are in the grip of that anguished concern for each other which admits no substitutes, and in which the vocabulary of love—glance, caress, kiss, silence—has taken on another and higher meaning. Siegmund and Sieglinde are face to face, and the music outlines them with supremely erotic tenderness. At this new, personal level, the suffering of love is a premonition of bereavement, a recognition of the irreplaceability of another life, in which the self and its glance have become the focus of commitment. At this higher level, the suffering of love is also a vindication: a sign that the lovers have risen above the natural order and possessed themselves of the individuality and the freedom which justify the trouble of existence, and of which bereavement is the price.

There is a premonition of this higher state in *Das Rheingold*. Although the giants are initially attracted to Freia as a personification of love in its natural form, one of them, Fasolt, is afflicted by her beauty. He cannot, in the end, relinquish her, until she is hidden from view. The hair which shines above the piled-up hoard represents the incarnate object of love—that which is caressed by the lover for whom natural appetite has been transcended into personal tenderness. Freia's hair can be hidden only by the Tarnhelm, the thing which hides the individual behind an infinity of disguises. But Freia's glance—her *Blick*—remains, the direct expression of that individual self for which there are no substitutes and no disguises, and which is the focus of Fasolt's desire. It is at this point that Ex. 6a sounds in the orchestra, completed by Ex. 6b in its shortest possible statement. Only one thing can take away the glance of Freia, namely the thing which was forged by renouncing love. Freia is exchanged for the Ring. Fasolt seizes the Ring from Fafner, with the cry: 'Back, thief! the Ring is mine—it is due to me for Freia's glance' (*Mir blieb er für Freias Blick*). This episode shows the meaning of the Ring: it is the spell which undoes love, by dissolving everything desired—even the object of love—in the stream of substitutes.

Fasolt's premonition of suffering is verified immediately: he is murdered for the sake of this object without a use. This is not merely because the Ring is wanted by Fafner: it is because it has already colonized the soul of Fafner, telling him that the only love known to him—brother love—can be exchanged for something better. In the fate of the giants we see, in fact, the artful way in which the political and the spiritual are fused. Of all the treaties and bargains struck in *Rheingold* it is only that between Wotan and the giants which has a genuine moral basis. Freia is promised in reward for a creative act, whereby something of value is brought into the world: Freia is the price of labour. Fasolt's touching description of the need of 'Uns armen' for woman's beauty and charm, which the gods enjoy in abundance, makes it clear that the giants worked so hard precisely because love was to be their wage. Freia is not promised in exchange for an object, but in exchange for labour, and this labour embodies the soul of the giant, all that is 'properly his'. The Ring, therefore, is no mere trinket, but the means to transfer the goal of labour from use to exchange—from the intrinsic value of love, to the instrumental value of power. A creature whose essence is labour can accept this transfer only by losing his soul. He has wasted his self on a thing with no use.

In referring to love and power I am using the language of Wagner and his contemporaries. But the point can be put in a more up-to-date idiom. The Ring comes into being because Nature has been repudiated. It is the mark and product of a primordial alienation, a loss of that innocent contentment in which life is an end in itself. It casts its spell over all desire and all aspiration, so that everything—the Ring included—is demoted from end to means. That is what power amounts to: a *perpetuum mobile* which feeds on itself and knows no point of rest. The forging of the Ring involves, therefore, a universal rest-lessness, which can be overcome only in the individual soul, by regaining, though at a higher and more self-conscious level, the sense of one-ness that was lost when the Natural order was left behind.[8] This higher unity occurs through love, which is, in Wagner, the symbol of every condition that can be understood and valued as an end in itself. The passage from Nature through power to love therefore has the structure of Hegel's dialectic: it is a passage from innocent one-ness and contentment, through alienation and separation, to a higher and freely chosen unity, in which the experience of value is regained. What is un-Hegelian in Wagner is precisely that which distinguishes him from all the Young Hegelians: namely, his profound pessimism—or rather, his profound realism—which leads him to understand the final goal as simultaneously freedom and nothingness. Death knowingly accepted is the end of love and love's redemption.

If the Ring is crystallized power, however, why is it so useless to those who gain control of it? Nobody who possesses the Ring is able to keep it, or to use it to ward off danger. It is taken from Alberich by Wotan, from Fasolt by Fafner, from Fafner by Siegfried, from Brünnhilde by Siegfried; it is also the cause of Siegfried's death, against which it offers no protection. In what then lies its power—the power which is supposed to offer world-domination to the one who wields it? Only one protagonist uses the Ring to gain power over others, and that is Alberich. By renouncing love he has already prepared the way for this power. He views others as instruments, means to his ends; hence he can avail himself of the gold—not only by forging it into the Ring, but also by using the Ring to enslave his fellows. What confers power on Alberich is not so much the Ring as the spiritual process—the self-alienation—which enables him to forge it. Only someone who had undergone that process—Mime, for example, or Hagen—could use the Ring as Alberich uses it, in order to enslave the world. For the free being the Ring is inert, a mere trinket.

Moreover, the possession of the Ring does not protect Alberich against those who live in the world of freedom and personality, as Wotan does. For—as the drama reveals—these free beings have a capacity to relinquish power. Only love, freely given, can satisfy their need for others, and their salvation consists in understanding that love demands mortality and therefore the acceptance of death. The Ring cannot protect Fasolt from Fafner, since the giants live in a world of brute strength, without intelligence, and even instrumental power has no clear meaning for them. Hence, having gained the Ring, Fafner can do nothing with it. He merely sleeps on the hoard, with no conception of its value.

Nor can the Ring protect Fafner from Siegfried, who is immune to its charm. Yet it does protect Fafner from both Alberich and Mime, because they live in the world of instrumental values, where the power of the Ring prevails. In an important sense, nevertheless, the power of the Ring remains, like the gold from which it was made, illusory. We can understand this illusory quality if we return to the parallel with money—pure 'exchange-value'. Money is entirely useless, except in so far as it can be exchanged for something useful. In an emergency you cannot eat it, fight with it, or shelter beneath its roof. Nor can you exchange it for love, kindness, friendship or anything else that is needed for self-growth and self-knowledge. Purchased love is not love but prostitution. Only when dealing with those who want money—who are themselves prey to the illusion of its usefulness—does money become useful, and only because it can be exchanged for other things. Its utility lies in the socially sustained illusion of its utility. Upon this illusion the institution of exchange is founded. Money therefore has dominion only where people measure the value of everything in terms of what can be exchanged for it—in other words, only where nothing has value, but everything has a price.

Of course, that indictment is exaggerated. Nevertheless it was repeated and refined by the Young Hegelians, and bequeathed by them to Marx and Wagner. Moreover, it enables us to see more deeply into the Ring and its meaning, since it suggests another aspect of that impersonal power which prevails in Nibelheim. There is a 'power illusion', which parallels the money illusions studied by nineteenth-century economists—that is to say, an illusion of power which makes power real. It is exactly this that has been described by the witnesses to totalitarian government: a habit of fear and evasion, from which power arises 'by an invisible hand' —power which belongs to no one and which oppresses everyone, including those who appear to wield it.[9]

Such is the power of the Ring, which while nominally Alberich's, is in fact dispersed through the capillaries of Nibelheim, and perpetually regenerated from the illusion that someone—someone else—possesses it. Wagner gives us a masterly portrayal of this illusory power, self-generated by those who fear it, in the passage which follows the Wanderer's departure from Mime's hut. (*Siegfried*, Act 1.) Mime stares out into the sunlit forest, dazzled by the light, and promptly gives way to his fear of Fafner the dragon. The music, playing with the magic fire motive and using keyless augmented chords, conveys the nature of Fafner's power, which is the phantom product of Mime's emotion. The real power which steps from behind the veil of illusion is not Fafner, but Siegfried, the hero who knows no fear. A profound inner drama is contained in this musical transition, and also in the ensuing scene, in which Mime tries to teach fear to the hero, but alerts him instead to the mystery that sleeps in the heart of things, and which it is his personal destiny to awaken.

Example 14

But what of the curse? The dramatic logic of this is evident: Alberich exchanged love for the Ring, and did so by a curse. That he is robbed of the Ring, with which his soul is mingled, is the worst thing that could happen to him. So he says, in effect, to Wotan. Hence he must transfer the burden of the curse (which is the loss of love) to all who try to exploit his property. In the new world of exchange and mutation, the curse becomes transferable. It haunts the cycle thereafter, reminding us that nature has been deflected from its course, that all is unsettled and at odds with itself, that the cry from the deep must be answered, if the world's equilibrium is to be regained.

The curse acts at all four levels of the action: mythical, dramatic, political and spiritual. Curses have a particular importance in myths, for they attach the will of absent people to present objects—they symbolize the traps that are everywhere laid for the unwary, the inexplicable danger by which we are always surrounded, as we encroach on what has been fought for and died for by people whom we shall never know. A curse activates and makes present some part of the immeasurable suffering that precedes us. Dramatically the curse is attached to a specific character and his projects. It is the means whereby Alberich's will and bitterness are projected forward through the drama, so as to poison everything that happens. This bold conception would have been impossible to realize with the force that Wagner intended had he not hit upon a brilliant musical idea, which is worth analysing if only because it again shows how the music welds the political and the spiritual into a single movement. The curse motive is built up, both melodically and harmonically, from thirds (Ex. 14). Here is how I would describe it: over a prolonged but muffled F sharp pedal on the timpani the melody rises from F sharp through the triad of A minor to E. These four notes form a half-diminished seventh—the chord which, suitably inverted and spaced, is the famous Tristan chord.[10] The melody drops an octave, and spells out the triad of C major, the F sharp still sounding in the bass. All three notes of the C major triad are then sounded in the orchestra, using clarinets in the lowest register and bass

Example 15   *Example 16*

Example 17

clarinet. The resulting contaminated sound is poisoned still further by the F sharp pedal below. This, surely the murkiest C major triad in all music, sets up a bitter conflict in the ear of the listener, which continues as the triad is 'resolved' on to a discord—the dominant seventh with minor ninth on F sharp—so enabling the music to settle on B minor for Alberich's blood-curdling prophecy. The motive divides into two parts: the half-diminished chord (A minor plus F sharp), and the C major triad, both over an F sharp pedal. The first chord forms a harmonic condensation of the curse motive, and one that frequently reappears. (See Ex. 4 above.)

The chord contains a tritone clash—C and F sharp—which is spelled out more overtly by the second half of the theme. This tritone becomes a central motive of evil in *The Ring*—as in the dragon's motive (Ex. 15), and Hagen's motive (Ex. 16). Extract it from the curse-chord, and what is left is a perfect fifth. The dialogue thus established between fifth and tritone is one of the leading ideas of *Götterdämmerung*, the fifth being associated with the Gibichungs, and the tritone with Hagen, in rhythmic patterns which emphasize their disturbing identity-in-difference. In the magnificent scene in which Brünnhilde and Siegfried swear on Hagen's spear, the melody, taken over by Brünnhilde, is harmonized over a succession of curse-chords. It first rises a fifth, and then settles on the curse-chord in its original key (Ex. 17). The falling fifth—E to A—is at once answered in the bass by the falling tritone—C to F sharp. The entire passage is constructed by the dialogue between

Example 18

these two intervals, miraculously woven into a musical structure in which heroic defiance and sneering venom move in mutual excitement. The curse never sounds in this passage: but it is there in the music, whose harmony and melody are both determined by it. Even what is most free and defiant—and surely there is nothing more defiant, more full of spirit, than this melody given first to Siegfried and then to Brünnhilde—has now been ensnared by the curse.

I give the example as one of many, in order to illustrate the way in which Wagner, by exploiting the musical potential of his motives, moves forward on the political and the spiritual levels simultaneously. The workings of power are displayed here, both in the public sphere of the Gibichung household, poisoned by the presence of Hagen, and in the inner sphere of Brünnhilde's passion, where her heroic defiance is negated by the catastrophe that has undermined the public world. The pedal note of F sharp is of some significance in understanding the dramatic potential of the curse motive, it being identical with G flat, the first note of Alberich's cry of woe in its B flat minor version—B flat minor being the key of Alberich's most important music, as in the inspired prelude to Act 2 of *Götterdämmerung*, just as its relative major, D flat, belongs to Wotan. Keys had an enormous significance for Wagner; instead of reiterating a leitmotive, he would sometimes return to the key in which it first appears. (This often happens with the E major associated with Brünnhilde, and with Siegfried's C major.) The penultimate appearance of the curse begins with the curse-chord at its original pitch—an A minor triad over an F sharp pedal—as Brünnhilde, in her final soliloquy, informs Wotan that she knows and accepts what must be. Here the curse-chord is used to introduce the 'fate' motive (Ex. 21), in distorted and non-resolving harmonies (Ex. 18). The F sharp pedal continues until E flat sounds below it, the F sharp becoming G flat, the first note of the curse in a new statement. The curse-chord

Example 19

sounds now as a G flat minor triad, rendered unstable by the major sixth in the bass. This miraculously resolves to the Rhinedaughters' praise of the gold in its original harmonization, recalling, in the A flat triad over an E flat bass, the key structure of the first scene of *Das Rheingold* (Ex. 19). Then, with a slight shift in the harmony, we find ourselves in D flat, for 'Ruhe, ruhe, du Gott!' (The curse occurs one final time, at its original pitch, as Hagen tries to snatch the Ring and is dragged to his death by the Rhinedaughters.)

This whole extended movement is condensed into the final cadence of *Götterdämmerung*, in which the curse-chord is treated as the subdominant minor—here as G flat minor, resolving through that mischievous added note, on to the D flat major of the tonic (Ex. 20). This—Wagner's favourite cadence (see especially the final bars of *Tristan*)—epitomizes the story of *The Ring*: the resolution of Alberich's curse by Wotan's acceptance that all must end. Key, harmony and musical movement all emphasize this spiritual process, which occurs not merely in the depths of things but throughout the observable cosmos. By purely musical means, Wagner has made the curse penetrate the world of his drama, and also work for and achieve its final quiescence.

That is one small instance of a general observation about *The Ring*. Whenever the action seems incomplete, contradictory or mysterious the

Example 20

puzzle is resolved by the music, so that we feel, even if we do not understand, the rightness of what is happening on the stage. It is primarily through the music that Wagner is able to project the cosmic drama of Alberich and Wotan into the background, so that it becomes part of everything that happens, to be re-enacted in the story of Siegfried and his death. In conclusion, therefore, I shall briefly attempt to show why the story of Siegfried is, as Wagner intended it to be, the focus and resolution of the drama.

At several points in the cycle Wotan and Alberich confirm their mysterious identity—the first is Licht-Alberich, the second Schwarz-Alberich. They arise from the same psychic condition, which is the separation of the individual from nature, and his need to affirm himself against it. Each acquires power by usurpation; and Wotan, in stealing the Ring, makes Alberich's crime his own. Wagner's conception parallels the story of man's Fall. Just as in the political realm, leisure, law and citizenship are made possible only at the cost of exploitation and exchange, so in the private sphere, personal freedom is dependent, in the end, on the apt deployment of power, and all that power implies by way of disloyalty. Even our highest emotions are polluted by the lust for substitutes, and when Siegfried receives from Hagen the drink that will wipe away the memory of Brünnhilde, the action makes explicit what is implicit in love itself.

The inner identity of Wotan and Alberich illustrates Schopenhauer's description of original sin as the 'crime of existence itself'. If we see the gods and Nibelungs in that way, then we will locate the moral centre of the drama where Wagner located it—in the story of Siegfried's death. The myth which frames this story and exalts it to an archetype is only a projection into cosmic regions of the light generated by the Walsung's lonely tragedy. This light is reflected in Wotan, whose character is bestowed by his equally lonely obsession with the mortals whom he has

Example 21

fathered, hoping to borrow and make use of their freedom.[11] That Wotan is unfree in all the respects in which his mortal offspring are free is a corollary of his nature as a psychic residue. In effect he is their creation, made real by their suffering and by their (ineffective) prayers to him, and—in a spectacular inversion of Christian doctrine—Wotan must be redeemed by them, and redeemed precisely by sharing their mortality.

The logic of this becomes clear in Act 2 of Walküre, in Brunnhilde's encounter with Siegmund. The goddess, having announced the hero's death, is overcome by his selfless love and grief; as a result she identifies with his fate, so jeopardizing and ultimately losing her godhead. The idea came from a hint in one of the Eddas; but the realization of this extraordinary change of heart—or rather acquisition of heart—is one of Wagner's most inspired achievements. Here the verse makes a decisive contribution to the *Legendenton*, to borrow Schumann's apt expression: the avoidance of pronouns; the sequence of pregnant questions; the slow, magnificent unfolding of Siegmund's destiny like a great curtain being drawn back from the icy stars—such things recall the mystery of the Eddas, and also the Greek tragic stage. The opening motive (usually known as the 'fate' motive—Ex. 21) is a perfect condensation, in music, of man's relation to the gods: an infinitely sorrowful 'why?' And the motive that follows (Ex. 22) is not merely a natural continuation of this question, but also, through its constantly evolving harmony and melodic drive—its almost unbearable search for an answering phrase—a confirming, substantiating, and making concrete of the metaphysical puzzlement.

Ex. 22 is a question, but also a yearning, and by giving it to Siegmund, and repeating it always with softer orchestration, Wagner illustrates two things: first the structure of man's relation to God, in which yearning and interrogation are the crucial ingredients; second the evolution in time of our predicament, the working of the great question

Example 22

Example 23

into the heart of what is most personal—into love itself. At the same time the question never loses its cosmic character, suggesting always that in death we face the mystery of creation, the illuminated edge between being and nothingness. (Hence Ex. 22 reappears in the prologue to *Götterdämmerung*, accompanying each Norn as she passes the rope of fate to her sister.) The 'fall' of Brünnhilde into the world of mortal sympathy occurs when she suddenly takes up the motive, now inseparably joined to another in the bass associated with Wotan's frustration (Ex. 23).

It is now Brünnhilde's turn to be penetrated by a metaphysical question, as she announces the immutable law of the gods, knowing it to be a sham: 'You saw the Valkyrie's withering glance: With her you now must go!' This is set to Ex. 22, constantly punctuated by the memory of Wotan's suffering (Ex. 23), reminding us that Brünnhilde is also Wotan's other self. The climax comes when Brünnhilde tells Siegmund that the one who sent him the sword now sends him death, at which Siegmund gives way not to despair on his own account but to pitying love for Sieglinde, in a version of Ex. 6b (Ex. 24)—the whole passage shifting between D flat major and B flat minor, as if to remind us of the cosmic contest which is being played out in this intimate sphere. And then Siegmund turns on the Valkyrie with the cry 'Shame on him who bestowed the sword, if he give me shame, not victory!' This

Example 24

Example 25

Example 26

pierces Brünnhilde, since she is, in a sense, the very person whose will is being so acutely criticized. At this Ex. 24 is joined to a vigorous ascending chromatic scale, which recalls Wotan's anger at Fricka's victory and his mental bequest of the world to Alberich (Ex. 25). Brünnhilde responds with her own amazed and brooding question —troubled beyond measure at the thought that someone might care more for a mortal woman than for all the joys of immortality. Examples 22, 23 and 25 are combined, and Ex. 22 elaborated (Ex. 26) to form the passionate denunciation which Siegmund then hurls at Brünnhilde and by implication at all the gods. Because Ex. 22 is always elaborated, but never answered, the music, which becomes ever more excited, with a wholly credible sympathy for Siegmund's predicament, passes the hero's defiance into the soul of Brünnhilde. In preventing him from killing Sieglinde, she acts as the immortal projection of his mortal will. From this moment the forces are in place that will lead to her own mortality.

Example 27

Example 28

Example 29

Ex. 22 is later varied, to form the subject of the fugal chorus sung by the Valkyries in their vain attempt to protect Brünnhilde (Ex. 27). In this ironed-out and reharmonized version, the motive at last finds an answering phrase (Ex. 28b). This foreshadows Brünnhilde's pleading with Wotan, to grant that her incarnation in the world of mortals will also set her on the path of redemption (Ex. 29). The completed melody sounds softly on the bass clarinet, as Brünnhilde steps forward to receive what is at first a punishment, in retrospect a redeeming gift (Ex. 28). The very fact that the passage is wordless, reminds us that we have been brought to this wholly convincing turn of events by the musical elaboration of Siegmund's defiance.[12]

Why does this concluding scene resolve the drama of *Die Walküre*? Why do the emotions of two doomed and mortal lovers find their quiescence between god and god? *Die Walküre* makes sense, it seems to me, only as a preparation for new life; all the protagonists, mortal or immortal, are committed to this life as the one thing that will validate their striving. This is explicitly conveyed in the scene between Brünn-hilde and Sieglinde, when the Valkyrie hands over the fragments of the sword—the god's broken promise, which can be redeemed only by a man. And then, at the end of the opera, after all these tragic conflicts have been not so much solved as dissolved in Brünnhilde, and are now held in solution in her, the drama returns to the same emotion: the emotion of the 'womb of time'.

A secret lies buried in the heart of things and awaiting discovery: the fruit of an obscure cooperation between god and man, in which the destiny of each is at stake. The unawoked wisdom of the world has come into being from transactions in which god and man, mortal and immortal, are equally necessary and equally compromised. That idea, and its realization in music in which magic, wonder and grief are woven inextricably together, provides the most sublime moment of *The Ring*, the point between two worlds, where destiny is handed on from god to mortal—a moment whose authority, artistic, moral and metaphysical, ought not to be questioned by anyone who understands music.

At the end of *Die Walküre* the divine has been made flesh, and sleeps in vacant anticipation. The awakener is the individual, the free being who realizes his freedom in the outward-going energy of love. *Siegfried* is a series of awakenings, as one by one the characters of the drama are confronted with their own predicament, and forced, too late, to acknowledge it. The last awakenings are the most significant. First Wotan's awakening of Erda, who in turn awakens Wotan to the intransigence of fate. Second, the scene between Brünnhilde and Siegfried, in which the hero is awakened first to fear and then to love, while Brünnhilde is awakened first to the radiance of mortal life, and then to the fateful love which is its consequence. In their mutual awakening, the two lovers achieve the personal union which is the mortal incarnation of divinity—the flow of free emotion which occurs when individual love defies its mortal destiny, and briefly affirms itself as pure personality and will.

The magnificent prelude and summoning of Erda in Act 3 of *Siegfried* are vitally necessary even at the most superficial level of the action. Until Wotan's will has been shown once again to be deeply at variance with itself, still struggling in the midst of resignation, it will seem as though he merely decides to be angry with Siegfried and to block his passage. But in that case his gesture would be spurious. Wotan has understood that Siegfried's freedom will be a reality only if the hero defies the God of whose plans he is the unwitting residue. In a sense, therefore, Wotan offers his spear to be shattered by Siegfried. But the

anger that Wotan expresses in this scene is real, for it is a last surging
of his divine autonomy, a final futile resistance to the knowledge that
his will must now be surrendered. It is also part of the process whereby
the destiny of the world is transferred from god to man.

We should see this encounter in terms of Wagner's inversion of the
Christian doctrine. God needs man for his salvation. In order to create
the individual whom he needs, God must incarnate himself, and bestow
on a mortal the apartness from nature which belongs in essence to the
gods. God thereby endues man with freedom and individuality: the
divine spark that shines in every human glance, but never in the eyes of
an animal. In the world of mortals, however, freedom is a prelude to
love, and therefore to a return to the natural order. Hence it demands
the downfall of the gods. The eye which Wotan had sacrificed in order
to obtain dominion over the world is now looking at him from
Siegfried's head. In other words, the need for Siegfried—for redemption
at a mortal's hands—arose at the very moment of seizing power (an
Ur-moment lost in the depths of things).

Siegfried's emergence as an individual coincides with the neutral-
ization of Wotan's will and hence with the spiritual nemesis of the gods.
As Siegfried emerges on to those strange heights, having unknowingly
robbed the world of force (the giants), and law (the spear), and bearing
only the dangerous link (the Ring) which once united them in conflict,
the old order of things is at an end. Now there is only the individual,
without god, without community (except a community founded on
broken oaths and contracts). His alone is the task of personal redemption, through recognition of the other and of himself in the other. This
brief moment of individuality, when all that we have received from the
gods is transferred downwards (but only at the summit) into human life
itself—this final self-recognition of man as the root cause and reason of
all that surrounds him—is the last, tragic, uncertain gift of history, the
soul's sudden awareness as it falls from the brink. And it is here that the
real drama—the drama of the individual—begins.

I shall conclude by summarizing what Wagner has achieved at the
point when Siegfried and Brünnhilde awaken to each other, so as to
begin their rash defiance of the world. Wagner has created a drama in
which those forces which constrain our freedom are fully personified.
First there is nature and species-life: that which refreshes us, and which
also sets impassable limits to what we can be. Second, there is authority,
law and civilization: forces that exist both around us and within, and
which inspire us to transcend mere nature, in search of personality,
freedom and love. Third, there is power, intrigue and exploitation:

forces which also defy nature, but which set themselves against the order of personality.

If we were to look to a philosopher as authority for this three-fold division of the human predicament, it would not be Feuerbach or Hegel or even Schopenhauer, but the thinker who inspired them all, namely Kant. Wagner has found the way to dramatize, through myth and music, the predicament of humankind as modern man receives it and as Kant described it. As persons, we exist apart from nature; we can abuse our apartness by taking the path of instrumentality and power; or we can strive for a kingdom of ends, a world of intrinsic values, each member of which is an end in himself. Unlike Kant, however, Wagner believed that the critical moment in the development of personality is the erotic: the point at which sympathy for another person is precisely fed by nature, so as to translate the great force of species-life into a project in which freedom and personality are fulfilled and also jeopardized. It is in this project that I come face to face with what I am, both for myself and for the other.

But the project is fatally qualified by species-life, and also by the temptation to reject love and its uncertainty for the trodden path of power—as Hunding does—or the more insidious path of exchange. Many playwrights have explored the trials and illusions of erotic love. But words confine us to a specific dramatic situation, in which the protagonists are those who are speaking now. In *The Ring* Wagner animates his characters with music that has acquired its meaning from sources outside them—from the nature and the temptation with which they are simultaneously at war. This musical material—transformed and transcended into a new and wholly personalized idiom—shows what cannot be said: it displays the individual, in the highest form of love, as fatally ensnared in forces which lie beyond the province of his will. This is our predicament, which compels us to accept what nature and power refuse: death not passively submitted to, but willed.

If we see the cycle in that way, then its culmination in the story of Siegfried and Brünnhilde is entirely logical. Siegfried, for all his mythic and medieval trappings, represents a distinctly modern project. He is born, raised and brought to manhood as an isolated individual. He finds love and self-knowledge only through the encounter with a woman more solitary than himself. Everything that gives sense to our life on earth—custom, community, religion and obedience—has been excised from Siegfried's world. Indeed, he himself has destroyed them. He smashes the spear of Wotan, not knowing its cosmic significance but only its significance for him, and so ends the rule of the gods. All those things upon which we unknowingly depend for our personal fulfilment —law, custom and obedience, to name but three—have vanished.

The consequent urgency of erotic love, as our last remaining refuge, is the starting point of Siegfried's drama. But love between mortals cannot sustain itself, outside the laws, treaties and institutions of the world that has vanished. Mortality asserts its sovereign power, which is the power of forgetting. Having shattered Wotan's spear, Siegfried enters a world where all oaths are broken and all promises forgotten; where the moral law has lost its influence, and every attempt at transcendence leads sooner or later to disaster. This is our world—the world since Enlightenment—and it is brilliantly dramatized in *Götter-dämmerung*. Just as *Siegfried* was a series of awakenings, so is *Götterdämmerung* a series of oaths, each one broken in the very act of making it. The oaths take us through all the old comforts of humanity—community, tribal loyalty, household, friendship, marriage—as well as through the dark workings of an implacable revenge. But the real meaning of Siegfried's life is hardly touched by them. Only as he dies, surveying his path to self-discovery, does he remember the moment of personal transcendence which is the meaning of all that he has done both before and since.

The drink of forgetfulness, given by Hagen to Siegfried, stands proxy for something else. In *Götterdämmerung*, as in *Tristan*, magic potions signify our subjection to forces which operate from a region outside our control—forces which enter through the body, and dictate to the soul from an unknowable place beyond it. In an illuminating article,[13] Michael Tanner describes the drink given to Siegfried as a dramatic condensation of a long process of corruption: and this is evidently true. (The journey down the Rhine takes only a few minutes of music: but we must understand those minutes musically, not temporally.) But there is something more, something contained in the very idea of magic as Wagner conceives it. This something more is the fact from which modern tragedy derives: that the most important things, those things in which the spirit has invested everything, those things which really are the self, in so far as we understand it; that those very things may disappear, eroded by a force which we neither control nor understand, and yet which operates in us. Hence it is important that a drink should cause Siegfried's faithlessness—for drink, the symbol of all intoxication, enters us from outside, and at the same time operates from within, as though it had *become* the spirit in the act of overcoming it.

The first effect of the drink is to provide Siegfried with a substitute for his love. Siegfried follows in Alberich's footsteps, along the way of all flesh. But he has not yet fallen to Alberich's level. For he is not aware that he has exchanged his beloved and therefore his identity. Nor does he ever become aware of this. Those who find the character of Siegfried unsatisfactory are often troubled by the unconsciousness that obliterates such vast areas of his psyche. But the missing consciousness is supplied at another level by the music, which shows a hero realizing himself as a free individual, while entirely at the mercy of forces that are hidden from his innocent gaze. The interpretation that I have proposed suggests a solution to the final puzzle of *The Ring*—the raising of Siegfried's dead hand, so as to withhold the Ring from Hagen. As the miracle occurs, the sword motive sounds in the orchestra—a reference to Siegfried's will, which he put in to the Ring, first in winning it, second in giving it as a love-pledge to Brünnhilde, and finally in wresting it from her by force. Some part of Siegfried's will survives in this ring, unpurged by his extinction—namely the part that committed itself to Brünnhilde with an 'eternal' promise, a promise that reaches beyond death in just the way that we now witness. (This is why Brünnhilde is already 'intimate' with the miracle, and might even seem to be its author.) All else has been extinguished—the winning, the wresting: these were events in time, whose significance has been superseded. Only the bestowing of the Ring in the vow of love lifted it above the order of time and destruction: hence the curse motive did not sound in that passage, and the lovers willingly and exultantly accepted their deaths as they pledged their love, so making clear that the curse cannot harm them. When the dead hand rises, it is to execute the inextinguishable meaning of the vow, and to summon Brünnhilde to death beside her husband. This is the purified remnant of Siegfried's will, from which all the dross of mortality has been purged.

The scene reminds us of the meaning of mortmain in law: the will which survives in an object after the conscious life that ordered it has fled. The 'dead hand' survives in our loves, too, but only for the shortest time—which is why Brünnhilde must die before the magic of forgetfulness takes over. The beauty of Siegfried's dead gesture is that it contains everything in him that could have survived as an object of Brünnhilde's love—all that his will had meant by way of giving and renunciation. Siegfried's life-project has been finally accomplished, and the old order—the order that intended Siegfried and was also fulfilled in him—must now come to an end.

Notes

1 For more on this theme see Georg Simmel, *The Philosophy of Money*, tr. T. Bottomore, D. Frisby and K. Maengelberg, London 1978, pp. 376–7, and Roger Scruton, *Sexual Desire*, London 1986, pp. 156–60.

2 Wagner himself commented upon this transformation in 'Uber der Anwendung der Musik auf der Drama' (1879), in *Gesammelte Schriften und Dichtungen*, ed. Wolfgang Golther, Berlin 1913), vol. X, pp. 189–90. The passage is summarized in Ernest Newman, *Wagner as Man and Artist*, London 1925), pp. 238–9.

3 William Mann, 'Down with visiting cards', in John DiGaetani, ed., *Penetrating Wagner's Ring*, London 1978, pp. 303–6.

4 *Opera and Drama*, in *Richard Wagner's Prose Works*, ed. William Ashton Ellis, St. Clare Shores, Mich. 1972, vol. 2.

5 Deryck Cooke, *I Saw the World End: A Study of Wagner's* Ring, Oxford 1979, Chapter 3.

6 Ernest Newman, *Wagner Nights*, London 1949, reissued as *The Wagner Operas*, London 1961.

7 Wagner has something to say about the two kinds of love in *Opera and Drama*, §352: 'The nature of woman is love; but this love is one of conception, and of unreserved devotion in conception. Woman only attains to full individuality at the moment of this devotion . . . The look of innocence in the eye of the woman is the endlessly clear mirror in which the man can perceive only a general capacity for loving, until he has been able to discern his own picture therein.' The whole passage which follows (to §362) helps to illuminate what the later operas of Wagner dramatize: the need in sexual feeling for individual love and a self-transcending act of possession of the kind that only free and responsible individuals can engage in.

8 The Ring is therefore a potent symbol of the regime of mass consumption, which is rapidly destroying the natural world. It is one of the oddities of the now standard Marxisant productions of Wagner's drama that the natural world is routinely banished from the stage. For this neutralizes one of the most important political messages that the work conveys: namely, that power divorced from love is an ecological catastrophe.

9 The locus classicus here is Václav Havel's essay, 'The power of the powerless' (tr. Paul Wilson, in John Keane, ed., *The Power of the Powerless: Citizens Against the State in Central-Eastern Europe*, London 1985), though of course the spiritual condition that he relates has been foretold many times: by Kafka, Orwell and Dostoevsky among others.

10 See the discussion by Carl Dahlhaus, in John Deathridge and Carl Dahlhaus, *The New Grove Wagner*, London 1984, pp. 120–1.

11 On one reading of *The Ring*, therefore, Wotan is its central character, even if one who spends much of his time in retirement. His lack of freedom, seen as an inevitable consequence of his great project to establish a cosmic rule of law, is brilliantly explained and explored by Philip Kitcher and Richard Schacht, in *Finding an Ending: Reflections of Wagner's Ring*, Oxford 2004.

12 Porges gives a beautiful description of the melody in Ex. 28 in his account of Wagner's rehearsals. See Heinrich Porges, tr. Robert L. Jacobs, *Wagner Rehearsing the Ring*, Cambridge 1983, p. 72.

13 'The total work of art', in Peter Burbage and Richard Sutton, eds, *The Wagner Companion*, London 1979.

11

True authority: Janáček, Schoenberg and us

There is an experience that is familiar to all of us, and central to the value of art, which we might characterize as a sense of necessity, of an absolute rightness in some artistic gesture, a perception that 'it could not have been otherwise'. We have this experience, even though we know full well that it *could* have been otherwise, that, in the very detail that strikes us as imbued with an ineluctable necessity, the artist is exercising complete freedom of choice, and lesser talents might have proceeded in quite another way without disaster. Hence our recourse to figurative language: we are not speaking of a real necessity, but of a necessity of the heart—a necessity that seems to reveal an order and rightness whose meaning lies in us. This experience is, we might say, an encounter with authority, and it has much in common with encounters that command obedience in life.

Kent says to Lear: 'You have that in your countenance which I would fain call master.' 'What's that?' asks Lear, and Kent replies: 'Authority'. In art as in life authority answers our questions: it is the self-authenticating presence that silences doubt. During the first decades of the last century composers and critics were full of such doubt and anxious to discover the authority that would overcome it. It is a cliché to say that the tonal language had become a cliché; but like every cliché it has a core of truth. After Wagner and Debussy it seemed impossible to return to the diatonic melodies and tonal polyphony of the romantics: these things had lost their innocence, which meant that they had ceased to be genuine expressions and become sentimental, parts of a complicitous game of pretence. Tonality was kitsch.

'Kitsch' is a Central European word for a phenomenon that flourishes everywhere, but which reached a poignant self-awareness in Central Europe at the end of the nineteenth century. For many artists of the late Habsburg Empire kitsch was the artistic nemesis of the Austro-Hungarian settlement, the proof that a civilization had been eaten away by emotional termites, and stood veneering its own emptiness and on the brink of collapse. Nothing in the decaying order had real authority; everything was a laughable pretence—such was the message of Robert

Musil and Karl Kraus. The artistic revolutionaries did not seek popularity, since it was precisely the kowtowing to popular culture, they thought, which had cheapened the artistic language, and brought it down to the commercial level. They wanted to *command* respect, not to court it.

Schoenberg perfectly exemplifies this attitude, both in his compositions and in the theoretical writings through which he explained and rationalized the twelve-tone technique. Schoenberg also illustrates an important distinction—that between the person with authority and the authoritarian. The authoritarian is the one who hides behind rigid edicts and peremptory commands. He fortifies himself with systems, rules and rubber stamps, in order to conceal the arbitrariness of his actions.[1] The authority, by contrast, is the one who spontaneously does what is right, and whose actions and example elicit our approval because they seem to emerge ineluctably from a free and understanding nature. The contrast between the two kinds of character is displayed, it seems to me, in that between Schoenberg and Janáček.

Both Schoenberg and Janáček were great teachers, and both divided their lives between composition and public-spirited musical enterprises. Both were theorists, and both bequeathed to posterity deep and difficult textbooks on the nature of harmony.[2] And both were Central Europeans, caught up in the turmoil of events that led to the collapse of the Austro-Hungarian Empire and to the political vacuum into which Nazism and Communism poured their nihilistic poisons. And although Janáček belonged to the generation prior to Schoenberg, he was a late developer, and found his musical identity at the same time as Schoenberg.

The contrast between the two composers illustrates a wider division within the civilization from which they both emerged—the division between the centralizing, cosmopolitan culture of Vienna, and the national revivals that had become the principal source of light in the Slavonic and Hungarian provinces. Schoenberg's sense that tonality was exhausted, and that the romantic language at which he was so consummate a master had nothing more to say, reflected the parochial concerns of Vienna, where a tired cosmopolis, presided over by a tired Emperor, had consumed without remainder its inherited capital of hope. Nothing was left, the intellectuals believed, save officialdom, anonymous routines and the impersonal jurisdiction that was spread over a vast hinterland of strangers. By contrast, Janáček's ability to catch from his native Moravian air the freshest tonal harmonies, and the palpitating fragments of original and life-enhancing melody, reflected the hopes and longings of a new country—or rather a country newly discovered, rejoicing in the sense of locality, of being here and now and not (like Vienna) anywhere and anywhen.

The impenetrable bureaucracy of Kafka's *Trial* and *Castle* reflects the old order of Vienna in terminal decline—an order in which inviolable procedures and inscrutable laws conceal the arbitrariness and will-lessness of the power that imposes them. The hollowness of this cosmopolitan order is placed dramatically before us also by Musil, in *The Man without Qualities*. Musil shows the individual conscience, surrounded by a society kept in place by empty routines. In this demoralized order the conscience becomes subjective, vacillating, pro-foundly unsure of anything save its own impressions. The man without qualities is in fact a man without substance, a subjectivity without a self.

In *Young Törless* Musil, himself born in Bohemia, describes the youth of a cosmopolitan aesthete, educated in a military school which stands so much apart from the surrounding farms and villages that their inhabitants appear, to the boys who stare from the windows, scarcely human. Only once, when Musil refers to one of these troglodytic creatures as bearing a name which, in the local language, means 'he came hurrying', do we have an inkling that this is a place where Czech is spoken (for presumably, though the author does not say so, the name is Pospíšil). Musil's despair at the emptiness of cosmopolitan Vienna goes hand in hand with a refusal to acknowledge the existence of anywhere else. His sights pass from everywhere to nowhere, without finding the somewhere that counts. And the everywhere and the nowhere are one, namely Vienna, on the brink of self-destruction.

It is this nowhere that is rejected by the 'good soldier Švejk' in Jaroslav Hašek's eponymous epic, even though, being a native of Prague, he has no somewhere to offer in exchange for it, apart from his local pub. Janáček also rejected both the everywhere of old Vienna, and the nowhere to which it led. But his somewhere was both imagined and peopled, for him, with real characters and emotions, rooted in the soil. Nothing was further from his heart than the cynicism of Hašek; he had re-imagined Moravia not as it was, but in a higher and purer version of itself, a version in which the locality and its people were idealized as objects of love. Two momentous results of this were his folk-song arrangements and his speech melodies. Both of these fed his conception of music, as an expression of feeling, intimately tied both to speech and to dance: to be judged like speech for its truth, and like dance for its life. Hence music, for Janáček, could not be detached from its social context—any more than speech or dance could be detached. Music is a form of immediate communication and togetherness, and its roots are to be found in a people, a place and a time.

Of course, such an attitude is possible only in certain places and at certain times. Janáček was the heir of Smetana and Dvořák, and the active participant in a movement of national revival that reached to the humblest levels of society—even to the housemaid, Marie Stejskalová, whose garrulous reminiscences, recorded by Marie Trkanová,[3] give such a vivid picture of the changes through which the people of Brno, and the Janáček household in particular, then lived. It was, for a brief while, possible to regard folk song and folk poetry, folk festivals and folk religion, as genuine expressions of community, in which all the sacred episodes—youth, courtship, marriage, childbirth, nurture, mourning—were sincerely expressed and marked with the stamp of a place and a time.

No such thing was true of Vienna. In place of folk music and folk dances there was the music of the café and the dance-hall—some of it sophisticated, in the manner of the Strauss family, much of it degenerate. The sentimental song and the waltz had seized the popular imagination, and serious composers had become wary of 'the spirit of the people' when its voice was so often near to schmaltz. Only Mahler would sometimes risk it—and he drew as much on his native Moravia as he did on Vienna in his invocations of the people. As for Schoenberg, it is very clear from his theoretical writings that he blamed the decay of tonality as much on the eruption of its debased popular forms as on the exhaustion of post-Wagnerian harmony. The people appear in his music not as a self-renewing moral community, but as a bewildered crowd. Indeed no work of art matches *Moses und Aron* in this respect—a portrait of the crowd as a degenerate monster, a collective denial of God, wandering in need of a redemption that must come, if it comes, from outside. For Janáček the imagined community was not a crowd at all, but a kind of person, not the recipient of redemption but its source.

As theoreticians neither Janáček nor Schoenberg is an easy read. But there is an immediate and all-important distinction between them: Schoenberg is abstract, generalizing, systematizing, whereas Janáček is intuitive, concrete, and reluctant to explain. He is concerned above all with how we hear music, and with musical relations as they are experienced. His theory of the moment of chaos, which ensues when the notes of one chord hang over into the beginning of the next, and so form a binding or *spletná*, is a theory of what we hear, a kind of deep psychology of musical connection. Likewise, his theory that common chords can retain their identity even when 'thickened' with other notes, or even when another and rival chord 'percolates' into them—this is again a theory of what is heard, and a very interesting one. Chords, for Janáček, were musical individuals, whose identity was not cancelled when they were sounded simultaneously, but which continued to shine through the changed harmonic texture. The common chords of the major and minor scales never lost their truth for him, for it was a heard truth—a truth of phenomenology. The triads have an innocent life of their own, and if, in vulgar contexts, they can be abused, the fault lies in the contexts, not the chords. It would never occur to Janáček to dismiss a chord on the ground that it had 'become banal'. But this is what Schoenberg did, in relation to the diminished seventh.[4] No chord, for Janáček, was banal in itself, or incapable of being refreshed by returning it to its source, in the music of humanity. Throughout Janáček's music we find the simplest of tonal harmonies, juxtaposed with harmonies taken from the modernist repertoire, used not in any system-building or rule-governed way, but because they sound right —both musically and emotionally. The chord, for Janáček, is both a complete individual and also a plastic and adaptable material, capable of ever new uses and combinations.

'Sounding right' is not the same as 'being right' in accordance with some rule or system. For the authoritarian personality, however, nothing short of a system will do: without it he feels entirely unprotected. It is in this way, I believe, that we should understand Schoenberg's break with tonality. Schoenberg saw tonality as a system—a set of grammatical rules, which had exhausted its expressive potential. The solution was not to add new chords and new melodic and rhythmic shapes to the system, for this could never remove the fundamental pollution, which lay in the system itself. The rules, which had once set us free, were now constraining us, forcing us towards falsehood and schmaltz. So it is the rules that must be changed. We must devise a new system for the combination of tones, a new musical grammar, which would enable us to do the same kind of thing that tonality enabled us to do, but without making the tonal sounds. Thus emerged the serial technique, and composition with twelve tones, each treated as equal, so that none could emerge as a tonic, and no chord could be sidetracked into the old patterns of functional harmony.

This famous experiment was also an act of aggression. Schoenberg hated the audiences of contemporary Vienna, and he despised the easy-going recourse to the common chords of the tonal tradition. Although, as his arrangements of Strauss waltzes indicate, he had an ironical and sophisticated love of the old Viennese culture, he was also appalled by the sight of ordinary human enjoyment. He devised erudite concerts at which clapping was outlawed, and in which works of music were displayed like patients on an operating table, to be attended to in the same frame of mind as a surgical operation.

Furthermore, Schoenberg's new system was designed to have the same trans-national character as the one it replaced. Music was not to be renewed, as Janáček sought to renew it, by being returned to a community and a locality where song and dance still lived. It was to be reconstructed in the terms laid down by the old imperial idea, but somehow rescued from the decadence and exhaustion of empire.

Schoenberg thereby opened the way to what could be called the routinization of modernism. To write music, on the Schoenbergian model, it was not necessary to look for the community to which your music was addressed, and from whose heartbeats you took your primary inspiration. It was enough to devise a system, a code, which would cancel the arbitrariness of the sounds, by organizing them in accordance with another, however inaudible, grammar. The method could be applied anywhere, and in any frame of mind. And so long as the old expectations, enshrined in the experience of tonality, were frustrated, and so long as the inner logic of the result could nevertheless be revealed to the rational and enquiring mind, the result would be music—new, meaningful music, cured of banality by being rescued from the crowd. This was the aspect of Schoenberg's thinking which had the most lasting effect. And in the hands of Adorno, who saw the break with tonality as continuous with a rejection of the entire 'bourgeois' order, the defence of atonality became a moral and political duty, a way of capturing music for the fight against ideology, false consciousness and the fetishism of the consumer society.[5]

Schoenberg's approach to music made listening hard. But it made composing easy. Only a few practitioners of serialism had the genius of Schoenberg or Berg, who were able to reconcile the mad mathematics of the system with another and more musical organization, which had nothing to do with the serial order (except when the serial order was itself founded, as in Berg's Violin Concerto, on tonal principles). For lesser talents, the adherence to the *a priori* system failed to conceal the arbitrariness of the result. Nevertheless, they were fortified against criticism by the erudition of their theory. For many decades after Schoenberg's triumph it was difficult to criticize the modernist experiments: each came fully armed in theory, and the more arbitrary the sounds, it was implied, the deeper their true musical meaning, as revealed by the theory. Moreover the adroit propaganda of Adorno and Ernst Bloch, which had identified atonality with left-wing politics, and its opponents with the Nazi critics of *entartete Kunst*, made it risky to question the prevailing orthodoxy.

Thus it was that a whole generation of critics failed to notice that many of the modernist sound effects had themselves become banal—far more banal than the diminished seventh chord, since they belonged to no coherent language that could inject them with musical meaning. A sufficient dose of Milton Babbitt and Luigi Nono will convince the average listener that tonality is not a system in the sense that the serial method is a system. It does not proceed from a set of *a priori* rules for the organization of notes, but from an empirical understanding of the way things sound, and of the gravitational forces that set up mutual attraction and repulsion between the degrees of a scale. Such rules as can be given for tonal composition are not rules of grammar, but *a posteriori* generalizations, records of past successes, which together form a tradition, rather than a language or a code. Being rooted in the way things sound, tonality is infinitely open to experiment. If the diminished seventh sounds banal, then drop it, or change the context so that it regains some of its freshness (as in Berg's *Lyric Suite*, first movement, bar 15): that, surely, is the correct response to Schoenberg's strictures.

The same should be said of the fundamental building blocks of tonal harmony. If the major triad is a cliché, then try spreading it over five octaves, as Janáček does; try thickening it with the discordant second sounding quietly in the alto, and the tonic and mediant clustered in the bass, as in so many places in Janáček's lyrical operas. Or try using it as Janáček does in Ex. 1, from the last and greatest episode in the *Diary of One who Disappeared*, in which a D flat major triad, second inversion, underpins a pentatonic melody, with the tonic itself left out of the chord but appearing only as a passing note in the melody. If the change from major to minor sounds too cheap, remake the minor third as part of a whole-tone sequence, as in the next strophe of the melody from the *Diary*. (Ex. 2.) And if you need to stand at one remove from the key for a moment, without sliding into another, use whole-tone chords, as Puccini does in *Madama Butterfly*, or as Janáček does, for example in Ex. 3, from *On an Overgrown Path*. There is nothing daring about these experiments; nor do they imply some new harmonic system. But they have a naturalness and freshness that rescue them from Schoenberg's dismissive strictures.

Example 1

Example 2

Example 3

Purists will not be satisfied. They will point out—and rightly—that the great achievement of the Western musical tradition has been to produce organized and extended musical structures, in which musical material is not merely stated, but developed melodically, harmonically and rhythmically to create an impression of organic growth, and the sense of an ending. Of course, Schoenberg was wrong to think of tonality as a set of rules, even more wrong to think that he could find an equivalent in his permutational system. But he was not wrong to think of tonality as permitting large-scale relations and audible development, or in identifying these features as fundamental to the power of classical music. What does Janáček offer us instead? And if he offers nothing except brilliant flashes and enigmatic fragments, why should we take him as our model? Why not follow Schoenberg at least in this: in searching for a comprehensive musical order which will facilitate the great arches of musical thought that are familiar to us in Mozart and Brahms?

It is wrong to suggest that Janáček's music contains no development: as John Tyrell has argued, the paradigm of theme and variations is always at work in his musical thinking.[6] The concluding song of the *Diary* provides a vivid illustration, and it is worth pausing to examine it (Ex. 4). The theme is stated in its quasi-pentatonic version, in D flat major. The first variation follows at once in D flat minor, but with that strange whole-tone accompanying phrase (which seems to imply a D natural by way of completing the scale, and which is therefore in tension with the melody). The piano varies this phrase and then, in a diminished version, establishes it as a running whole-tone background to the melody in its original version, this time in canon with the bass line. The melody is repeated in unison, with a new variant of the concluding phrase. The accompanying figure is now transposed to the bass, with the melody, in a new variant, sounding in E major/minor, until the piano breaks in with a magical abbreviation of the theme in demi-semi quavers, now in A flat minor, the crucial concluding phrase being used to take the music into its sublime peroration in E flat major, in which the various fragments are rearranged as a surging accompaniment. The song is a masterpiece of musical organization, all the more remarkable in that the material from which it is built is chosen not for its structural potential, but for its independent expressive power: the folk-like melody—which has already appeared in the context of Zefka's seductive appeal—and the three-note phrase with its repeated note and whole-tone prolongation.

The critic will not be satisfied with such examples. This is organization, but organization at the micro-level: what about the larger scale? Janáček's instrumental works rely on repetition, ostinato and accompanying figures; the melodic lines are short, often curtailed before their implied point of closure; keys may be sustained (as in the example given) for no more than a few bars, and modulations are rapid, unpredictable and transitory. There is little in the way of counterpoint,

Example 4

and the whole effect is one of episodes and interruptions, as in the string quartets and the *Sinfonietta*, with timbre, colour and rhythm displacing argument and structure from the foreground. Are these not signs that

Example 5

musical structure, and long-term development, have yielded place to momentary heart-beats and expressive gestures?

It is a real question. But it also suggests the true nature of Janáček's achievement, in cutting the living parts of tonality from the parts which had ossified or died. If the only way to continue the great tradition of structural hearing and thinking was by means of the caricature proposed by Schoenberg, in which intellectual order replaces the order perceived by the ear, then this was a sign that the architectonic tradition was dead. But it was not a sign that tonality was dead, only that tonality must be severed from the architectonic project, and remade as a more plastic and impressionistic idiom. That was what Janáček did.

The architectonic tradition, as we find it in Brahms, for example, depends upon lengthy themes, carefully prepared changes of tonal centre, contrapuntal organization, and a direction of phrases, melodies, sections and movements towards a goal. Janáček rejected all those features. His musical practice, like his musical theory, concentrates on the atomic particles of musical meaning: chord-sequences and melodic phrases, together with the multi-layered rhythmic organization that he called *sčasování*. His themes are short, pregnant gestures; shifts of key are abrupt and colouristic, seldom fully prepared and seldom establishing a true tonal centre. (Notice, for example, that the *Diary* is notated without a key signature save for no. XX and the piano peroration to no. XXI, both of which are given the signature of A flat. This is indeed the key around which the work revolves, but the music settles in A flat only fleetingly, and always with sidelong glances to rival tonal centres.) Organization depends upon repetition and small-scale variation rather than counterpoint, and the emphasis is on beginnings rather than endings. The Janáček theme is typically moving away from rather than towards its most vital moment—in just the way that human gestures erupt and then dwindle—as in Examples 5 and 6. (Note the wholly characteristic one-beat empty bar which comes at the end of these melodies, and in which they die away. This bar is an integral part of the

Example 6

Example 7

Example 8   *Example 9*

melodic structure, like the bar of silence that concludes Beethoven's
Fifth Symphony.)

Janáček's figures tend to contain repeated notes, as in Examples 7, 8
and 9, creating two beginnings without an ending. His melodies tend to
set out, in Slavonic fashion, from the downbeat; his greatest moments
are announcements rather than conclusions, like the trumpet call that
summons back the introductory fanfare of the *Sinfonietta* to end the
work—to end it, in fact, as it began. And even in the final bars he may
start something new—as in the conclusion of Act 2 of *Kat'a*, in which
the music suddenly slips out of the composer's favourite erotic region of
D flat/A flat, and ends on a radiant E major chord, but one in which we
hear a new beginning, as the mediant weaves in and out of major and
minor, planting seeds of tragedy in the midst of joy.

This emphasis on beginnings means that cross-rhythms arise as
spontaneously in Janáček as they do in ordinary life. Phrases burst out
and cut across each other like speech in the marketplace. The typical
Janáček sound reminds one less of a carefully disciplined gathering, in

which each person is dedicated to the collective task, than of a passionate and intimate conversation, in which voices break out under the pressure of some inner urgency and in which harmony is achieved in spite of the many voices and not because of them. This is dramatic music par excellence, and it is organized according to dramatic rather than symphonic demands. This is as true of the string quartets and the *Sinfonietta* as it is of the operas and the *Glagolitic Mass*. And because Janáček was a great dramatist, his music hangs perfectly together, achieving heights of expression which entirely justify the passage-work that leads towards and away from them. In a sense he was the opposite of Wagner. While Wagner achieves dramatic intensity by symphonic means, Janáček achieves symphonic intensity through drama. It is thus that we hear, for example, the great second act of *Kat'a*, and the equally sublime peroration to the *Makropulos Case*.

This has, I believe, a great bearing on Janáček's importance for us, in our current historical predicament. Schoenberg's experiment with serial organization was an attempt to reconnect modern music to the great tradition of symphonic utterance. The new music was to be as organized and as authoritative as the tonal symphony, with the same kind of organic interdependence among its parts, and the same depth of structure. It was to be an exercise in sustained musical thought, inviting the same intense, objective and analytical audience that might listen in silence to a symphony of Brahms. The assumption was that the traditional concert audience would be reborn, and music once again assume its place at the heart of the metropolitan culture. The enterprise failed not merely because the serial system remained a merely intellectual device, with no ability to address the ear, but because the audience to which Schoenberg addressed himself could not be created anew. It belonged to a particular cultural moment, and that moment was passing. The routinization of modernism in our time reflects this fact. The modernist novelties are not the spontaneous results of a dialogue between composer and audience: they take place in a void, like abstract thought-experiments, appealing more to curiosity than to an established emotional need. Only by elaborate artifice, involving state patronage, a carefully nurtured establishment of insiders, and the cooperation of the critics of the quality press, can something like a modernist audience be brought into being.

The transformation of the audience that was occurring in Schoenberg's day reflected the increasing mobility of society, the ready availability of music, the democratization of taste, and the shortening of attention span that is the inevitable concomitant of modern life. The great chamber works of Brahms are addressed to people who move more slowly, and at a greater distance from one another, than we do. They contain tenderness, longing and passion: but all are recollected in tranquillity, and set at a distance by the patient musical thought that sits, as it were, in judgement upon them. A modern composer could not write in such a way; to do so would be to falsify the rhythms of his psyche. Tenderness, longing and passion still exist; but they are intense, momentary and, as it were, thought-resistant. You can stay at Brahms's level of musical objectivity only if you purify music of its reference to life, and remake it as an intellectual exercise. And you can fortify this exercise with theories and commentaries and systems and rules, but it will never achieve the authority of art. Instead it will be an author-itarian mask, behind which lies a frozen or an anxious sensibility.

It is in these terms that we should understand the achievement of Janáček. His venture towards the folk culture of Moravia was not just a repudiation of metropolitan Vienna; it was an attempt to create a genuinely modern music that would be connected to our spontaneous ways of understanding musical form. Janáček's interest in speech melodies, *nápěvky*, derived from the view that the true units of musical meaning exist at the micro-level. As he put it, the whole state of the organism, and every phase of spiritual activity, may be revealed in speech melodies.[7] If we need to revitalize tonality, then we should look for those points where life and melody coincide. It is here, in speech melody, that musical discovery and musical invention must begin.

Moreover, the elements of musical order still retain their appeal. Even in the accelerated conditions of modern life—and especially in those conditions—people understand repetition; they understand the rhyth-mical figure; they respond to the pure intervals of fifth and fourth; their attention can be captured by strophic melodies and dance rhythms. To use these as your raw materials is not to cheapen music but to begin from the point where music makes contact with life. Of course, there is always a risk of banality; but one reason for returning to the old folk culture is that it shows the basic musical devices in their pure and uncorrupted form, before becoming banal through the loss of their real-life context. It was this pure material that was reworked by Janáček, and which set limits to his style without cramping it. He wrote in such a way that, even in the midst of the most angular phrases and dissonant harmony, he could regain at a step the lilt of a folk melody and the clarity of a tonal chord. And because he was a natural dramatist, he was prepared for the great change that came over the audience in the twentieth century—the change from cool, objective listening to audiovisual involvement. The *Diary* illustrates this perfectly: a song-cycle which can be staged, with off-stage chorus and an opportunity for theatrical lighting—a song-cycle in the tradition of the monodrama.[8]

The gains, for Janáček, were not merely aesthetic. At the same time as capturing a new kind of audience, he was able to communicate a moral vision. In contrast to the despair and emptiness expressed by Schoenberg's *Erwartung*, for example, the operas of Janáček are vindications of human life. His characters—his women especially—are real, lovable and the objects of a most compelling sympathy. This sympathy animates the music, and forms a kind of halo around the characters as they move on the stage. Even a tragic fate like Kat'a's seems to confirm the value of the life that leads to it. For it provides Kat'a with the opportunity to capture our hearts, to show that she is what she ought to be, and suffers through no fault of her own.

There are those who find, in the instrumental music as much as the operas, a message of rebellion—a desire to cast off the strictures of an oppressive religious morality, to live freely and to love by impulse, as Janáček was to imagine himself loving the reticent Kamila Stösslová. They see those frightening stepmother figures—the Kostelnička and Kabanicha—as embodiments of a sclerotic moral order, against which the young heart makes its futile bid for freedom. And they connect all this with the composer's life in the obvious ways that that life suggests. Did he not say, in response to the critic who welcomed the *Glagolitic Mass* as an affirmation of Christian faith, that he was no believer?

And yet the ear tells quite another story. We meet Kat'a first in intimate conversation with Varvara, telling the girl about her life before marriage, and how the church was the most important part of it: 'Já k smrti ráda chodila do kostela'—leading at once to the tenderest of music in which you hear the character-forming force of Kat'a's piety (Ex. 10). All that precedes this passage is a supreme vindication of Janáček's account of *nápěvky*. Kat'a's whole organism, and all the phases of her spiritual life, are contained in the little bursts of ingenuous melody that she breathes above the orchestra. The music tells us that Kat'a's religion has been an education of the emotions, a preparation for the very passion that would have fulfilled her, had life been kind, but which will in the event destroy her. Moreover, the only explanation that Boris gives of his love for Kat'a, when confiding in Kudrjáš, shows that he too sees Kat'a's piety as the centre of her being and the source of her irresistible appeal: 'if only you could see her at her prayers, what an angelic smile plays on her cheeks, and the light which shines from them!' And again we hear what is being said far more clearly from the

Example 10

music than from the words. Boris has been lifted out of the ordinariness of his being by this encounter with the spark of God in Kat'a. (It was Janáček who said of *From the House of the Dead*, that it endeavours to show the 'spark of God' even in the lowest of human life.)

To put the point directly: Janáček was aware that a folk culture cannot exist without religion, that religion is not so much a set of doctrines as a habit of worship and devotion, and that its meaning lies in the practices which instal it in human hearts. If we must go to folk culture for our paradigms of passion, then we must also acknowledge that passion is here dependent on a religious context. This truth is brought home in another way by *The Makropulos Case*. Emilia Marty's longevity has deprived her of passion because all piety has died in her. By playing at God she has lost Him. Alone of the characters on the stage, she is without the spark of God—and miraculously regains it as she dies.

Janáček's invocation of the Marian processional at Frydek in *On an Overgrown Path* shows how deeply, for him, was the Moravia of his childhood woven with folk religion. The dramas of Jenůfa, Kat'a and the young man who disappeared involve the impact of life in its new and mobile forms on characters shaped by faith and prepared for passion by pious routines. One by one the characters in the Tsarist gulag portrayed in *From the House of the Dead* reveal the spark of God that glows in them, and which was planted in some forgotten childhood. The masterly libretto that Janáček wrote for this opera owes its success precisely to the religious impulse which it allows to shine through the music and cancel the sense of failure.

I mention this because it brings to the fore the underlying realism of Janáček's vision. He did not sentimentalize the folk culture whose melodies and rhythms he drew upon, but saw it as a whole—a complete form of life, in which the consolations of community were obtainable only because the discipline of religion has been internalized by those admitted to membership. Consolation has a cost, and it is a heavy one. The discipline of religion may be a source of joy; but it also turns temptation into tragedy. To put it in another way: religion in Janáček is not abstract, theological or universal. It is local, immediate, the voice of the very community that is being invoked by the music. Its meaning does not lie in doctrine: its meaning is the individual life lived under its aegis—a life that may be tragic as well as fulfilled, and in which tragedy and fulfilment derive from a common source.

Again there is an interesting contrast with Schoenberg, in whose works religion plays a large and imposing role, but for whom faith was a matter of abstract doctrine addressed to a wandering people, a crowd without a place or a time of their own. The failure of Schoenberg's Moses to communicate this theological faith to a people bent on idolatry parallels the failure of Schoenberg's abstract serialism to win an audience. Neither Moses nor Schoenberg is able to win through to the human heart, since the heart is fulfilled not by abstract laws or a universal culture but by the concrete customs of a community rooted in a place and a time.

The sceptic will say that, even if Schoenberg has no authority for us now, the same must be true of Janáček. For the community that he invokes in his music has long since vanished from the world. Folk music is a thing of the past and pop, our modern vernacular, is without roots in any real community. In a world in which the sexual revolution has made all options easy and affordable the very possibility of a drama like Kat'a's is ruled out. In such a world alienation is the fundamental fact, and whatever we think of Janáček as a composer his is a supremely unalienated music—a music of acceptance, at every point affirming that life is worthwhile. The modernist avant-garde does not presuppose the background of naive social order that is assumed by Janáček; it is not addressed to a community but to individuals, who experience through the music the alienation that reigns in their hearts. In so far as we notice a genuine modernist audience emerging in our conditions it is an audience of sceptical individualists, urban, agnostic and unattached, who look on the world of Janáček as a curious survival beyond its proper time.

Such a sceptical rejoinder is, however, too quick. The community invoked in Janáček's music no longer existed at the time when he wrote. And it had always been, in part, an 'imagined community', brought alive by its own story-telling, and dependent on literary make-believe, combined with subsidies from Vienna. The national revival in the Czech lands was a work of the imagination, and from the beginning music had played a vital part in the project. Janáček's music, like Dvořák's, was not derived from the community portrayed in it: it was an attempt to create that community as an artistic and musical idea. And that, in part, is why it is so inspiring, and why it still has such authority for modern people. They hear in this music the working out of an ideal—not a metaphysical or mythical ideal, but an ideal of community. Janáček's authoritative gestures are really gestures of sympathy, reminding us of our human potential. We too, while the music works on us, rise above our self-involvement, and reach outwards to others, idealizing them in our surge of fellow-feeling.

Here, I think, lies the significance of Janáček's principal devices: repetition, rhythmic figures, folk melodies, *nápěvky mluvy* and altered diatonic harmonies. All of these are addressed directly to the ear; they are anti-theoretical, even populist in their meaning. Even if it is only a few musically educated people who appreciate this music, the image it creates is of an inclusive community, united by a common culture and a common moral code.

Whether you can write music in this way now is, of course, a controversial question. But I shall conclude with a few observations. First, art is an act of communication, which makes no sense without a real or imagined audience. And in imagining the audience you are imagining the community which idealizes them and to which they aspire. In a world of short attention-spans and information overload this audience cannot be captured by Schoenberg's method. It is still questionable whether the avant-garde can obtain a real audience; too often those present in the concert hall seem like a pseudo-audience, if not an audience of pseuds. The true goal, by contrast, is to win the audience over, to make them part of a shared imaginative project.

Secondly, we should respect the devices that Janáček used. Repetition, dance rhythms, diatonic harmonies, speech and folk melodies are the perennial symbols of a shared and settled form of life, and an available prophylactic against solipsism. As for dissonance, we should take a lesson from Janáček, Bartók and Stravinsky, contrasting the dissonant chord with the chord that wholly or partially resolves it. Schoenberg sought to reject this contrast. He hoped for 'the emancipation of the dissonance', in which no chord would be heard as intrinsically more harmonious than any other. But by emancipating dissonance you lose it. Dissonance is what it is because of the contrast with consonance, and it is only through this contrast that it brings its own distinctive life to the musical line.

Finally, music without melody lacks the most important dimension of musical significance. Music is not a 'sound effect', but an expression of life, and melody is the principal sign of this. Melodies are the true musical individuals, the actors on the stage of music, whose life-stories are told by the notes. Janáček sets an irreproachable example. His melodies, taken from the rhythm of human speech, and at the same time imbued with a tradition of song and dance, were entirely unsentimental—images of sincere human utterance, as though compelled from the heart rather than put together from a repertoire of formulae. Such melodies have been within the reach of composers even in the most recent past: witness Britten's *Curlew River*, the Triple Concerto of Tippett, or Messiaen's *Harawi* songs. Are we to assume that the store of melody is finite, and that we have scraped the barrel clean? Surely not.

I do not doubt that the problems posed by the attempt to follow Janáček's example are at least as great as the problems posed by the attempt to follow Schoenberg. But we should not be deceived into thinking that the radicalism of Schoenberg's formulae is a reason for adopting them, rather than rejecting them. It is reasonable to be sceptical towards the dogma that tells us to throw away tonality and to defy the musical ear. For this dogma is rooted in the theory of music rather than in the sound of music, and is addressed to the task of justifying avant-garde music in the way that Mark Twain jokingly justified the music of Wagner, by arguing that it is better than it sounds.

Notes

1 Such is the authoritarian personality, famously diagnosed by Schoenberg's disciple and fellow authoritarian, Theodor Adorno. See *The Authoritarian Personality*, New York 1950.
2 See Arnold Schoenberg, *Harmonielehre*, 3rd edn, Vienna 1922, and Leoš Janáček, *Úplná nauka o harmonii*, in *Hudebné teoretické dílo*, ed. Zdeněk Blazek, Prague 1974, vol. 2. This volume also contains the important text, 'Můj názor o sčasování', in which the composer gives his theory of rhythm as a multilayered structure. Janáček's theories are well set out in Michael Beckerman, *Janáček as Theorist*, New York 1994.
3 See Marie Trkanová, *U Janáčku*, Prague 1959.
4 See *Harmonielehre*, 3rd edn, Vienna 1922, pp. 288–9.
5 See *The Philosophy of Modern Music*, tr. A. G. Mitchell and W. V. Blomster, New York 1973.
6 See John Tyrell's article on Janáček in the *New Grove Dictionary of Music*.
7 Bohumír Štědron, *Janáček ve vzpomínkach a dopísech*, Prague 1946, p. 138.
8 The monodrama was popular in Central Europe throughout the nineteenth century, usually with a spoken text over a piano accompaniment. Somehow this combination does not work today, although the monodramas by Zdeněk Fibich to texts by Vrchlický would have been known to Janáček.

12

Thoughts on Szymanowski

In this chapter I consider two early twentieth-century masters, Skryabin and Szymanowski. The first is, in my view, one of the greatest of modern composers, while the second, who followed in Skryabin's footsteps, deserves almost as high a reputation. Szymanowski attempted to come to terms with the problem that exercised Schoenberg, while rejecting Schoenberg's search for a *theory* with which to solve it.[1] The problem was that of redeeming a musical idiom from its inherited decadence; of purging its super-abundance of cliché, and preventing its lapse into emotions that can no longer be genuinely felt. It is partly because of his highly original manner of confronting this problem that Szymanowski deserves our respect.

Szymanowski was a Polish composer, but perhaps only in the sense that Chopin was a Polish composer. We should not be misled, either by his nationality, or by his nationalism, into thinking that his music must be understood as the expression of a burgeoning national consciousness. Chopin was strongly attached to Poland, and celebrated its native music in many of his compositions, and in particular in the exquisite mazurkas, through which he created a musical idiom that was to have a profound influence on both Skryabin and Szymanowski. However, the musical significance of Chopin's experiments lies not so much in their Polishness, as in their contribution to the development of the romantic keyboard.[2] Chopin added to the harmonic and thematic repertoire of Schumann only those elements of Polish sentiment which could be heard to develop—in a new and surprising direction—what was already there. Polish folk music was a stimulus to Chopin; but the structure of his musical thought is to be understood in terms of the larger tradition of piano writing to which he belongs.

Likewise with Szymanowski, whose most self-consciously Polish works must still be understood, not as attempts to discover a purely Polish idiom (comparable to Bartók's purely Hungarian idiom), but as off-shoots of the musical thinking which grew in cosmopolitan Europe. The same applies, I believe, to Skryabin. While many of his contemporaries tried to make sense of his astonishing idiom by describing it as

Russian—or at any rate as Slav—his music obeys a logic which can be understood neither in terms of the idioms of Russian folk music, nor in terms of the music of the nationalist composers who were his contemporaries. Of course, the insensate extremism of Skryabin's metaphysics is very Russian, as is the apocalyptic longing for 'world conflagration' which inspired his symphonies. This peculiar longing has been a vital element in much that is good in Russian culture, as well as in much that is disastrous. Nevertheless, Skryabin is not a Russian composer in the way that Musorgsky, Tchaikovsky or Shostakovitch are Russian. His art, like Chopin's, and also like Debussy's (and who could be more French than Debussy?), must be understood in terms of the development of Romantic keyboard music, and in particular in terms of the new harmonic possibilities which the piano presented to its most thoughtful exponents. It is part of Skryabin's genius that he did not allow his overblown emotions to corrupt his music. On the contrary, it was through the finesse and discipline of his art that he was able to contain and resolve the discordant mania of his soul. (Cf. Pushkin: 'Madam, my writings are genteel, but my heart is completely vulgar'.) Skryabin's later music displays an impressive struggle to contain and give form to his decadent emotions. It is the true expression of the 'elegant soul' which Sabaneev attributed to him, and which triumphed first in his art, and also in his life, over the extravagant self-indulgence which warred with it.[3]

Like Skryabin, Szymanowski was born into the milieu of the *szlachta*, isolated from the popular movements and the political developments of his time. His education was refined and indulgent, allowing complete freedom for the development of his talents. Both composers dedicated their lives to composition, and lived, in consequence, in constant debt. Both men saw the external world as an arbitrary, indulgent parent, who sometimes gave, sometimes withheld, and whose concerns were of a separate order from those of music, and largely inscrutable. This similarity of spirit is matched by an unmistakable similarity of musical inspiration. Although Szymanowski was by no means an imitator, it could be said that the influence of Skryabin over his music is that of a master, not a colleague. The influence is apparent already in the early piano music. The opus 4 Études, for example, show a detailed derivation from Skryabin, both in structure and in harmony. Even the justly famous third Étude, in B flat minor, involves a remaking of melodic and harmonic devices already used by Skryabin – in the B flat minor study, op. 8 no. 11 (the resemblance of which to Szymanowski's has already been noted by Jim Samson[4]), but also, perhaps more importantly, in the beautiful slow movement to the F sharp minor Piano Sonata (no. 3).

The influence here is not confined to melodic line or harmonic progression: there is a resemblance of what, for want of a better term, I shall call 'musical personality'. The disposition of notes on the keyboard, the movement of the musical line, the 'feel' of the chords in the fingers, and the peculiar resonances of the fourth, the tritone, the open fifth, and the major seventh—all these acquire, from the very first of Szymanowski's experiments in piano writing, a significance that closely parallels their significance for Skryabin. There are, of course, important points of difference. In particular, Skryabin's piano music follows a steady path of logical development; it is informed, if not by theory, at least by system, so that each new piece extends and develops the language of the preceding one, and the sequence as a whole gradually moves towards, and also justifies, one of the most original styles in all keyboard writing. While there is development—or at least, considerable movement—in Szymanowski's keyboard style, it is also true that there is not the same effect of system, and therefore not the same attempt to follow through the harmonic and melodic implications of individual ideas.

The comparison may be usefully extended to the orchestral works. It is undeniable that Szymanowski explored the range of dissonance to its furthest reaches, and employed harmonies that were well beyond Skryabin's in their defiance of the innocent ear. Nevertheless, his harmonies are, in one way, less daring than those of *Prometheus*, or of the late Skryabin sonatas. For their dissonant quality is part of the colour, rather than the structure, of the music. In Skryabin, there is an harmonic order which, even when it stretches tonality to the limit, retains the two guiding principles of tonal structure: the principle of progression, whereby chords arise out of, resolve into, and diverge from one another; and the principle of resonance, whereby melodic line and harmonic progression are mutually dependent, with the shape of the melody dictating, and also dictated by, the underlying harmonic movement.

Skryabin's 'mystical' harmonies do not belong to the common Western repertoire. But they are, in their own way, functional, inheriting tensions and resolving or augmenting them in ways that make sense only in the longer musical term. Hence they impose large and often barely tolerable harmonic and melodic obligations. The composer must shape progression and melody in accordance with their imperatives. He must approach them by sequences which are compelled by a musical

Example 1

logic in which dissonance is actually required. I believe that, even in the Messiaen-like prodigies of *Metopes*, and the densest superimpositions of *King Roger*, Szymanowski never undertook risks of so high an order.

The resemblance to Skryabin is also revealed in Szymanowski's melodic lines. Jim Samson has again perceptively pointed to Szymanowski's indebtedness to an important *Grundgestalt* of Skryabin's music: a sequence of rhythmically characterized ascending leaps, followed by a stepwise chromatic descent.[5] (Ex. 1 reproduces Samson's examples, together with an example of my own, in which the basic 'cell' of this structure is displayed, and also its ultimate source in the opening motive of *Tristan und Isolde*.)

This is but one of many extremely important resemblances between the melodic thinking of the two composers. However, I think that it would be wrong to place too much emphasis on these resemblances. In art difference is more important than similarity. And here the difference is great. While Skryabin is through and through an integrated composer, deriving his abstruse harmonic experiments from a sense of the melodic relations between tones, and his melodies from the musical space created by his chords, Szymanowski remains a composer of motive and colour, whose thinking is not truly permeated by melodic principles.

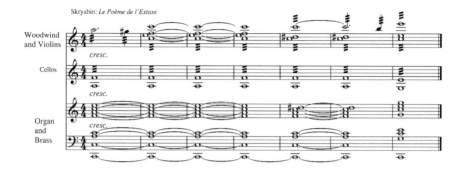

Example 2

The influence of Skryabin is perhaps most apparent in the colour and the mood of certain middle period works, in particular, in the Third Symphony (*The Song of the Night*), whose resemblance in texture and atmosphere to *Le Poème de l'Extase* is remarkable. The chromatic and insistent melodic line, the shimmering orchestral colour, the growling organ pedal—all these, which are structurally decisive features of the Szymanowski, derive from the closing section of Skryabin's poem (and, indirectly, from Strauss's *Also sprach Zarathustra*). Most important of all is the sense of Skryabin's music as being constantly driven towards a climax, falling back only to take breath, and again rushing into frenzy. When the accumulated wave finally breaks, Skryabin produces one of his most magnificent resolutions. (Ex. 2.) Here huge beautifully spaced brass chords are backed by organ over a low C pedal and percussion, while tremolando strings and woodwind carry the movement to its peak. The harmonic structure is of an extended IV–I progression, in C major. The subdominant chord is 'coloured in', first with a major seventh, and then with a minor seventh, so displaying an exaggerated tension which endures and diminishes, until the final release into C major.

It is interesting to find a complex reminiscence of this passage in the conclusion to *The Song of the Night*. The music works towards its final culmination in Skryabin's manner, with constant feints at a climax, interspersed by breathy hesitation and dazed voluptuousness. When the culminating point is reached, at bar 495, we are assailed by an overwhelming chord, orchestrated in a manner strongly reminiscent of the Skryabin. (Ex. 3.) Again there is a choir of brass, backed up by organ over a pedal note of low C. The melodic line is carried by high

Szymanowski, *The Song of the Night*

Example 3

tremolando strings, together with woodwind, while massive trilling
percussion (complete with bells and piano) gives a tumultuous character to the movement.

Szymanowski does not resolve the chord, but allows it to dwindle,
gradually adding new and colouristic harmonies, while retaining the
pedal note on low C until bar 526, when the orchestra and chorus,
having lingered in the harmonic region of C major for almost twenty
bars, finally subsides with a brilliantly orchestrated C major sigh. The
effect of this is of a vastly extended and heavily burdened IV-I cadence,
the climactic chord—itself straight out of the Skryabin repertoire
—being given a subdominant character by virtue of the pedal on the
tonic note of C.

Such comparisons show Szymanowski to be deeply influenced by
Skryabin, precisely when he is attempting to give form to the state of
mind, and the musical language, which he had appropriated as his own.
The Song of the Night is the major expression of Szymanowski's
orientalism,[6] and one into which he put all his meticulous knowledge of
orchestral atmosphere. It is both highly personal in its meaning, and at
the same time flagrant in its desire to open that meaning to its audience.
Unfortunately, however, once the comparison with *Le Poème de
l'Extase* is made, it seems to show the relative weakness of Szymanowski's idiom. *The Song of the Night* does not match the architectonic
brilliance of Skryabin's poem, with its relentless energy, and its superb
arch of consecutive harmonies. *Le Poème de l'Extase* has a structure of
struggle and resolution, which is foretold in the opening bars. (Ex. 4.)

Example 4

Here the passage from the whole tone chord to the relaxed C major
provides a marked harmonic resolution, closely related to the progression from 'Skryabin sixth' to tonic, as in the conclusion to the *Satanic
Poem*, op. 36. And this progression through atonal regions into plain
C major provides the dominating movement of the symphony. (Mac-
Donald has argued that Skryabin had to 'earn' the right to C major;
that he had somehow to graduate towards this key from such darker
regions as G flat.[7] On the contrary, it seems to me, Skryabin's
accomplished use of the C major tonal region was a recurring feature of
his idiom, and one that made a considerable impact on Szymanowski.)

Even *Prometheus* shows the same sense of resolution, moving slowly
out of its penumbra of fourth-built chords into a magnificent conclusion in F sharp major. By contrast *The Song of the Night*, although it
ends in a heavily emphasized C major, does not really resolve. It does
not have the harmonic impetus of the Skryabin, and nothing which
precedes the climax necessitates the movement into C. Szymanowski's
firm pedal-based tonal structures seldom seem to be compelled by any
harmonic logic: the harmonies which precede them are obliterated, but
not quietened, by the tonal utterances. When tonality reaffirms itself in
Skryabin, it is because it has been summoned up by atonal passages
which seem to yearn for it. The effect is so powerful as to provide one
of the major justifications for the finicky perfumes of accumulated
fourths.

Of course, Skryabin's piano music shows a movement away from the
idea of tonal resolution towards that of a Schoenbergian 'unity of
musical space'. But often, as in the augmented E major chord that
concludes *Vers la Flamme*, chords which are by no means part of the
tonal directory are used in a manner that creates a strong suggestion of
tonal resolution. And equally, when there is not even a hint of tonality,

Example 5

Skryabin is seldom without the logic of tonality—the logic that enables us to hear a chord as compelled by, and answering to, those which had preceded it.

Musicologists have attempted to analyse this 'logic of tonality' in ways which do not suppose that only strictly tonal music can possess it.[8] But it seems to me to be a defect in many of these analyses—a defect not unrelated to their implicit claim to a 'scientific' rigour—that they can, in the end, be applied equally to the music of Skryabin and Szymanowski. Consider, for example, the concept of 'pantonality' advanced by Reti. This seems to encompass equally the shifting tonal foundation in the music of Szymanowski, and the uncompromising logic of Skryabin's eighth sonata, which neither alludes to tonality, nor defies it, but simply reproduces its underlying dynamic compulsion.

A more important criticism emerges, I believe, from the comparison with Skryabin. It seems to me that—with some exceptions to which I shall shortly return—Szymanowski's style creates a need for melody which he cannot satisfy. This is not to say that there are no melodies in Szymanowski's music. On the contrary, there are very many, perhaps even too many. It is rather that the melodies are often lacking in vigour and appeal: they have a studied, abstract quality, which it is hard to describe, but easy to hear. Consider the two melodies in Ex. 5, from *The Song of the Night* and the *Fontaine d'Aréthuse* (no. 1 of *Mythes*, for violin and piano, justly famous for its lovely impressionistic harmonies). These are beautifully crafted ideas, without a hint of banality, and rich in implications. And yet they leave the listener cold. We are not absorbed by them, and cannot hear them as constituting the essence of

Le poeme de l'extase

Example 6

Skryabin. Somata no. 7

Example 7

the musical movement. On the contrary, it is an important feature of the style exemplified in these works that we generally hear the musical movement to progress independently of the melody, the melody being, as it were, superimposed upon a separate dynamic idea.

I do not wish to imply that all melodies must be diatonic, or borrow the logic of the diatonic scale. On the contrary, one of the great achievements of twentieth-century music has been to overthrow that idea, giving us melodies derived entirely from the whole-tone scale (Debussy), or catchy phrases which defy tonality altogether (Berg in *Lulu*). Nevertheless, it seems to me that, in the sense in which Debussy and Berg produced atonal melodies, which may stand alone as the expressions of an integrated musical movement, the two examples from Szymanowski fail to be melodies.

Once again the comparison with Skryabin is useful. The opening theme of the *Poème de l'Extase—con voglia languido* (Ex. 6)—although of indeterminate key, is an exquisitely turned melodic fragment, which can stand as self-sufficient and also grow and develop (the hints of B major/minor are entirely negated both by the harmony and by subsequent developments). Throughout his career Skryabin organized musical movement according to melodic principles, whether tonal (as in the melody which provides the energy of the *Divine Poem*'s first movement), or atonal (as in the theme, Ex. 7, from the extraordinary seventh sonata). By virtue of his melodic emphasis, Skryabin is able to engage the listener in the movement of his music, to create as an inner necessity the transition from disharmony to disharmony, which can exist as movement only in the ear of the listener who is persuaded so to hear it. In comparison with Skryabin's melodies, even the much praised aria of Roxana (*King Roger*, Act II) fails, it seems to me, to persuade us of its ineluctability—a point that is vividly illustrated in Kochanski's transcription for violin and piano.

It should not be thought that Szymanowski could simply by-pass melody and its function. On the contrary, as I have indicated, his music creates a need for it. Melody provides the inner dynamic to a musical line, by making the listener a willing participant in its movement: through melody, you are the music, while the music lasts. A melody is heard therefore to yearn towards its own continuation; it provides, indeed, the musical encapsulation of the idea of yearning. For Szymanowski, whose ruling preoccupation was the expression of yearning, melody became a potent symbol of musical 'charm'. The idea of charm, in all its resonances, is one without which the content of Szymanowski's major works could not be described. Charm has for Szymanowski all the resonances that 'mystery' has for Skryabin: the force which beckons onwards, promising ineffable gifts of experience and knowledge.[9]

Charm is symbolized in the Shepherd-Dionysus of *King Roger*, who, in describing his god as *piękny jako ja*—lovely as I am—makes in his own image a god of pure come-hitherish-ness. The shepherd is the dramatic embodiment of the musical meaning for which Szymanowski searched. The promise of charm is the promise of an indefinite permission, whose meaning is unambiguously erotic. It is this yearning that provides the passion behind Szymanowski's music.

Such a yearning stands in need of melody: the voice that calls from heart to heart. Szymanowski's stylistic achievement consists in devising effective substitutes for melody—devices that gave to his music both immediate delightfulness and dynamic compulsion. Three features stand out as particularly important in this achievement: colour, motive, and pedal-based ostinato.

First, colour. Skryabin once said of himself that, unlike Richard Strauss, he wrote symphonic music in which all the voices are distinguishable. The same might have been said by Szymanowski, who was so great a master of orchestral colour as to be able to multiply voices indefinitely, while still guaranteeing their discernibility. In his middle period, this agility with colour took on a new meaning. Colour became the essential ingredient in the musical 'beckoning', the feature which lured the audience into the music. Although Szymanowski could hardly be said to have evolved anything like Schoenberg's *Klangfarbenmelodie*, it is nevertheless true that he used colour in a novel way, as a basic unit of musical structure.

It is hard to define 'colour'; the term denotes a feature of music that

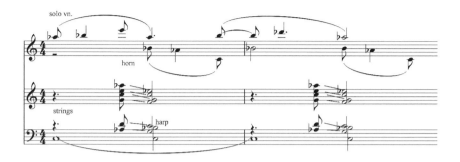

Example 8

condenses many dimensions into a single *Gestalt*. To put the matter crudely, colour is whatever changes in a transcription that leaves harmony and melody intact. Szymanowski was a master at erecting blocks of colour, which grow and melt into each other, and which shift through the spectrum with all the enticing quality of a Schubertian melody. Thus a kind of 'colour melody' emerges, which depends not so much on the horizontal relation between tones, as upon the overlapping and interrupting of colour areas.

An example is provided by measures 27–41 of *The Song of the Night*. Here a solo violin keeps up a soaring pseudo-melody (Ex. 5), over a slowly shifting background of orchestral colour. Three bars consist of tremolando strings and piano, with decorative runs on clarinet and celesta, over a pizzicato bass. The next three bars involve a punctuated tremolando motive on the strings, with a rippling arpeggio figure from the piano, above short, muffled chords on the harp. A solo viola, emerging from the first colour block, melts into this second block, while the clarinets fade away. Clarinets and flutes then return with runs that lift the colour into a new region, the tremolando confined to the lower strings, and with a throbbing motive on woodwind and celesta; a second solo violin briefly enters, doubling a fragment of the 'pseudo-melody' an octave below; the whole slips discernibly into a fourth block of colour, in which plaintive horn calls sound out over glissando strings and muffled harps and timpani (Ex. 8). Each of these colour blocks recurs with thematic significance later in the work. Many further examples can be found, especially in the two violin concertos, which exhibit extraordinary subtleties of orchestration. One of the reasons for the comparative unpopularity of Szymanowski's piano and chamber works is the absence of the vast palette from which he could compose

Example 9

these striking effects. In these 'colour melodies' he effectively abrogates melody, by providing a potent alternative with which to present the essentials of musical charm. We should not be surprised to find, therefore—as I have already noted—that the transcription of Roxana's aria for violin and piano seems, in comparison with the original, so singularly drab and unfeeling. The charm of this melody is inseparable from the colour tapestry into which it is woven.

I now turn to motive. The first Violin Concerto—which illustrates perfectly Szymanowski's use of colour—is also the finest example of his second stylistic device: the replacement of melody by abbreviated and repeatable motives. This concerto shows Szymanowski's orchestral technique at its finest, it also shows a novel kind of melodic radiance. While the composer had created, in the Second Symphony, a style which permitted the bold, leaping melodies at which Richard Strauss excelled, and while the symphony as a whole is a creditable approximation to Strauss's idiom, the impression of tunefulness very quickly fades, leaving behind only a sense of clever pastiche. The Violin Concerto is a different matter. From the electrifying opening bars, with their tight harmonies and fluttering upper parts, the listener is completely absorbed by the musical movement. We hear a new kind of melody, which is both compelling in itself, and also in its turn compelled by a highly logical harmonic structure. The tuneful quality is derived entirely from the abbreviated statement of motives in rapid succession.

Some of these motives are given by Samson[10] and it can be seen that none of them could survive alone as thematic material. Yet, when combined in the rapidly shifting structure of the concerto, each seems to sing out with an individual voice. In particular the climactic phrase in Ex. 9, in which Szymanowski's favourite colouristic device of parallel sevenths is used to create a thrilling tension, seems to seize the whole orchestra, and drag it from harmony to harmony with something like the force of a Wagnerian *Leitmotiv*.

In order to build from such fragments Szymanowski dispenses entirely with classical requirements of structure, and divides the concerto itself into small continuous sections. This provides a free-flowing form, in which motives can be thrown together *ad libitum*, the rhapsodic solo violin part creating the thread upon which the sections are hung. The result is one of Szymanowski's most successful creations, with an energy and purity of line that are entirely his own, and perhaps unique in his output.

I turn now to the pedal-based ostinato. I believe that this is the key to Szymanowski's style, both in its successes and in its failures. Leaving aside the first Violin Concerto and the Second Symphony, which are structurally and thematically isolated from the body of Szymanowski's work, the principal device which Szymanowski uses to inject energy and continuity into his musical structures is that of a prolonged, powerful and intricately orchestrated ostinato, usually over a firm pedal point, and often concentrating around a definite tonal centre. The existence of the pedal point is all-important, serving to balance the vagrant harmonies of the upper parts, and providing an overall pastiche of harmonic structure.

Extended ostinato is by no means peculiar to Szymanowski: it provides one of the principal resources of Stravinsky's 'barbaric' style and has become a cliché in the works of John Adams. The combination of ostinato and pedal point is nevertheless of particular importance in Szymanowski's music. It is the antidote to music's 'charm': a symbol of the deeper musical and emotional foundation, upon which all extravagances eventually depend.

The pedalled ostinato is given dramatic significance in the opera *King Roger*, the first and third acts of which are almost entirely constructed by means of extended pedal points, involving octaves and fifths in the bass register. (A glance at the bass line of the score will establish this.) Above this pedal the music plays out its turbulent, anxious and voluptuous emotions, like a wind-blown tree firmly rooted in the landscape. If we wish to see that tree when the wind has ceased to blow, then we should turn to the *Stabat Mater*. It is in these two works, I believe, that Szymanowski reaches the culminating point of his artistic endeavour, and achieves the musical resolution to the yearning of his earlier works. In order to understand them it is helpful to return for a moment to Skryabin.

The Russian composer was conscious of the relation between the emotions conveyed by his music and the languours and passions of sexual desire. In conversation with Sabaneev he recounted that, 'I have known (since my early days as a composer) that the creative act is inextricably linked to the sexual act. I definitely know that the creative urge in myself has all the signs of a sexual stimulation . . .'[11] As is well known, the drafts of *Le Poème de l'Extase* were called 'poème orgiaste', an expression which Skryabin was disposed to gloss in terms of the experience of orgasm. It seems to me that this unsurprising revelation gives the listener a far clearer understanding of those extraordinary musical directions—*avec une douce langueur de plus en plus éteinte, avec une douceur de plus en plus caressante et empoisonnée*, etc.—than any number of loathsome ruminations by Mme Blavatsky.

Like Skryabin, Szymanowski made no secret of the erotic nature of his inspiration, and, in the First Violin Concerto and *The Song of the Night*, he allows it all to 'hang out'. At the same time, his music exhibits an increasing struggle to quieten this erotic fervour, to bring it down from the perfumed realm of deception and 'charm'. No art can exist on a diet of pure voluptuousness. When detached from the concrete experiences of creation and re-creation, voluptuousness evaporates, leaving a bleak and frozen heart. This is indeed the true nature of decadence. What is decadent cannot truly be felt; it exists as dream and illusion, as self-intoxication, but not as a warm response. Every voluptuous feeling, every mystical experience, therefore stands in need of the real activity upon which it is predicated: without that reality, it withers and dies.

Skryabin's salon mysticism reaches the point of attenuation, the point beyond which no artistic expression can proceed without lapsing into bombast and exhaustion. Szymanowski too had reached that point, and his vapid sensuality could no longer be sustained, having no roots in reality from which to take its being. It is this, I believe, which explains his attempt to rediscover in himself a 'Polish' soul—a soul that would be rooted in the uncomplicated passions of a people bound by circumstance. In *The Song of the Night* Szymanowski had swooned his last. His search for a more robust style was an inevitable result of his desire for a real emotional foundation.

Undeniably his renewed acquaintance with the music of Stravinsky and Bartók was vital for the development of his later music. But their influence is due to the fact that they correspond to a spiritual need. If we were to search for the true theme of *King Roger*—whose boyish and schematic libretto suggests a vast effort of concealment—then we should pay considerable attention to the 'search for roots' to which I have referred. Szymanowski averred that the question of *King Roger* was the question of his continued artistic existence. I believe that he was right, although not for the reasons that he himself put forward.

Ostensibly *King Roger* concerns a perennial conflict of values, and also a conflict of civilizations. It has been argued—in recognition of the

enormous influence exerted over Szymanowski's thinking by Nietzsche's *Birth of Tragedy*—that the fundamental opposition in *King
Roger* is that between Apollo and Dionysus: between discipline and
release.[12] And no doubt that was part of Szymanowski's meaning.
However, if we ignore the highly academic stage conception—a kind of
Baedeker guide to the monuments of European culture—we find
something rather more specific. The drama is only passingly Nietz-
schean. At the abstract level it has a clear religious connotation.
Christian civility encounters oriental yearning; out of their conflict a
pastoral paganism is born, in which erotic longings combine with a
Homeric attachment to sun and soil. But even this metaphysical
Aufhebung out of Christianity into paganism is not, I think, the true
subject-matter of the score. The erotic component is by far the most
important constituent of Szymanowski's paganism. The appeal of the
shepherd's 'religion' to King Roger is not separable from the appeal of
the shepherd. His message is all 'charm', and beyond this all is 'secret'.
Words like '*tajny*' and '*tajemnica*' appear monotonously, when the
shepherd and his apologists have to declare their intentions. Of course,
there are echoes here of Skryabin's 'mystery'. But this is surely the most
commonplace of mysteries. The shepherd is charm concealing a
secret—the 'dirty little secret', as Freud characteristically put it, under
clothes.

It is a secret into which Roxana has already been initiated, and only
King Roger, it seems, has yet to learn. His uninitiated state is one with
his sexual incompetence—to which he confesses at the beginning of Act
II. It is in search of initiation that he undertakes his 'pilgrimage' to the
shepherd's shrine. But what does he find there? Only an indefinite
longing, an empty stage, an altar upon which a vague and unfocused
apotheosis is to occur. Roger rushes into this illusion with suicidal
passion, while the orchestra encourages him with a familiar C major
chord. But what has he encountered, and why? His yearnings have no
fulfilment, no accomplishment, no definition. The cry 'To on!'—'It is
he!'—with which he greets the shepherd, says far more about his
passions than his final flourish. If his surge of emotion appears like
religion, this is only because, in the state of sexual frustration into
which the vanishing shepherd provokes him, the king would go to any
lengths—even to that of self-immolation—to give substance to his lust.
The closing C major is intended to sound like a resolution. But it is in
fact no such thing. Like the closing cadence of *The Song of the Night* it
is a shimmering radiance, a musical whiteness, in which there is nothing
to discern. The senses turn away dazzled and bewildered. To find the

meaning of this 'resolution', we must therefore look to the musical discourse which it interrupts.

It is difficult to describe with any precision the content and atmosphere of the literary works which Szymanowski composed and projected. But it is certain, from surviving accounts of them, that they exemplified the same feverish voluptuousness as his music.[13] The structure of the opera is dictated by the libretto, which the composer completed from the sketch given to him by a far from enthusiastic Iwaskiewicz. It is certain that the final version follows the logic of Szymanowski's literary inspiration—fulsome, indeterminate, crucially unfocused. For this reason it is necessary to look behind the structure to the musical expression. The music is, in fact, quite at variance with the ostensible meaning of the text. *King Roger* exhibits a musical idiom which denies the decadent yearnings of its protagonist. Szymanowski is in the grip of a new emotion, which shapes the music, and which overthrows the dominion of his voluptuous style.

This new idiom opens the opera, with a magnificent choral prelude, set in the Byzantine cathedral that symbolizes the concentration of successive cultures. The style is deeply influenced by Renaissance polyphony, and by Polish—or at least Slavonic—melody; its harmony is unashamedly rooted in the open octave and open fifth. The idiom represents a great clearing away of superfluous colour, an attempt to achieve what Dr Johnson called 'bottom'. Extended pedal points emphasize stability, while the voices mingle in a finely wrought interdependence. Nothing in the opera rivals the poignancy or the grandeur of this opening chorus, which exerts its discipline throughout the first act, constantly recalling the orchestra from its colouristic flourishes to more solid and more urgent emotions. Its order transforms the music, so that, when it brings the first act to a close, pianissimo, in C minor, the effect of resolution is entirely persuasive.

The new voice is banished from the second act, in which all is charm and illusion; but it returns briefly in the third act, where again the plangent voices of the choir are heard, this time ostensibly in praise of Dionysus, but in fact reiterating the same fifth-based harmonies that had dictated the logic of the choral prelude. Once again an organ provides support, with the familiar pedal point on bottom C. However, it is distorted by chords of deliberate atrociousness, which finally drown the choral voice and make way for the Dionysiac 'mystery', in which nothing is truly considered and nothing, therefore, resolved.

The voice of the choir is the voice of community, the voice which denies that 'secret' world of absolute permission for which the decadent yearns. Because it permits everything, the decadent illusion also permits, and necessitates, nothing. This is the meaning of the 'bottomless' intoxication of Roxana's aria, into which Szymanowski condenses the 'charm' from which he also withdraws. Roxana dances off into nothingness, for nothingness is what she represents. Her reappearance is mirage-like, as is that of the shepherd. The real 'happening' which these impostors endeavour so wildly to conceal takes place, musically speaking, in the chorus: it is the happening with which the opera opens, and out of which it grows. In short, it is the musical rediscovery of community.

King Roger marks Szymanowski's final breach with the muse of Skryabin, whose journey to the limits of self-intoxication had become doubly impossible. Szymanowski could no longer ally himself with the swooning eroticism of his master; at the same time his music had moved of its own accord towards a language which defies the sexual crescendoes of the First Violin Concerto and *The Song of the Night*. The new language of pedal point, open fifth, and plangent Slavonic vocal lines, is the language of reality. It is the voice of community, and of the renunciation which makes community possible. It persistently interrupts the perfervid sexuality of Szymanowski's former idiom, and reminds us of the emptiness of a desire founded in permission alone. This new voice calls faintly at first, but insistently, from the religious experience that King Roger, the character, rejects, but which *King Roger*, the opera, affirms.

It cannot go unremarked that *King Roger* was composed during an important period in the history of modern Poland, when the Polish national spirit was at last beginning to realize itself in political institutions. Szymanowski was aware of the disparity between his cultivation of a 'mysterious, liberating charm',[14] and the emerging spirit of nationalist Poland. And he wrote illuminatingly of the difficulties facing the nationalist composer, at a time when the true spirit of the people, once enshrined in the spontaneous songs and dances of a rural culture, had been buried beneath the 'popular music' of the towns.[15] At the same time he was aware of how distant the truly modern artist — such as he undeniably was — had become from anything that could be called 'the spirit of the people'. He expressed this awareness in a letter:

I am more deeply and sincerely a patriot than many. However, I realize one thing as deeply as is possible: that in the present historical and cultural epoch, that sort of artistic breed represented by myself is not only superfluous, but almost injurious . . . There remains only one thing: to shake off one's personal life, and stand alongside the lowliest of the devoted, honest workers, striving

Example 10

Example 11

to build up the nation from its foundation. For such an artistic luxury as myself, Poland has neither the time nor the need.[16]

We know that the political turmoil of inter-bellum Poland was not calculated to induce self-knowledge in those who took part in it.[17] This deference towards the 'people'—whether or not in their fictional embodiment as 'devoted, honest labour'—has a meaning which is not political but religious. Thus we should not be surprised to find that it is in the *Stabat Mater*—arguably Szymanowski's finest work, and the one whose influence lives on in Górecki, Penderecki and the two Panufniks (Andrzej and his daughter Roxana)—that this new sentiment, and new musical idiom, reached its culmination.

Szymanowski chose to set an old Polish version of the text, thus emphasizing that, for him, this act of worship is also a return to historical and communal identity. The harmonic basis again lies in pedal point and open fifth, although Szymanowski continues to allow himself massive resources of orchestral colour. But the most significant fact about this work is its utterly persuasive melodic line. From the very opening theme (Ex. 10) a new kind of 'invitation' is displayed, which is not the invitation of charm. This modal theme, which balances A minor against A/E major, in an invigorating paradox, is richly Polish. At the same time it shows a craftsmanship and logic that distances it completely from the world of folk music.

Szymanowski's melodies begin to exploit the questions and answers of traditional tonality: as in the phrase marked A in Ex. 11, from which the last movement generates its atmosphere. The example reminds one of the distinction between motive, as employed in the First Violin Concerto, and melodic phrase. The melodic phrase, while itself integral to a melodic line, is endowed with some special poignancy of its own, which causes it to stand out from the remainder of the melody. Skryabin was master of such melodic phrases, as in the justly famous melody from the slow movement of the op. 23 sonata, with its 'dying fall'. The *Stabat Mater* contains many such phrases, and the duet for alto and clarinet provides a striking example of novel harmonic organization. It is hard to find fault with this style, or with the use which Szymanowski makes of it.

The *Stabat Mater* has a serenity that is absent from the earlier works, expressing a religious experience that gathers the individual into the maternal arms of custom. After the *Stabat Mater*, however, Szymanowski's music shows a decline. With the exception of the Kuprian songs, the *Veni Creator Spiritus* and certain other works which try to match the inspiration of the composer's choral idiom, the later style is harsh and unyielding, notwithstanding Szymanowski's avowed intention to make his art more accessible to the people. This transformation should be understood as one both of spirit and of style. The melody of Ex. 10 displays the extent of Szymanowski's acquisitions from the repertoire of folksong. But this kind of folklore is little different from that of Chopin's mazurkas. It involves accommodating an existing and highly accomplished style to folkloristic material. In the course of doing so, the composer raises the material to an artistic station where it could not otherwise freely breathe.

By incorporating folklore at this level Szymanowski was in effect interiorizing its moral idea. He was building into his innermost inspiration the reference to that tragic community whose religious yearning provides the ultimate relief from solitude. In two articles published in 1928–9 on the subject of Romanticism in music,[18] Szymanowski argued for a thorough-going rejection of all Romantic idioms, all Germanic and absolute strains in music, and for the development of a new anti-Romantic realism. He expressed the belief that a return to the local consciousness of folk art would provide the modern artist with that bridge to the sentiments of the people which religion alone could not provide. In the later work, therefore—in *Harnasie*, and in the Fourth Symphony—Szymanowski aimed for a style that did not incorporate, but rather grew out of, folk music in the manner of Bartók. He wished folk music to constitute the substance of his style, rather than a piquant addition to it.

Bartók had derived not only rhythm and melody, but also harmony, from a folk tradition in which he saw the most potent musical thoughts lying dormant. The idioms of Hungarian music suggested to him a new musical world, lying largely outside the classical tradition, but by no means incompatible with it. For Bartók, therefore, folklore became a structural and stylistic principle. Szymanowski's attempt to match this achievement caused, I believe, a kind of musical collapse. What he first heard in the voice of Polish music was the plangent religion of the *Stabat Mater*—the religion which was to endure into our time, and to bring about (with the election of Pope John Paul II) the final collapse of communism in Europe. What Szymanowski tried then to hear, however, was the rumour of some deeper, more primitive force, a force beyond religion and culture, lying—like the 'religion' of the shepherd—in landscape and climate alone.

In fact he heard no such thing, because there is no such thing to be heard. Instead he simply fitted out his ostinato style with a new percussiveness; he acquired Bartók's *martellato* idiom, and adopted a frenzied idiom which lacked both the charm of his earlier works and the serenity of his vocal masterpieces. Of course, a major influence here was the Stravinsky of *Les Noces* and *Le Sacre du Printemps*: Stravinsky as armchair anthropologist. But it is interesting to note that Szymanowski's initial response to these works was very far from the nagging freneticism of *Harnasie*. The first effect of *Les Noces* was to inspire the remarkable *Słopiewnie* op. 46, in which Szymanowski copies Stravinsky's basic idea. *Słopiewnie* is a setting of nonsense words, chosen for their atmosphere rather than for their literal meaning, in an idiom which hints at an intense 'folk-experience'.

But Szymanowski borrows nothing besides that one idea: the rhythmic and percussive character of the Stravinsky work seem to have had no effect on him. Instead, he produces songs of a lyricism which he was to rival only in the *Stabat Mater*. Here we see the new melodic idiom at its most haunting (Ex. 12), in music that is nothing if not profoundly religious, and the more so on account of the 'abstract' character of the words.

Of course, it could be argued that such works as *Les Noces* and *Le Sacre* are more hyper-civilized than barbarous, and that 'barbarism' and folklore were, for Stravinsky, the product of an imaginary world, whose boundaries were the walls of a St Petersburgh drawing room, and whose source was, not popular culture, but academic anthropology. At any rate, it is hard to think of Stravinsky as finding a real musical root in folklore, or a musical thought deriving purely from primitive melos. In this he was unlike Bartók, but very like Szymanowski. In pursuing this pilgrim's path, the Polish composer was led towards another hyper-civilized abstraction, this time without the

Słopiewnie

Example 12

charm that had redeemed his earlier works. Szymanowski follows, in the end, the erroneous path of King Roger, exchanging for the true community of Catholic Poland a fantasy community of pagan shepherds.

Community is made possible only by the deepest attachment to place and time. Such attachment is not a fact of nature, but a gift of civilization; it grows, in the end, from religious sacrifice, and from submission. Without common worship, place, time and community are fragile and evanescent. It should not surprise us to find, therefore, that in the 'barbaric' works, Szymanowski's melodic inspiration again deserts him. He returns to the motive style (as in the repeated minor third which opens the Second Violin Concerto), or to those beautifully crafted pseudo-melodies that had perfumed the 'oriental' works (as in the slow movement of the Fourth Symphony). There is much in the later music of interest and beauty. Nevertheless, it seems to me that Szymanowski, who rose to self-knowledge by the sheer energy of his musical genius, declined again into the mere competence from which he began. The impoverished musical thought of the later compositions suggests a lack of conviction, a loss of faith. But (to parody a remark of Bernard Shaw's) Szymanowski's journey from decadence to barbarism passed through a glorious period of civilization.

Notes

1 Szymanowski recognized many dangers in the tendency of his contemporaries to embed their music in a nest of theory, and to mask stylistic uncertainty behind a myth of 'historical inevitability'. See Karol Szymanowski, *Z Pism*, ed. T. Chylinska, Kraków 1958, p. 105.

2 This was not the view of Szymanowski, who revered Chopin as the first composer to capture the uniqueness of the Polish soul in music. See the article on Chopin from *Skamander*, 1923, in *Z Pism*, *ibid.*, translated in *Szymanowski on Music: Selected Writings of Karol Szymanowski*, tr. and ed. Alistair Wightman, London 1999, pp. 177–95.

3 Leonid Sabaneev, *Reminiscences of Skryabin*, quoted in F. Bowers, *Scriabin*, Tokyo and Palo Alto 1969, vol. 1, p. 148.

4 Jim Samson, *The Music of Szymanowski*, London 1980, pp. 29–31. In *Music in Transition*, London 1976, the same author has given a valuable account of Szymanowski's place in the development of twentieth-century harmony.

5 *Ibid.*, pp. 108–9.

6 A term which I by no means intend in the disparaging sense of Edward Saïd's seminal work *Orientalism*, New York 1971.

7 Hugh MacDonald, *Skryabin*, Oxford 1978, pp. 17–18.

8 Thus Hindemith, for example, and Reti, in many works. See especially Rudolph Reti, *Tonality-Atonality-Pantonality*, London 1958.

9 In *'Wyclowacza rola muzyki'* (The educational role of music)—*Z Pism*, *op. cit.*, p. 214—he refers to the 'mysterious, liberating, charm of music' (*tajemny wyzwalający czar muzyki*). These words are importantly connected, as I argue below, with the 'question' of *King Roger*.

10 *The Music of Szymanowski*, *op. cit.*, p. 89.

11 Quoted in F. Bowers, *op. cit.*, vol. I, p. 293.

12 See especially the persuasively documented article by Paolo Emilio Carapezza: 'Re Ruggero tra Dioniso e Apollo', in 'Studi in onore di Cesare Brandi'; *Storia dell'arte*, 38–40, Firenze 1980.

13 The plot of *Efebos*—a novel of sultry and ecstatic homosexual passion—is recorded by Janisław Iwaszkiewicz: *Spotkania z Szymanowskim* (Meetings with Szymanowski), Kraków, 1947. See B. M. Maciejewski: *Karól Szymanowski*, London 1967, p. 62. It seems that a draft of the novel has recently been discovered.

14 See note 9 above.

15 See 'The educational role of musical culture in society' in *Z Pism*, *op. cit.*, translated in *Szymanowski on Music, Selected Writings of Karol Szymanowski*, tr. and ed., Alistair Wightman, London 1999, pp. 289–317. Szymanowski shared some of Adorno's revulsion towards mass culture (see Chapter 13, below), and admired both Stravinsky and Bartók for their attempts to disinter the buried voice of the folk culture, while remaining largely sceptical that it could really be done.

16 Letter to Zdzisiaw Jachimecki, 29 January 1920, quoted in Alistair Wightman, 'Szymanowski's Writings on Music', *Res Facta*, vol. 9, Warsaw 1982.

17 See Czeslaw Miłosz, *Native Realm, a Search for Self-Definition*, New York 1968.

18 *Z Pism*, *op. cit.*, pp. 139–69.

13

Why read Adorno?

Adorno's studies of Mahler, Zemlinsky, Schoenberg and other composers who shaped his musical sensibility were major contributions to
the understanding of modern music, and his attempt to understand
kitsch and its significance is a landmark in social criticism. But his lack
of clarity, his jerky and unsequential style of analysis and his attempt to
politicize the entire discussion of modernism in music, so as to force it
into a neo-Marxist framework that has lost whatever plausibility it
might once have had, place great obstacles before the reader. The least
we might say is that his contributions to musicology are flawed by a
narrow-minded obsession with ideas whose time has passed. Yet that is
not how Adorno is seen. Although Richard Taruskin, in his *History of
Western Music*,[1] treats Adorno with the impatience that he invites, this
is a rare departure from the now routine adulation that is bestowed by
the American musicological establishment. In this chapter I will try to
explain this adulation, and to show what might still be rescued from
Adorno's attack on mass culture.

One thing is certain: Adorno owes much of his success to his
Marxism, and to his membership of the Frankfurt School in exile
during the Second World War. His criticism of popular music is
presented from an avowedly left-wing perspective, as part of the
cultural critique of capitalist society. And it is directed against the mass
culture of America by an exile from Nazism, who sees the battle over
culture as continuous with the larger political conflicts that divided the
modern world: conflicts between left and right, between socialism and
capitalism, between autonomy and totalitarianism, between the emancipated awareness promised by a Marxist critique and the false
consciousness of the consumer society.

In the first instance, therefore, we should see the adulation of Adorno
as politically inspired. Adorno's cultural critique engaged with the
dominant conflicts of a highly politicized world, and he defined his own
position in terms of them. He showed American musicologists that you
can despise popular culture and still believe in the ideological rescue of its
captives. You can be a cultural elitist and yet on the side of the underdog.

T. S. Eliot, in his *Notes Towards the Definition of Culture*, expressed an attitude to mass culture similar to Adorno's. But he failed to identify himself as a man of the left. He did not deploy Marxist categories; nor did he advocate either the overthrow of the capitalist system or the emancipation of the proletariat. On the contrary, Eliot defended high culture as the citadel in which the past and its treasures are sequestered, maintained by people conscious of their membership of an elite, who must nevertheless cultivate within themselves the kind of humility and self-sacrifice that have been associated with the Christian religion. His stance was consciously reactionary, and his social doctrine (in so far as it existed) conservative. As a result Eliot's book has had little impact on the academic establishment in America, and the critique of mass culture has proceeded as though it were a left-wing monopoly.

Yet Eliot was a modernist, who believed modernism to be continuous with the great traditions of European artistic expression. He vindicated the artistic experiments of the twentieth century far more persuasively than Adorno, who wrote of them through clenched teeth, spitting out his venom at every musician who could still feel the allure of tonal harmony. As the greatest of modernist poets writing in English, Eliot has a claim to our attention far beyond that established in his essays, while Adorno ought to have been regarded with a certain scepticism, precisely because of the vehemence with which he defended an artistic revolution to which he proved himself incapable of contributing—as his few sterile compositions show.[2] However, Adorno was on the left, Eliot on the right—and this alone was sufficient to guarantee an influence to the one that was denied to the other.

It seems to me, therefore, that there is no way of understanding Adorno's influence that does not see his leftist posture as crucial. Adorno's critique of mass culture began life as a critique of the 'culture industry' that exploits the tastes of the simple-minded. Ordinary Americans, in Adorno's view, were oppressed by the music that they had been misled into liking, just as they were oppressed by advertising, by the consumer culture, by Hollywood, by the idols of the market-place—in short by just about everything that appealed to them. A critique of their musical culture was primarily a critique of the capitalist system which had confiscated their inner freedom.

Having made this routine Marxist move, Adorno felt that he had done all that conscience required, by way of accepting the society that had welcomed him as an exile from the Nazis. There was nothing henceforth to impede his attack on the 'regressive' nature of American music making, which he prosecuted with a no-holds-barred antagonism that has few parallels outside the world of political and religious diatribe. 'Regressive listeners' 'are confirmed in their neurotic stupidity . . .'; they 'behave like children. Again and again and with stubborn malice, they demand the one dish they have once been served.' 'Types arise from the masses of the retarded who differentiate themselves by pseudo-activity and nevertheless make the regression more strikingly visible . . .' Those quotations from 'On the Fetish Character of Music and the Regression of Listening' are entirely typical of the relentless contempt for ordinary humanity that animates Adorno's prose; and there is no gainsaying the fact that it is only a leftist who could get away with writing in this way. We are confronting that mysterious asymmetry of blame, which enables people on the left to express the basest emotions without the slightest concern for their language and which accuses all others of guilt by association—the accusation that Adorno placed immovably on Wagner. And when, in his later writings, Adorno turns his guns not only on music and the cinema, but on all the ordinary forms of leisure with which Americans express their contentment with the world as it is—dismissing even DIY as a form of 'pseudo-activity' and a sign of inner enslavement[3]—ordinary left-liberal readers, instead of throwing the book across the room and closing forever the chapter that they had opened on Adorno, struggle instead to reconcile what they read with the now obligatory 'postmodern' perspective, according to which pop culture is a legitimate field of study, and judgement a thing of the past.[4]

Now I believe that Adorno, bad manners apart, was right to care about the decline of popular taste, and right to think that it matters what we listen to and how. But I believe that he arrived at this position from the wrong premises, and in the wrong frame of mind. His writings also cast an interesting light on the agenda of neo-Marxism in our time, and on the vision of human beings that underlies the liberationist movements of the Sixties—movements of which Adorno himself did not approve, even though they often made use of what they thought to be his arguments.

Culture, according to Marx, belongs to the institutional and ideological superstructure of society. It is the by-product of economic processes which it does not seriously influence. The ideological battles are so many 'storm clouds in the political sky': history is unaffected by them, since it is driven by economic forces and the inexorable laws of their development. Against that vision, which seems to relegate culture and the arts to the historical sidelines, the Frankfurt school (Horkheimer and Adorno in particular) argued that a properly theoretical approach to

criticism would undermine the false consciousness that facilitated
'bourgeois relations of production', and so contribute to loosening the
grip of the capitalist economy. The enslavement exerted by capitalism is
exerted at every level—the mental, institutional and cultural as much as
the economic—and by adopting a critical stance at each of these levels
we facilitate resistance overall. Hence even the Enlightenment, which to
most of us represents an enormous gain in moral, political and spiritual
freedom, is, for Adorno and Horkheimer, a cunning device for tying
humanity to the machinery of bourgeois production.⁵ The freedom it
seems to offer is in fact a pseudo-freedom, and its critical stance merely a
way of perpetuating bourgeois attitudes to social life.

If the Enlightenment is rejected, then on what principles should our
criticism be based? Adorno took his cue from the theory of 'commodity
fetishism' expounded in *Das Kapital*. According to Marx the capitalist
economy generates powerful illusions in the minds of its participants,
and these illusions are ideological—which is to say that they obscure
the realities of social and economic power, and shore up the 'false
consciousness' of its victims. The exchange-value of a commodity in the
capitalist economy seems like a force contained within the commodity
itself—a magnetic charge which causes it to move in the market as
though compelled from within. In fact, according to Marx, exchange-
value is the result of human labour and the energy visible in the market
belongs not to goods but to those who produce them. Hence in a
capitalist economy the causal power of labour is objectified, attributed
to commodities, which become 'fetishes', animated not by any real life
of their own but by the emotions of those who fall under their spell.

The refutation of the labour theory of value left that argument
without any serious foundation in economics and returned it to its
original source in the philosophy of the Young Hegelians. It is in fact a
survival of the idea of fetishism that Marx had earlier taken from
Feuerbach's debunking of religion.⁶ For Adorno, however, the concept
of commodity fetishism provided the key to a comprehensive cultural
critique. In a capitalist economy, he suggested, people are enslaved not
by others but by themselves, falling victim to the charm with which they
invest the commodities that glitter all around them. Their 'false
consciousness' exposes them at every turn to the same enchantment,
and their real freedom is confiscated by the illusory freedoms of the
consumer culture. In the course of his critique Adorno expanded the
concept of fetishism to include every way in which capitalism displaces
long-term interests with short-term desires, so that pleasure becomes
the enemy of freedom.

Worst among the fetishes that bewilder the victims of capitalist production are those of the culture industry, as Horkheimer and Adorno described it. Mass culture is a commodity whose function is to neutralize the critical spirit and to induce an illusory acceptance of an illusory world. It is an 'ideological' product in Marx's sense—a veil drawn across the social realities, so as to present a comforting illusion in their stead. In other words, mass culture is part of the false consciousness of capitalist society, and Adorno set out to show how its devices short-circuit the path to emotional truth, leading always to clichés and a kind of routine sentimentality. His hope was to contrast the creative logic of the masters, who wrestled with realities, found the style that comprehended them, and never shirked the pain of a real musical argument, with the kitsch that looks for the short cut to comfort, as a popular song slops home to the tonic chord. The cultural fetish is marked by its 'standardized' nature, its routine presentation of predigested material, and its refusal to question its own status as a commodity.

Adorno connected the theory of commodity fetishism with that of reification, as this had been developed by György Lukács.[7] 'Reification' (*Verdinglichung* or *Versachlichung*) denotes the way in which people allegedly lose their subjective freedom by investing it in objects outside themselves. Marx, in his early criticism of Hegel, had argued that private property condemns everyone—those who possess it as much as those who do not—to a state of alienation. By owning a thing I place my will in it. I become what I own, and that which I begin by possessing ends by possessing me. Private property transforms all personal relations into relations of things. Friendship is replaced by contract, enjoyment by use, and love by the household, which is a structure of property relations—relations whose most significant terms are things. Lukács amplified that argument to form a general critique of capitalist society. As their freedom is spilled out and ossified in objects, he argued, people are reified: their freedom is transferred to, and captured by, the objects that represent them. Institutions, laws, relationships—all are prone to reification, which voids the world of human meaning, by putting mechanical relations between objects in place of free relations between people. Art too is reified, becoming an ornamental addition to the bourgeois inventory, and so losing its authentic nature as a critical instrument.

Bringing together the two ideas of commodity fetishism and reification we conclude that, in a capitalist culture, free relations between subjects, on which our human fulfilment depends, are overlaid and replaced by routine relations between objects. What a grand way of putting the point—the way of German philosophy from Fichte to Husserl: in the mass culture of capitalism subjects become objects and objects become subjects! No wonder Adorno believed that he had seen through the veil of mass culture to the underlying reality. And he extended the jargon of subject and object into the study of the classical tradition. Here is how he applied it to Bach, for example:

Bach . . . renounced his obedience, as antiquated polyphonist, to the trend of the times, a trend he himself had shaped, in order to help it reach its innermost truth, the emancipation of the subject to objectivity in a coherent whole of which subjectivity was the origin. Down to the subtlest structural details it is always a question of the undiminished coincidence of the harmonic-functional and of the contrapuntal dimension. The distant past is entrusted with the utopia of the musical subject-object: anachronism becomes a harbinger of things to come.[8]

That passage makes a perfectly standard observation—namely, that in Bach the logic of counterpoint and that of functional harmony coincide, so that neither seems to be imposed upon the other. But this observation is tortured into philosophical jargon, so as to imply that Bach was somehow announcing the 'utopia of the musical subject-object'.[9] Such a reworking is typical of Adorno's sleights of hand. The jargon merely *evokes* a conclusion that Adorno fails to prove, namely that Bach is great because his music is on the right side of history—the side that seeks utopia, and which preserves, in objective form, the real freedom of the subject.

Why was writing of the kind that I have just quoted so influential? This question returns us to the revolutionary spirit of the Sixties and Seventies. The advocates of 'liberation' were aware in their hearts of the benefits that they had received from the capitalist economy. They belonged to a generation that enjoyed freedom and prosperity on a scale that young people had never previously known. To dissent from the capitalist order in the name of freedom seemed faintly ridiculous, when the contrast with the Soviet alternative was so vividly apparent. What was needed, in order to vindicate the new spirit of revolution, was a doctrine that would show capitalist freedom to be an illusion, and which would identify the *true* freedom that the consumer society denied. That is what Adorno, Horkheimer and Marcuse provided. Adorno's attack on mass culture belonged to the same movement of ideas as Marcuse's denunciation of 'repressive tolerance'. It was an attempt to *see through the lies*. The theories of fetishism, reification,

alienation and repression that circulated in the wake of 1968 all had
one overriding aim, which was to show the illusory nature of capitalist
freedom, and to perpetuate the thought of a critical alternative, of a
liberation that would not lead merely to another and darker form of the
'state capitalism' which supposedly ruled over East and West.

And here I should like to add a note of blame, since it seems to me
that Adorno and Marcuse massively deserve it and Lukács yet more so.
By constantly notching up the critique of American capitalism and its
culture, and making only muted or dismissive references to the real
nightmare of communism, those thinkers showed their profound
indifference to human suffering and the unserious nature of their
prescriptions. Adorno does not explicitly say that the 'alternative' to the
capitalist system and the commodity culture is utopia. But that is what
he implies. And utopia is not a real alternative. Hence his alternative to
the unreal freedom of the consumer society is itself unreal—a mere
noumenon whose only function is to provide a measure of our defects.
And yet he was aware that there was an *actual* alternative on offer and
that it involved mass murder and cultural annihilation. For Adorno to
dismiss this alternative merely as the 'totalitarian' version of the same
'state capitalism' that he had witnessed in America was profoundly
dishonest.

Having said that, I want to acknowledge that the Frankfurt critique
of the consumer society contains an element of truth. It is a truth far
older than the Marxist theories with which Adorno and Horkheimer
embellished it. Indeed it is the truth enshrined in the Hebrew Bible,
reformulated time and again down the centuries: the truth that, in
bowing down to idols, we betray our better nature. The Torah sets
before us a vision of human fulfilment. It tells us that we are bound by
the law of God, who tolerates no idolatry, and wishes for our absolute
devotion. By turning to God we become what we truly are, creatures of
a higher world, whose fulfilment is something more than the satisfaction of our wishes. Through idolatry, by contrast, we fall into a lower
way of being—the way of self-enslavement, in which our appetites
shape themselves as gods and take command of us.

Of course, Adorno did not believe in God and had little time—less
time than his hero Arnold Schoenberg—for the teachings of the Torah.
But his attack on mass culture should be seen in the Old Testament
spirit, as a repudiation of idolatry, a reaffirmation of the age-old
distinction between true and false gods—between the worship that
ennobles and redeems us, and the superstition that drops us in the ditch.
For Adorno the true god is utopia: the vision of subjects in their

freedom, conscious of the world as it is, and claiming that world as their own. The false god is the fetish of consumerism—the god of appetite, who clouds our vision and confiscates our inner autonomy.

And here is where Adorno profoundly differed from the revolutionaries of the Sixties, even while speaking a language which they thought they could use. The advocates of 'liberation' were seeking another form of society, in which people would be truly free—free precisely because they had torn away the veil of illusion to begin the construction of a less oppressive world. But the redemption that Adorno promised was not to be achieved by social reform: it was a personal salvation, a turning away from fantasies, on a voyage of self-discovery. Through fixing his mind on utopia, a person is put in touch with his subjectivity, and acquires true discipline of spirit. Such a person has no motive to avoid hardship and suffering: for he knows that these are the proof of human freedom. Nothing is more repugnant to him than the false consolations of the fetish, which beckons from the land of illusions, and which, by denying tragedy and suffering, denies and destroys the higher life. But the consolations of Cythera stand condemned by the same moral decree, and a 'liberation' which adds sex, sin and idleness to the list of consumer products is merely another name for the old enslavement.

To put the point more exactly, Adorno's outlook is not that of the revolutionary seeking the overthrow of capitalism, but that of Hegel's 'beautiful soul', condemned to live in an idolatrous world, while working always to retain the spiritual discipline that defines his moral apartness. The Hegelian jargon of subject and object points to the real message of Adorno, which is not about the conflict between capitalist 'relations of production' and some emancipated alternative. It is about art, and the difference between true art and its idolatrous substitutes. True art matters because it puts us in touch with what we really are, and enables us to live on that higher plane where freedom and fulfilment are given. But we are surrounded on every side by pseudo-art—by sentimentality, cliché and kitsch. And this pseudo-art ties us to the world of 'reifications', in which things with a value are replaced by things with a price, and in which human life loses its worth, to become a thing of repetitive appetite.

Such, as I understand it, is the burden of Adorno's critique of mass culture. Like other such critiques, from Ruskin and Arnold to Eliot and Leavis, it is downstream from the Old Testament condemnation of idolatry. And like them it contains a core of truth. The problems stem from Adorno's use of the Marxist language, and from the resulting implication that he is shaping a *political* alternative to 'bourgeois' society, identifying defects that could be overcome by a Marxist revolution. The only revolution that Adorno can envisage is one that takes place in the world of culture itself—not a political but an aesthetic revolution, an attempt to understand utopia through art. Moreover, art that places itself directly in the *service* of revolution, like the propaganda art of Brecht and Eisler, surrenders—according to Adorno—the only kind of truthfulness of which art is capable. The utopian urge must be vindicated within art itself, through an internal revolution in the forms of creativity. 'Direct protest is reactionary'.[10] It is precisely in this way that Adorno was able to belong to the revolution of the Sixties, and also to slip out from under its grip, so as to return to the meditations which really interested him, concerning the fate of tonality, the nature of mass culture, and the reign of kitsch.

What of truth is left in those meditations, and how should we respond to them now? Lay aside the Marxist mumbo-jumbo, and you find, in Adorno's writings, three residual ideas which are of enduring interest. First, there is the attempt to give a general theory of kitsch, and a justification for avoiding it. Secondly, there is an assault on American popular music in general, and on jazz and the jazz-driven song in particular. Thirdly (and derivatively) there is the attack on tonality and the defence of the Schoenbergian alternative. In each case, it seems to me, Adorno has put his finger on something of great importance, which needs to be rescued from his particular way of discussing it.

First kitsch. The theory of the cultural fetish is designed as an explanation of this phenomenon, which remains as mysterious today as it was in Adorno's youth, when the word was invented. In the last analysis, however, the idea of a fetish gets us nowhere. What is the difference between a Bellini Virgin and a votive fetish of the Mother of God? Simple: the one is art, the other kitsch. Without the Marxist theory, now thoroughly refuted, the idea of the fetish simply reduces to that of kitsch, and so partakes of the mystery that it was designed to remove.

Hermann Broch has argued that the kitsch object comes about because of the '*Kitschmensch*' who chooses it.[11] A new human type has emerged, for whom commitment, responsibility, heroism and heartfelt love are all to be avoided, on account of the suffering that they entail. The world of the *Kitschmensch* is a heartless world, in which emotion is directed away from its proper target towards sugary stereotypes, permitting him to pay passing tribute to love and sorrow without the trouble of feeling them. Kitsch arises when the self replaces the other as the centre of attention, and when a narcissistic haze settles over the moral life. The world of kitsch is a world of trinkets, which we cling to as proof that we can be good without effort and loved without pain. By contrast, every true artistic gesture constitutes an appeal to our higher nature, an attempt to affirm the other realm in which moral and spiritual order prevails. Others exist in this realm not as compliant dolls but as spiritual beings, whose claims on us are endless and unavoidable.

And here, I believe, is the truth in Adorno's complaint against mass culture, or at least a certain *kind* of mass culture—that its pleasures are too easily obtained and obtained without effort. There is next to nothing to *live up to* in the world that it invokes, and what it offers is not judgement but an easy-going endorsement of all that we are. Its pleasures are often addictive, to be obtained at the touch of a switch. Distinctions which are forced on us by art, between true sentiment and false, between reality and fantasy, between sincerity and pretence, are down-played in the world of the *Kitschmensch*.

Why this is so is another matter: the phenomenon of kitsch seems so difficult to analyse, and its historical genesis so hard to explain, that we must rely, in treating of it, on our immediate intuitions. Maybe one day the sentiments that I have expressed in the last three paragraphs will be received with bafflement or incomprehension; maybe it is only for a few more years that the instincts can be relied upon in the students of art, literature and music, that will enable the critic to assume an immediate understanding of kitsch and a ready ability to identify its instances. But one thing is certain, that we get nowhere either in the explanation or the criticism of this phenomenon, by referring it to the 'commodification' of art under capitalist conditions, or to the 'fetishism' that is encouraged by the culture industry. Kitsch has been the standard form taken by art under communist regimes, it was sprayed into every mental space by Mao's Cultural Revolution, and if it attaches to commodities this is merely because art is a commodity like any other.

But this brings me to Adorno's assault on American popular music, on jazz and the harmonic and melodic devices of American song. Like many Marxist thinkers (Marx included), Adorno had a tendency to think in dichotomies: autonomy or reification, freedom or oppression, utopia or ideology, art or kitsch. Indeed, this dichotomizing is intrinsic to the approach to social criticism which Adorno and Horkheimer called 'negative dialectics'. Every social phenomenon should be understood through the tendency that it negates. The American song is not art in the manner of Schubert or Brahms, still less in the manner of Schoenberg or Berg: its every feature spoke to Adorno of big business, celebrity singers and mass entertainment. Hence it could not be art. And if it wasn't art it had to be kitsch, and part of the false consciousness of capitalist exploitation.[12]

At the same time American songs were and are music of the people: the music that they make spontaneously when the spirit moves them to dance or sing. So why are they so very different from the folk music that has inspired the great composers and provided them with an enduring repertoire of natural rhythms and melodies? This question points to an interesting piece of cultural history. During Adorno's youth composers and musicologists set out to collect and preserve the folk music of Europe. Janáček wrote down the songs and dances of Moravia and found in them inspiration for his own brand of speech-melody; Cecil Sharp collected in pubs and fairs the tunes that were to generate the modal harmonies and plangent melodies of the Vaughan Williams symphonies, while beneath the fake dance rhythms and creamy chords of 'salon gipsy' music, Kodály and Bartók discerned polytonal and polyrhythmic structures that miraculously coincided with their own stylistic innovations. All over Europe the music of the people was being discovered by serious composers and used to give a kind of democratic endorsement to their modernist experiments. Stravinsky, Szymanowski, Canteloube, Albeniz, Respighi—composers from every European country joined in the rush. It was as though the past of European music was being discovered precisely in order to break with it. For no sooner was our folk music captured on the page, dusted off and universally admired for its melodic invention, than it died. Those performers heard by Janáček, Sharp and Bartók were already old, and no young person could be prevailed upon to sing with them.

The explanation has something to do with industrialization and the loss of status of the rural way of life. But it also has much to do with the conquest of Europe by America. The musical idiom which had poked its head through a window in Dvořák's *New World Symphony*, had now stormed through the door. Not jazz only, but the entire tradition, from the Negro Spiritual, via the Blues and the Minstrel Shows to the Music Hall, the Broadway musical and beyond. Europeans had begun to be captivated by that 'Great American Songbook' which has been so expertly assembled by Terry Teachout in his poignant articles in *Commentary*.[13] There has never been anything in the world like this—a tradition of song which is open at every point to outside influence, which absorbs every competing idiom into itself so that it is in effect without competition, a great 'yeah-saying' to the modern world and everything in it, which is also a day-to-day reminder of the human heart. Is it really true, as Adorno implies, that this is a fake art, the kitsch image of the folk art which it displaced?

It is through music that America has had the furthest-reaching influence on other cultures; it is through music that the country came to self-knowledge and it is still part of the American character to fill every silence with a song. Scholars like Gunther Schuller have devoted many volumes to the mystery of jazz—how this unprecedented idiom emerged from African drum music, from the fusion of the pentatonic and diatonic scales, and from the four-square harmonies of the Baptist hymnal.[14] But the synthesis didn't stop with jazz. One after another the rival musics of the world were absorbed: the Shaker hymns and Afro-American field hollers, the marching bands of Central Europe, the fiddles and spoons of the celtic dances, the Spanish guitar and the Anglican organ. The classical orchestra too was conscripted, diverted by Hollywood into the great river of popular sentiment. Korngold brought the harmonies of Richard Strauss and the colours of Mahler; Gershwin added Stravinsky while Thelonious Monk and Art Tatum provided touches of Debussy and Ravel.

The influence went rapidly in the opposite direction too. The Central European cafés where Janáček and Bartók had collected folk songs were soon filled with the sound of jazz, and when the voice of the people is heard in the music of Martinů it may be in the style of a Moravian folk-song, but it is more often in the idiom of New Orleans. The new music of America was democratic and global, able to defeat any rival simply by its refusal to believe in rivalry, happily appropriating every sound that could be reissued as a song. And from Ives, through Gershwin, Copland and Bernstein to John Adams, Michael Torke and Steve Reich, American music has shown how to mix the idiom of popular music with the large-scale structures of the concert-hall.

One conclusion to draw from the history of American popular music is that we should take the word 'popular' seriously—far more seriously than it was taken by Adorno. *Pace* Adorno and Horkheimer, this music was not imposed upon the American people by an unscrupulous 'culture industry' eager to exploit the most degenerate aspects of popular taste. It arose 'by an invisible hand' from spontaneous music-making, with a large input from Afro-American music, both secular and religious. When that music later spread around the world it was not by some imperial venture of a conquering civilization but by the same process whereby it arose—the spontaneous taste of ordinary people.

The great days of American popular music may now be past: rock 'n' roll changed the Blues from a lyrical confession to a Dionysian display, and the long-term effects are now being felt, not only in America, but all across the world. Nevertheless, visitors to America are still astonished by the number of spontaneous musical episodes that they encounter: marching bands at football matches; barber shop singing; church choirs and 'praise dances'; jazz combos in the clubs and Blue Grass in the tavern. Churches in rural Virginia use the Baptist hymnal, with its wealth of Victorian parlour songs and its smattering of solemn numbers from the Geneva Psalter. Visiting 'witnesses' bring their backing on CD and croon out their love for Jesus in the idiom of Nat King Cole or Mel Tormé. The pastor will perform solo hymns to his own guitar accompaniment; groups of gospel singers from the black churches will come and go; and at Easter the little choir and their pianist might perform the 'Cantata for Holy Week' by Joel Raney, in which all the devices of American popular song are woven around the narrative of the crucifixion, in a kind of artless homage to J. S. Bach. This unpretentious weaving of music into the ordinary life of a religious community typifies the American manner, which prefers song to silence and loud praise to quiet prayer.

Like everything typical of America, this musical culture issues from the spontaneous interchanges of ordinary people. The American song exists because people have enjoyed it and asked for more. It is the musical expression of consumer sovereignty. And like everything typical of America it gets up the intellectual nose, precisely because it seems to leave no opening for the would-be priesthood. Intellectuals on the left have never been able to accept that the spontaneous choices of ordinary people might be the *final explanation* of their social world. Arrangements which arise by 'an invisible hand' from free choices that did not intend them are almost invariably seen by the left-wing intellectual as the expression of other and more sinister choices—the choices of those who benefit from the result. Animated by what Paul Ricoeur called 'the hermeneutics of suspicion', they have looked for the hidden power behind every custom, and the 'structures' that control every choice.

Thus was invented that supreme fiction of the Marxist worldview—the 'bourgeoisie', the class that supposedly benefits from every capitalist transaction, and which holds the whole system in place. This concept—in which the contempt of the French intellectual over centuries has been distilled—has no real application in America, notwithstanding Adorno's constant invocation of it. In small-town America everybody is a bourgeois if anyone is: and therefore no one is—the division between owners and producers makes no sense in a place where everyone is both. But to give substance to the charge of commodity fetishism, reification, false consciousness and the rest, it was important to identify the 'class' that benefits from these things, and whose domination is maintained in being against the real interests of the masses. Hence the American song, Adorno argued, be it by Gershwin or Berlin, by Jerome Kern or Cole Porter, is an instrument of capitalist exploitation. It is not the consumer or the producer who is really sovereign in this debased musical culture, but the 'owners of the means of communication', namely the capitalist class.

There is an undeniable streak of toe-curling kitsch in the American popular music of Adorno's day. For it is music that has escaped from the paddock of good taste into the open plains of common sentiment. But it is also, in its own way, the true record of a new moral order. This is music that incorporates the pains and joys of modern life. If it sounds so different from all the music that has gone before then this is because modern life—the life made in America—is also different from the life that has gone before.

Where a traditional folksong like 'Waley Waley' tells us of the unconsolable wretchedness of a woman betrayed, American popular songs provide us with the gentle remedies of modern life, as when Judy Garland sings of 'The Man That Got Away'. Such a song says goodbye to one man, by way of preparing the heart for the next, using the Big Band chorus in order to cheer the victim on. The small devices whereby ordinary people cope with ordinary disappointments are honoured in this music, which seldom if ever adopts a tragic tone of voice. Its attitude to rupture is typified by Hoagy Carmichael's nostalgic 'I Get Along Without You Very Well'; it uses homely images to normalize the excitement of falling in love—'If I Were a Bell' as sung by Blossom Dearie, or Irving Berlin's 'I'm Putting All My Eggs in One Basket'. It refuses to take a tragic attitude to unrequited desire (Rodgers' and Hart's 'Glad to Be Unhappy'), and it cuts down all experiences, whether of joy or sorrow, of embarrassment or humour, to a manageable size, making it clear that either they are within reach of us all or within reach of no-one.

If this music invokes the higher forms of passion, therefore, it also projects them into the background. The insinuating softness with which Peggy Lee sings of 'the days of wine and roses' and 'the door marked nevermore' is like the candlelit supper and the folded napkins—a way of invoking the unobtainable, and imbuing it with a fairy-tale glow. This is not for you, the music says; but only because it is not for anyone. Meanwhile, let's pretend. From Frank Sinatra to Barbara Streisand

America has produced a continuous stream of singers who know exactly how to represent in their tone of voice the ordinary American heart in its ordinary heartbeat, while adding just enough exaltation to make the heart miss a beat or two. Looked at in this way the American song has prepared mankind for the modern world of transitory attachments and temporary griefs far more effectively than has any other cultural innovation.

But if the American popular music of Adorno's day normalized those sentiments it also moralized them. While exploring the heartbreaks of infidelity and the excitements of seduction, it pointed gently in the direction of marriage, family and the future. Unlike the tragic ballads of old Europe it aimed for the 'happy ending', as boy and girl become man and wife. You may have fallen by the wayside, it said, but you can get back on the happiness train. The musicals of Rodgers and Hammerstein exported this American idea of available happiness, and it is to the American tradition of popular song that people all over the world still turn, when they wish to recapture their ordinary hopes.

It is undeniable that this musical tradition is full of kitsch and false sentiment. But there is another way besides Adorno's of looking at that fact. The American popular song arose from the spontaneous desire of ordinary Americans to celebrate the world that they themselves had created. It has never been a *critical* idiom, any more than the folk-music of old Europe was critical. It takes America as it comes, and its lyricism is a lyricism of acceptance. Kitsch is there in the music because kitsch lies all around. If this music were to make an effort to eliminate kitsch and false sentiment it would not be seeing through the lies but telling them. There is a kind of realism here, to which Adorno closed his ears, just as he closed his mind to the real function of song in the life of ordinary people—which is to help them to be at one with their social condition, and to normalize their sufferings and their joys. As their social conditions change, so do their songs; to the problem of divorce there is the remedy contained in Cole Porter's 1932 musical, whose title might have to be changed for modern audiences, *The Gay Divorce*; to the problem of gambling there is the light-hearted solution of Frank Loesser's *Guys and Dolls* (1950).

Adorno's blanket condemnation of the American tradition of popular song is of a piece with his criticism of the capitalist economy. His alternative is not another and better popular music. His alternative is utopia, and there is nothing to be done with utopia. Hence Adorno's attack on mass culture helped to kill off the critical attitude that he supposed himself to be encouraging. By implying that nothing could be

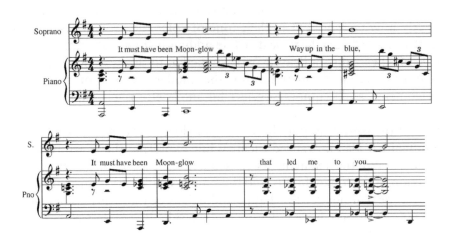

Example 1

said to distinguish Gershwin's 'Summertime' from a piece of kitsch like
'Moonglow' (Hudson, de Lange and Mills) (Ex. 1), Adorno showed his
real contempt for ordinary music lovers who, being human, are as
capable of aesthetic education as anybody else. But it is through such
examples that ordinary listeners can be led to distinguish genuine
melodic invention from the repetition of patterns, and the delicate use
of jazz harmonies to overlay voice-led cadences, as in the Gershwin,
from the softening of all structure by squidgy sevenths and ninths. (Let's
not mention the lyrics!)

   In other words, by teaching that popular music must be rejected in its
entirety, Adorno opened the way to the inverse attitude, that popular
music must be *accepted* in its entirety. A blanket criticism is no criticism
at all. Hence when pop dawned on the world of musicology it was as
a field of study in which the critic was denied a voice. It is precisely in
this way that Adorno has been useful to the postmodern musicologist.
By presenting judgement as a form of total condemnation, Adorno
consigned judgement to the dustheap. He presented the musicological
world with a dichotomy that facilitated the very view that he abhorred.
Either total condemnation, or 'anything goes'.

   It is only by making discriminations *within* the realm of popular
music that we can encourage young people to recognize the difference
between genuine musical sentiment and kitsch, between beauty and
ugliness, between the life-affirming and the life-denying, the inspired
and the routine—in short between The Beatles and U2. And once the

habit of judgement begins it will amplify its bounds until those who have known nothing but current pop music will be led by critical inquiry to the bright uplands of classical music, from where they will be able to look down on their earlier tastes and perhaps agree with Adorno in dismissing them, but in dismissing them kindly and with full awareness of their human strengths. And they might also become aware of the very real difference between the music that irritated Adorno, which was a music aimed at adults and designed to be sung, and the popular music that succeeded it, which is a music aimed at adolescents, and designed to be swallowed.

This brings me to the third important aspect of Adorno's thinking: the attack on tonality, conducted at many levels and in many places, and often understood as a defence of the modernist avant-garde against the late romantic orthodoxies of the early twentieth century. What should we make of this attack, a century on from Schoenberg's op. 11? To some extent that question has been absorbed into another, which is: what should we think of modernism, in the other arts as well as in music, now that its manifesto stage is over?

Adorno's claim in *The Philosophy of Modern Music* was that tonality had exhausted itself. And when an artistic idiom is exhausted the attempt to use it results in cliché and banality. Why should that be? Adorno does not give a clear answer, though his view echoes thoughts familiar from other contexts. The crucial idea is that of the cliché—a gesture, word or phrase which has been adopted for its ability to cast light on its subject, but which has lost that ability through too much use. This happens to figures of speech—'the apple of his eye', 'under the weather', 'making waves'—where what was once an illuminating association has become stale, losing the force of novelty. But what do we mean by 'stale', and why should staleness deprive an expression of its force?

We have no doubt that clichés are, in the artistic context, a fault: they show inattention, routine thinking, emotional laziness. They are a way of passing over things, without troubling to observe them. They show, in fact, the same defects as Adorno discerns in mass culture—a turning away from realities, so that pretend observation and pretend emotion stand in place of real engagement with the world. Reality has a cost attached; and the use of clichés is a sign that someone is not prepared to pay that cost.

Clichés dominate the world of advertising. They are an essential part of putting on sale those things which can only be sold through their meaning—like cosmetics and perfumes, idyllic destinations in the

Example 2

Example 3

tourist trade ('idyllic' being a cliché too), special occasions, evenings out and candlelit dinners in discreet surroundings. The advertising clichés produce what literary critics call a 'stock response': a reflex recognition of a repeatable dream. And it is undeniable that there are musical clichés too—chord progressions that have been too often used and which no longer surprise us, melodic devices (the upbeat in Mahler, for example) which launch us too easily and unthinkingly into the movement of the tune; the rhythmic clichés of the waltz and the tango. Such things can be used by a modern composer, but they must also be *rescued* from the inattention of the listener, by throwing them into sudden and unexpected relief. Thus Strauss, at the end of *Don Quixote*, rescues the V^7—I progression by presenting the bass of the dominant chord as the last of a series of chromatically related sevenths (Ex. 2); Berg in the Sonata op. 1, rescues the cliché of a dotted upbeat by stretching it across dissonant intervals on to a major seventh (Ex. 3); Ravel in *La Valse* rescues the rhythmic clichés of the waltz by piling them up in frenzied sequences, until it is clear that this is no longer a dance of mortals but a whirlwind of ghosts. Those approaches to musical cliché recall the treatment of verbal cliché by a writer like Samuel Becket, who uses clichés against themselves, forcing them to say something new by taking their literal meaning seriously.[15]

One interesting corollary of the view that tonality has declined to the status of a cliché is that tonality is not—despite the attempts by Schenker and his followers to prove the opposite—the equivalent in music of a transformational grammar.[16] The syntactical order of English, and its derivation from semantic structures, could not decline to cliché, since it provides the over-arching medium in which novelties and their degenerate forms both arise. Cliché is an *aesthetic*, not a syntactical, defect—a misuse of language that belongs to the order of style rather than that of grammar. And we must, if Adorno is right, say something similar about tonality.

But there is another corollary, with more serious implications for Adorno's critique. If tonality is not a grammar, then the faults that have arisen in the use of tonality will not be cured by inventing a new musical syntax. This new syntax will not in fact *be* a syntax in the linguistic sense, but a stylistic innovation, one that may be crystallized in rules and regularities, but which will be no more proof against cliché than a new fashion in dress is proof against the aesthetic defects of the old. Everything will depend upon the creativity and taste with which the new idiom is used—and the same goes for the old idiom too.

This is highly relevant to Adorno's defence of atonality against the champions of the tonal tradition. For it indicates that there is no guarantee that the faults that Adorno discerns in the tonal idiom will be avoided—or avoided for long—by adopting some rival musical 'syntax'. Indeed, just as the revolt against figurative painting soon produced abstract, cubist and fauvist cliché—indeed, abstract *kitsch* of the kind that decorates a thousand bars on the Mediterranean sea-front—so has the revolt against tonality produced a wealth of atonal clichés—cluster chords, explosions of cross-rhythms on the brass, exaggerated tessatura and a constant searching for effect which can be encountered in Birtwistle, Ginastera, Ferneyhough and many others. Adorno's defence of the avant-garde of his day was based on the view that 'standardization' could not take root in this idiom, which would always question its own status as a commodity and refuse to be driven by aesthetic routines. But the routines soon arose and, from the tin-cans of John Cage to the bombastic operas of Stockhausen, the musical landscape today is strewn with avant-garde kitsch.

Whatever we say about the atonal alternative, however, we must still confront the argument that the devices of tonal music are worn out, that tonality is no longer available to the serious musician, and that every attempt to write tonal music will end in cliché. What are the grounds for such a judgement? In the pre-war essay earlier referred to[17]

Adorno argued that the addiction to musical fetishes—by which he means the standardized effects of popular music—produces a 'regression' in the art of listening, what we might today call a shrinking attention span. People are content with snippets that they can hum or whistle, and—thanks to mechanical reproduction—will listen to a movement, a tune or a bar detached from the work to which it owes its significance. Inevitably, therefore, the old art of listening, which involves following a complex development over long stretches of time, gives way to an interest in catchy fragments, shortened sequences that can be detached from their context and repeated at will. And it is just such fragments, Adorno implies, that become clichés, which the ear of the listener and the mind of the composer prefer to the hard work of harmonic and melodic argument.

Now Adorno has a point here—a point that Walter Benjamin might have made (though he didn't quite) in his influential essay on 'The work of art in the age of mechanical reproduction'.[18] Whatever we think about tonality, there is no doubt that it has lent itself to a new kind of music, in which the lengthy paragraphs of the symphonic tradition have been replaced by the repetition of statically conceived cells—as in the ballets and symphonies of Stravinsky. The architecture of a Beethoven or Bruckner symphony, in which the modulation from tonic to dominant might take place over a span of many minutes, and in which every scale degree is conscripted to the task of transporting the material from one solid foundation to the next—this wonderful art-form is less and less present in the tonal writing of modern composers, and the 'developing variations' which Schoenberg discerned in the classical style and sought to revive through his serial language are now rarely encountered. The American popular song deploys the tonal language in a manner that is short-breathed and quickly exhausted; and the idiom of jazz, which has taken tonality in a new direction, and discovered harmonic sequences and dissonant cadences which have no place in the classical repertoire, has not produced any comparable expansion of the musical argument. On the contrary, where there should be development there is usually only improvisation, and where there might be the exploration of emotion and the building of character, there is usually a repetition of the same cheerful smile.

Of course, composers have used the jazz idiom in symphonic structures, and adapted it to the harmonic legacy of the classical tradition. But with a few exceptions, such as Gershwin's great *Rhapsody in Blue*, and the G major Piano Concerto of Ravel, the result has inherited the truncated and short-circuited character of the American songbook. The return to tonality by the so-called 'minimalists'—notably Adams, Reich and Torke—has emphasized the point. Works like Adams's *Harmonium* or Torke's colour poems are essentially static, using repetition and rhythmic pulse to generate a forward movement that is led neither by the harmony nor by the melodic voices. The experience of 'unfolding' which we associate with the great works of the classical tradition seems to have been lost, or at least hidden behind a solid metrical wall that will not melt at the touch of the harmonic wand, as bar-lines melt away in Brahms or Wagner.

Is it right, however, to generalize from such observations? As aesthetic judgements they are necessarily 'immediate' and 'singular', to use Kant's illuminating idiom.[19] They are not founded on rules but on the immediate experience of the particular case. Hence they do not authorize the blanket rejection of tonality that Adorno wishes to force on us. They are intrinsically vulnerable to the telling counter-example, just as Adorno's favoured atonal idiom is vulnerable to the proof that this idiom too is short-breathed and unable to construct a far-reaching argument. Indeed the complaint tells far more seriously against Adorno's alternative than it tells against the attempts at symphonic form by the tonal modernists—as in the Walton and Britten concertos, or the symphonies of Shostakovich. The best that the serial idiom has achieved in the direction of sustained argument is surely the Violin Concerto of Berg, which leans at every point upon tonal relations and reminiscences, to the point of belonging fairly within the tradition of voice-led harmony that Schoenberg, in his own Violin Concerto, had left behind. And as for that Violin Concerto of Schoenberg's—yes, it makes melodic sense. But it lacks the harmonic order that would enable us to hear it as moving through musical space in the manner of Schumann or Brahms.

If, however, the debate has to be conducted in that way, referring to example and counter-example, it is hard to see how it could be brought to a conclusion. Something is right in what Adorno is saying. But all attempts to pin the thesis down come up against the immovably singular nature of aesthetic judgement. And the failure of Adorno to produce any prescription, other than his entirely negative advocacy of atonality against the tonal cliché, leaves the matter hanging in the air. He intended his arguments to foretell the end of tonal music. But they could as easily be read as foretelling the end of music. For the shortened attention span and the emergence of addictive forms of entertainment are products of the new media rather than residues of the tonal tradition.

In the light of this it seems to me that we should retrace our steps and revisit the attempts by composers to learn from the example of song—both folk song and the jazz-influenced songbook. Although this means a return from large-scale forms to the strophic idiom of natural music, it also involves a return to the crucible of tonality, in which the tonal order is first crystallized from the soup of sound. That, it seems to me, is the direction taken by Debussy; and he was followed by Janáček, Dutilleux, Britten, Messiaen and many more—brilliant musicians who were led by their ears and not by theories, even if they were capable, like Messiaen, of theorizing at the highest level. It is true that, except in the field of opera, where they could rely on the short-term dynamic of song, they tended to produce short-breathed works. But they also have, to their credit, wonderful achievements of musical argument, such as the quartets of Janáček and Dutilleux, the *Turangalila Symphony* and *Transfiguration de nôtre Seigneur Jésus Christ* of Messiaen, and the Cello Symphony and Violin Concerto of Britten. Adorno might dismiss those achievements as belonging to the 'false consciousness' of the consumer society; to me, however, the falsehood belongs to Adorno, and the consciousness contained in those compositions is one that points to the truth.

Notes

1 Richard Taruskin, *The Oxford History of Western Music*, 6 vols, Oxford 2004.
2 That Adorno had genuine talent, however, is shown by his orchestration of pieces from Schumann's *Kinderszene,* in which he was free to rejoice in the tonal logic that he denied himself in his own compositions.
3 See the essay on 'Free time', reprinted in Theodor W. Adorno, *The Culture Industry: Selected Essays on Mass Culture*, ed. J. M. Bernstein, London 1991.
4 See, for example, the introduction by J. M. Bernstein to *The Culture Industry, op. cit.*
5 Max Horkheimer and Theodor W. Adorno, *Dialectic of Enlightenment*, tr. Edmund Jephcott, Stanford 2002.
6 See *The Essence of Christianity*, 1841, tr. Marion Evans, London 1856.
7 *History and Class Consciousness: Studies in Marxist Dialectics*, tr. R. Livingstone, London 1971.
8 'Bach Defended against his Devotees', in *Prisms*, tr. Samuel and Shierry Weber, Letchworth 1967, p. 142.
9 For the jargon, see the chapter 'Subject-Object' in *Aesthetic Theory*, tr. R. Hullot-Kentor, Minneapolis 1996.
10 *Aesthetic Theory*, p. 31. See also 'On the social situation of music', *Telos*, 35, 1978.
11 Hermann Broch, 'Einiger Bemerkungen' . . . in *Dichtung und Erkennenn*, ed. Hannah Arendt, Frankfurt 1976.
12 A similar dichotomizing can be witnessed in Clement Greenberg's essay 'Avant-garde and kitsch', *Partisan Review* 1939, at the time an important voice of American left-wing opinion.
13 Terry Teachout, 'The great American songbook', a series of articles in *Commentary*, 1999–2002.
14 Gunther Schuller, *Early Jazz: Its Roots and Musical Development*, New York 1968.

15 See Christopher Ricks, *Beckett's Dying Words*, Oxford 1995; R. Scruton, 'Beckett and the Cartesian Soul', in *The Aesthetic Understanding*, London 1982.

16 As maintained by Lerdahl and Jackendoff, *A Generative Theory of Tonal Music*, Cambridge, Mass. 1983, following the ideas of Schenker, Salzer *et al*.

17 'On the fetish-character in music and the regression of listening', 1938, reprinted in *The Culture Industry, op. cit.*

18 Walter Benjamin, 'The work of art in the age of mechanical reproduction', in *Illuminations*, tr. Harry Zohn, New York 1968.

19 *The Critique of Judgement.*

Bibliography

Adorno, Theodor W., *The Authoritarian Personality*, New York 1950.

Adorno, Theodor W., *In Search of Wagner*, Berlin 1952, tr. R. Livingstone, London 1981.

Adorno, Theodor W., *Prisms*, tr. Samuel and Shierry Weber, Letchworth 1967.

Adorno, Theodor W., *The Philosophy of Modern Music*, tr. A. G. Mitchell and W. V. Blomster, New York 1973.

Adorno, Theodor W., 'On the social situation of music', *Telos*, 35, 1978.

Adorno, Theodor W., *The Culture Industry*, ed. J. M. Bernstein, London 1991.

Adorno, Theodor W., *Aesthetic Theory*, tr. Robert Hullot-Kentor, Minneapolis 1996.

Al-Fârâbî, *Kitab al-mousiqi al-kabîr* (Big Book on Music), Cairo 1923.

Arato A. and Gebhardt, F., *The Essential Frankfurt School Reader*, New York 1978.

Aristotle, *De Anima*.

Aristoxenus, *Elementa Rhythmica*, surviving fragments of Book 2 translated in A. Barker, *Greek Musical Writings*, London 1989, vol. 2.

Bartók, Béla, tr. M. D. Calvocoressi, *Hungarian Folk Music*, London 1931.

Bartók, Béla, 'The so-called Bulgarian rhythm', in *Essays*, selected and edited by Benjamin Suchoff, London 1976.

Batteux, Charles, *Les beaux arts réduits à un même principe*, Paris 1746.

Beckerman, Michael, *Janáček as Theorist*, New York 1994.

Benjamin, Walter, 'The work of art in the age of mechanical reproduction', in *Illuminations*, tr. Harry Zohn, New York 1968.

Bennett, Jonathan, *Locke, Berkeley and Hume: Central Themes*, Oxford 1971.

Bennett, Jonathan, *Events and Their Names*, New York 1988.

Blackburn, Simon, *Ruling Passions*, London 1997.

Block, Ned and Fodor, Jerry, 'What psychological states are not', *Philosophical Review* 81 (1972), 159–81.

Bowers, F., *Scriabin*, Tokyo and Palo Alto 1969.

Bregman, Albert S., *Auditory Scene Analysis*, Cambridge, Mass. 1990, 1999.

Broch, Hermann, 'Einiger Bemerkungen Zum Problem des Kitsches', in *Dichtung und Erkennenn*, ed. Hannah Arendt, Frankfurt 1976.

Bücher, Karl, *Arbeit und Rhythmus*, Leipzig 1909.

Budd, Malcolm, 'Musical movement and aesthetic metaphors', *British Journal of Aesthetics*, 2003.

Burkert, Walter, *Homo Necans*, Oxford 1972.

Carapezza, Paolo Emilio, 'Re Ruggero tra Dioniso e Apollo' in 'Studie in onore di Cesare Brandi'; *Storia dell'arte*, 38–40, Firenze 1980.

Casati, Roberto and Dokic, Jérôme, *La philosophie du son*, Nîmes 1994.

Chernoff, John Miller, *African Music*, Chicago 1979.

Chion, Michel, *La voix au cinéma*, Paris 1982, tr. Claudia Gorbman, *The Voice in Cinema*, New York 1999.

Chomsky, Noam, *Language and Mind*, New York 1968.

Cone, Edward T., *Musical Form and Musical Performance*, New York 1968.

Cook, Nicholas, *A Guide to Musical Analysis*, London 1987.

Cooke, Deryck, 'Wagner's musical language', in P. Burbidge and R. Sutton, eds, *The Wagner Companion*, London and Boston 1979, pp. 225–68.

Cooke, Deryck, *I Saw the World End: a Study of Wagner's Ring*, Oxford 1979.

Cooke, Deryck, 'The musical symbolism of Wagner's music dramas', in *Vindications*, London 1982.

Cooper, Martin, *Beethoven: The Last Decade, 1817–1827*, London 1970.

Dahlhaus, Carl, *Esthetics of Music*, tr. W. Austin, Cambridge 1982.

Dahlhaus, Carl, *The Idea of Absolute Music*, tr. R. Lustig, Chicago 1989.

Davidson, Audrey Ekdahl, *Olivier Messiaen and the Tristan Myth*, Westport, Conn. and London 2001.

Davidson, Donald, 'The individuation of events', in *Essays on Actions and Events*, Oxford 1980.

Deathridge, John and Dahlhaus, Carl, *The New Grove Wagner*, London 1984.

Dennett, D. C., *Consciousness Explained*, London 1992.

Deutsch, Diana, 'Grouping mechanisms in music', in D. Deutsch, ed., *The Psychology of Music*, New York 1982.

Divenyi, L. and Hirsh, I. J., 'Some figural properties of auditory patterns', *Journal of the Acoustical Society of America* 64 (1978), 1369–86.

Dummett, Michael, *Frege: Philosophy of Language*, Oxford 1971.

Edwards, Arthur C., *The Art of Melody*, New York 1956.

Ewans, Michael, *Wagner and Aeschylus: The* Ring *and the* Oresteia, London 1982.

Feuerbach, L., *The Essence of Christianity*, 1841.

Fox Strangways, A. H., *The Music of Hindostan*, Oxford 1914.

Frazer, Sir James, *Totem and Exogamy*, London 1910.

Freud, S., *Totem and Taboo*, tr. J. Strachey, London 1913.

Frith, S., 'Towards an aesthetic of popular music', in Richard Leppert and Susan McClary, eds, *Music and Society: The Politics of Composition, Performance and Reception*, Cambridge 1987.

Gelfand, Stanley A., *Hearing: An Introduction to Psychological and Physiological Acoustics*, 3rd edn, New York 1998.

Gibson, J. J., 'The visual field and the visual world', *Psychological Review* 59 (1952), 149–51.

Girard, René, *La Violence et le sacré*, Paris 1972.

Goehr, Lydia, 'Being true to the work', *The Journal of Aesthetics and Art Criticism*, 1989.

Goehr, Lydia, *The Imaginary Museum of Musical Works*, Oxford 1992.

Goodman, Nelson, *Languages of Art: An Approach to a Theory of Symbols*, Oxford 1969.

Greenberg, Clement, 'Avant-garde and kitsch', *Partisan Review*, 1939.

Grosset, Joanny, 'Histoire de la musique: Inde', in *Encyclopédie de la musique et dictionnaire du conservatoire*, ed. A. Lavignac, Paris, 1913–31, vol. 1, pt. 1, pp. 287–324.

Guralnick, Peter, liner notes to *Elvis Presley: The Sun Sessions* CD (BMG/RCA 6414-2-R, 1987).

Guralnick, Peter, *Lost Highways: Journeys and Arrivals of American Musicians*, New York 1982.

Gurney, Edmund, *The Power of Sound*, London 1880, reissued Chicago 2003.

Hamilton, Andy, *Aesthetics and Music*, London 2007.

Hanslick, Edouard, *Vom musikalisch-Schönen* (Leipzig 1854, revised 1891; *The Beautiful in Music*, tr. Payzant, New York 1974).

Havel, Václav, 'The power of the powerless', tr. Paul Wilson, in John Keane, ed., *The Power of the Powerless: Citizens Against the State in Central-Eastern Europe*, London 1985.

Helmholtz, Hermann von, *On the Sensation of Tone*, tr. Alexander J. Ellis, London 1885.

Henderson, David, *'Scuse me while I Kiss the Sky: the Life of Jimi Hendrix*, Toronto 1983.

Holloway, Robin, *Essays and Diversions II*, London 2007.

Hornsby, Jennifer, *Actions*, Oxford 1980.

Horton, Julian, 'Schoenberg and the "Moment of German music"', *Musical Analysis* 24 (2005), 235–62.

Hutchings, Arthur, *A Companion to Mozart's Piano Concertos*, Oxford 1948.

Iwaszkiewicz, Janisław, *Spotkania z Szymanowskim* (Meetings with Szymanowski), Krakow 1947.

Janáček, Leoš, *Úplná nauka o harmonii*, in *Hudebné teoretické dílo*, ed. Blazek, Zdeněk, Prague 1974, 2 vols.

Johnson, Robert Sherlaw, *Messiaen*, 2nd edn, London 1989.

Kant, Immanuel, *The Critique of Judgement*, 1797.

Kim, Jaegwon, 'Events as property exemplifications', in M. Brand and D. Walton, eds, *Action Theory*, Dordrecht 1980, pp. 159–77.

Kitcher, Philip and Schacht, Richard, *Finding an Ending: Reflections on Wagner's Ring*, Oxford 2004.

Kivy, Peter, *The Corded Shell: Reflections on Musical Expression*, Princeton 1980.

Kivy Peter, '*Ars Perfecta*: Towards perfection in musical performance', in *Music, Language and Cognition*, Oxford 2007.

Köhler, Joachim, *Richard Wagner, Last of the Titans*, tr. Stewart Spencer, New Haven and London 2004.

Kurth, Ernst, *Romantische Harmonik und ihre Krise in Wagners 'Tristan'*, Berne 1920.

Le Huray, Peter and Day, James, *Music and Aesthetics in the 18th and Early 19th Centuries*, Cambridge 1981.

Lerdahl, Fred and Jackendoff, Ray, *A Generative Theory of Tonal Music*, Cambridge, Mass. 1983.

Lerdahl, Fred, 'Cognitive constraints on compositional systems', in John A. Sloboda, ed., *Generative Processes in Music*, Oxford 1988.

Levinson, Jerrold, 'What a musical work is', in *Music, Art and Metaphysics*, Ithaca, NY 1990.

Lévi-Strauss, Claude, *Le Cru et le cuit*, Paris 1964, tr. J. and D. Weightman, *The Raw and the Cooked*, London 1978.

Lipsitz, George, *Dangerous Crossroads: Popular Music, Postmodernism and the Poetics of Place*, London 1994.

Locke, John, *An Essay on the Human Understanding*, 1690.

Longuet-Higgins, H. C., *Mental Processes: Studies in Cognitive Science*, Cambridge, Mass. 1987.

Lukács, György, *History and Class Consciousness: Studies in Marxist Dialectics*, tr. R. Livingstone, London 1971.

MacDonald, Hugh, *Skyrabin*, Oxford 1978.

Maciejewski, B. M., *Karól Syzmanowski*, London 1967.

Magee, Bryan, *Wagner and Philosophy*, London 2001.

Mann, Thomas, 'The sorrows and grandeur of Richard Wagner', in *Pro and Contra Wagner*, tr. Allan Blunden, London 1985.

Mann, William, 'Down with visiting cards', in John DiGaetani, ed., *Penetrating Wagner's Ring*, London 1978.

Marcus, Grail, *Dead Elvis*, New York 1991.

Maynard Smith, John and Szathmáry, Eörs, *The Major Transitions in Evolution*, Oxford and New York 1995.

McGinn, Colin, *The Subjective View: Secondary Qualities and Indexicals*, Oxford 1983.

Messiaen, Olivier, *Technique de mon langage musicale*, Paris 1956.

Messiaen, Olivier, *Traité de rhythme, de couleur et d'ornithologie*, 8 vols, Paris, Leduc, 1996 onwards.

Miller, Geoffrey, 'Evolution of human music through sexual selection', in Nils Wallin *et al.*, *The Origins of Music*, Cambridge, Mass. 2000.

Millington, Barry, *Wagner*, London 1984.

Miłosz, Czesław, *The Captive Mind*, 1955.

Mocquereau, André, *A Study of Gregorian Musical Rhythm*, Richmond, Va. 2007.

Newman, Ernest, *Wagner as Man and Artist*, London 1925.

Newman, Ernest, *Wagner Nights*, London 1949, reissued as *The Wagner Operas*, London 1961.

Nietzsche, Friedrich, *The Birth of Tragedy out of the Spirit of Music*.

O'Callaghan, Casey and Nudds, Matthew, eds, *Sounds and Perception: New Philosophical Essays*, Oxford 2009.

O'Callaghan, Casey, *Sounds: A Philosophical Theory*, Oxford 2007.

Padel, Ruth, *I am a Man: Sex, Gods and Rock 'n' Roll*, London 2000.

Pasnau, R., 'What is sound?', *Philosophical Quarterly* 49 (1999), 309–24.

Pasnau, R., 'Sensible qualities: The case of sound', *Journal of the History of Philosophy* 38, (2000), 27–40.

Peacocke, C., *Sense and Content: Experience, Thought and their Relations*, Oxford 1983.

Peirce, C. S., Letter to Lady Welby, in *Selected Writings*, ed. P. P. Wiener, New York 1958, p. 406.

Pleasants, Henry, *The Great American Popular Singers*, New York 1974.

Porges, Heinrich, trans. Robert L. Jacobs, *Wagner Rehearsing the Ring*, Cambridge 1983.

Reti, Rudolph, *Tonality–Atonality–Pantonality*, London 1958.

Ricks, Christopher, *Beckett's Dying Words*, Oxford 1995.

Riemann, Hugo, *System der musikalischen Rythmik und Metrik*, Leipzig 1903.

Risset, Jean-Claude and Wessel, David L., 'Exploration of timbre by analysis and synthesis', in Diana Deutsch, ed., *The Psychology of Music*, New York and London 1982, pp. 25–58.

Rosen, Charles, Review of the *New Grove Dictionary of Music*, reprinted in *Critical Entertainments*, Cambridge, Mass. 2000.

Rosenthal, Ethel, *The Story of Indian Music and its Instruments*, London 1929.

Saïd, Edward, *Orientalism*, New York 1971.

Saïd, Edward, *Musical Elaborations*, London 1991.

Salzer, Felix, *Structural Hearing*, 2 vols, New York 1952–62.

Samson, Jim, *The Music of Szymanowski*, London 1980.

Schaeffer, Pierre, *Traité des objects musicaux*, Paris 1966.

Schenker, Heinrich, *Beethoven's Ninth Symphony*, tr. John Rothgeb, Yale 1992.

Schenker, Heinrich, *Free Composition*, tr. Ernst Oser, London 1979.

Schiller, Friedrich v., 'Kallias or concerning beauty: Letters to Gottfried Keller', in J. M. Bernstein ed., *Classic and Romantic German Aesthetics*, Cambridge 2003.

Schopenhauer, Arthur, *The Word as Will and Representation*, tr. E. J. F. Payne, New York 1969.

Schoenberg, Arnold, *Harmonielehre*, 3rd edn, Vienna 1922.

Schuller, Gunther, *Early Jazz: Its Roots and Musical Development*, New York 1968.

Schutz, Alfred, 'Making music together', in *Collected Papers*, vol. 2, The Hague 1964, pp. 159–78.

Scruton, Roger, *Art and Imagination*, London 1974.

Scruton, Roger, 'Beckett and the Cartesian soul', in *The Aesthetic Understanding*, London 1982.

Scruton, Roger, 'Expression', in the *New Grove Dictionary of Music*, ed. Stanley Sadie, London 1982 et seq.

Scruton, Roger, *Sexual Desire*, London and New York 1986.

Scruton, Roger, *Modern Philosophy*, London 1994.

Scruton, Roger, *The Aesthetics of Music*, Oxford 1997.

Scruton, Roger, *Perictione in Colophon*, South Bend, Ind. 2000.

Scruton, Roger, 'Confronting biology', in Craig Titus, ed., *Philosophical Psychology: Psychology, Emotions and Freedom*, Arlington, Va. 2009.

Sellars, W., 'Empiricism and the philosophy of mind', in *Science, Perception and Reality*, London 1963, p. 147.

Simmel, Georg, *The Philosophy of Money*, tr. T. Bottomore, D. Frisby and K. Maengelberg, London 1978.

Smith, Adam, *The Theory of Moral Sentiments*, London 1759.

Štědron, Bohumír, *Janáček ve vzpomínkach a dopísech*, Prague 1946.

Stove, David, *Darwinian Fairy Tales*, New York 2002.

Strawson, P. F., *Individuals*, London 1956.

Szabolcsi, Bence, *A History of Melody*, tr. Cynthia Jolly and Sára Karig, London and Budapest, 1965.

Szymanowski, Karól, *Z Pism*, ed. T. Chyliriska, Krakow 1958.

Szymanowski, Karól, *Szymanowski on Music: Selected Writings of Karól Syzmanowski*, tr. and ed. Alistair Wightman, London 1999.

Talbot, Michael, ed., *The Musical Work: Reality or Invention?*, Liverpool 2000.

Tanner, Michael, 'The total work of art', in Peter Burbage and Richard Sutton, eds, *The Wagner Companion*, London 1979.

Tanner, Michael, *Wagner*, Princeton 1996.

Taruskin, R., 'Resisting the Ninth', in *Text and Act*, Oxford 1995.

Taruskin, R., *The Oxford History of Western Music*, 6 vols, Oxford 2004.

Teachout, Terry, 'The great American songbook', *Commentary*, 1999–2002.

Till, Nicholas, *Mozart and the Enlightenment*, London 1992.

Tovey, Donald Francis, *Essays in Musical Analysis*, 6 vols, Oxford 1936.

Trkanová, Marie, *U Janáčku*, Prague 1959.

Tyrell, John, article on Janáček in the *New Grove Dictionary of Music*.

Vaihinger, Hans, *The Philosophy of 'As If'*, tr. C. K. Ogden, London 1932.

van Gennep, Arnold, *Les Rites de passage*, Paris 1901.

Wagner, R., 'Zum vortrag der neunten symphonie Beethovens', in *Gesammelte Schriften und Dichtungen*, zweite Auflage, Leipzig 1888, vol. IX, pp. 231–57.

Wagner, Richard, 'Über der Anwendung der Musik auf der Drama' (1879), in *Gesammelte Schriften und Dichtungen*, vol. X.

Wagner, Richard, *Opera and Drama*, in *Richard Wagner's Prose Works*, ed. William Ashton Ellis, St. Clare Shores, Mich. 1972, vol. 2.

Weiner, Marc A., *Richard Wagner and the Anti-Semitic Imagination*, Lincoln, Nebr. and London 1995.

West, M. L., *Ancient Greek Music*, Oxford 1992.

Wiggins, David, *Sameness and Substance Renewed*, Cambridge 2001.

Wittgenstein, Ludwig, *Philosophical Investigations*, tr. G. E. M. Anscombe, Oxford 1953.

Wittgenstein, Ludwig, *The Blue and Brown Books*, Oxford 1960.

Wittgenstein, Ludwig, *Lectures and Conversations on Aesthetics, Freud and Religious Belief*, ed. Cyril Barrett, Oxford 1966.

Wittgenstein, Ludwig, *Culture and Value*, ed. G. H. Von Wright, tr. Peter Winch, amended edn, Oxford 1980.

Wollheim, Richard, *Painting as an Art*, London 1987.

Wright, O., 'Arab music', sections 1–4, *The New Grove Dictionary*, ed. Stanley Sadie, London 1980.

Index of Subjects

absolute music 3, 50f
acousmatic hearing 5, 7, 11, 13, 22–3, 30, 58–9
African music 215
Afro-American music 215–16
alienation 144–5, 178–9, 208–9
All-India Musical Conferences 10
American songbook 18, 213–17
anti-semitism 119–21
Arabic music 14
aspects 39–41
atonality 12–18, 37, 64, 70–1, 220–4
audience 174–6, 179–80
auditory streams 22, 25–9, 57–8
Austro-Hungary 162–81
authoritarian 163, 166, 175, 181n
authority 162–5, 179

Baptist hymnal 215, 216
baroque 15, 67f
beat 65
Big Band 217
binaural beats 27–8
birdsong 5–6
Blues 14, 214, 216
bourgeoisie 216–17
Broadway 214–15

Cartesianism 35–6
categorical imperative 132
chant 77
charm 191, 197–8
Chinese music 11
Christianity 126, 128, 132, 152, 157, 176, 196, 205
cinema 29
classical style 15, 67f, 86ff, 90, 101–3
cliché 220–3
colour 191–3
commodity fetishism 207–9
communism 163, 201, 210, 213
community 163–81, 197–202
consumer culture 205–16
consumer sovereignty 216
curses 147–8

dance 9, 12, 47, 51, 53, 54, 55, 59, 60–3, 67–9, 76–9, 112, 164f, 180
Darmstadt School 79
decadence 195, 197f
dialectic 145
disco 68
double intentionality 43–5

economics 134
egalitarianism 119, 122, 123
emotion 52–3
Enlightenment 94, 109ff, 112, 116, 159, 207
Entäusserung 52
erotic love 140–4, 158–9, 196f
ethnomusicology 9, 14
events 5, 20–1, 25
evolutionary psychology 5–7, 22, 26
expression 3, 34–42, 49–56

false consciousness 206–9
fetishism 206–9, 210
figured bass 11
first-person case 34–6, 40, 42
folk song 62, 75, 164–5, 175, 178, 182–4, 198, 200–1, 214, 217, 225
folk stories 121–2
Frankfurt School 206f, 210
freedom 132–3, 156–7, 208–11
French Revolution 108, 122

'galant' style 86–7
Gestalt perception 22–3, 26, 39–40, 43, 44, 47, 57–9
Greek music 14, 60, 63, 110
Greek tragedy 126, 139, 152

hearing in 37f, 43f, 47f
Heavy Metal 17, 68
Hollywood 205, 215
hymns 62, 215, 216

ideology 9, 18, 167, 204–26
idolatry 210–11
imagination 41–2, 43–8

Index of Names